DEFIANT COURAGE

A WWII Epic of Escape and Endurance

Astrid Karlsen Scott and Dr. Tore Haug
Foreword by Harald Zwart

Skyhorse Publishing

Skyhorse Publishing books may be purchased in bulk at special discounts for sales promotion, corporate gifts, fund-raising, or educational purposes. Special editions can also be created to specifications. For details, contact the Special Sales Department, Skyhorse Publishing, 307 West 36th Street, 11th Floor, New York, NY 10018 or info@skyhorsepublishing.com.

Skyhorse® and Skyhorse Publishing® are registered trademarks of Skyhorse Publishing, Inc.®, a Delaware corporation.

Visit our website at www.skyhorsepublishing.com.

10 9 8 7 6 5 4 3 2 1

Library of Congress Cataloging-in-Publication Data is available on file.

Cover design by Rain Saukas

ISBN: 978-1-62873-664-9
Ebook ISBN: 978-1-62914-028-5

Printed in the United States of America

WITH LOVE
TO OUR FAMILIES:

Melvin McCabe Scott, Jr.
Susan, Eric, John
and their families

Wenche Haug
Carolin

CONTENTS

FOREWORD

TROMS, WAY above the Arctic Circle in northern Norway. Snow-capped mountains pierce the horizon and valleys open up to glaciers. It is March, 1943 and the dramatic landscape is slowly waking up from the third long, dark winter under Nazi rule. In this spectacular landscape one of the most amazing stories of World War II is about take place.

Twelve Norwegians have boarded a small fishing boat in Scotland. They have crossed the treacherous North Sea to get to their beloved country in order to fight the German invaders. It is not to be. Norwegian collaborators give them away. The boat is attacked and sunk with an explosion of eight tons of dynamite. Eleven of the twelve men are captured and eventually killed by the Germans, most of them after enduring horrific torture. But one man escapes.

The one who gets away is the twenty-five-year-old Jan Baalsrud. All Jan has to rely on is his moral fiber, his incredible strength--and eventually dozens of Norwegians willing to risk their lives to help him.

With a head start of only a hundred meters, shot in the foot and leaving a trail of blood in the snow, Jan embarks on one of the most legendary escapes of World War II. With the Gestapo on his heels, in storms and freezing cold, he swims across sounds, walks across mountains on foot, and skis to try to get to neutral Sweden. Along his route, he is housed, fed, and hidden from the Nazis by locals who know that the punishment for helping a fugitive is death.

As a Norwegian, I grew up with the story of Jan Baalsrud. When we were out cross-country skiing and fatigue got the better of us, we were always reminded of a man who never stopped and never gave up.

I remember seeing Arne Skauen's movie, *We Die Alone,* when I was very young and it left an unforgettable impression. How far can a man go to stay alive? How much can he take before he gives in? My generation has never come near the fear and terror our parents and grandparents experienced during World War II; we have not experienced war and have never been tested like they were.

My father was a prisoner in the Japanese concentration camps in Indonesia. The Dutch had colonized the country and when the Japanese moved in, those they did not kill, they threw into camps. My father has had a hard time telling me about it, but I understand that this was a defining period for him.

My grandfather was a Norwegian captain on a ship that sailed in allied convoys in German submarine-infested waters. He too was traumatized, although I've only realized this in recent years.

The stories of the men and women who made great sacrifices during all wars need to be told. We need to tell them to our children, and they need to tell them to theirs. But some stories resonate deeper than others--they speak to us on a profound level. Jan Baalsrud's story is in a class of its own.

This brings me to this book: A terrific piece of research and storytelling that brings us closer to the truth. Jan's story has been told many times, but never with the painstaking accuracy of this book. The authors manage not only to tell one hero's story, but also that of the many who helped Jan and became heroes themselves. Unsung heroes—until this book.

Tore and Astrid's years of research, and their meticulous focus on details and facts have resulted in a book that is free from sentiment and interpretation. It invites you to go trace Jan's footsteps and fill in your own emotions and terror. It is a riveting read.

I never met Jan Baalsrud personally, but I did meet many of those who helped him. When they me told about those days when they risked their lives to keep Jan Baalsrud alive, something happened in their eyes. Just like for my father and grandfather, these are not stories they visit without pain.

Harald Zwart

ACKNOWLEDGMENTS

THE MATERIAL in this book has been gathered from the following sources:

Jan Baalsrud's benefactors and the many others who were directly drawn into the happenings in 1943 reconstructed the dramatic events in minute detail.

Historians, authors and journalists shared with us their well-researched knowledge.

Jan Baalsrud's own report, written accounts from benefactors now deceased, and documents from the German war archives aided our search for the truth.

Nils Ivar Baalsrud, Jan Baalsrud's brother, lifelong friend and confidant, helped us understand Jan better. As a leader of the Jan Baalsrud Foundation for many years, Nils generously shared the information gathered by the foundation.

We also express our sincere gratitude to the following sources:

Karlsøy *kommune* and the International Sons of Norway for their grants in support of this work.

Christine Hansen, our editor. Your eye for accuracy and detail brought clarity to our words and your love for the people in this story helped to create a book which is a pleasure to read. Your dedication of long hours to meet the deadline is gratefully acknowledged.

Jan-Barman Jensen, District Manager for Braathen Airlines in Troms, we appreciate your generosity in obtaining complimentary flights to help us with our research.

Erland Rian, *Destination Tromsø*, we gratefully acknowledge your help with accommodations and transportation. Your interest in our work in its beginning stages was an inspiration.

Thank you, Holger Raste, reporter and authority on the Baalsrud story, for taking us in hand and guiding us in many of Jan's footsteps. You generously shared your innumerable articles about Jan Baalsrud and his benefactors with us; your information is liberally sprinkled throughout this book.

Author and research-historian Kjell Fjørtoft, we are grateful that you met with us repeatedly and answered our many questions. Your research and early articles on the Baalsrud story are responsible for much of the information included in the chapter, "The Fate of the Brattholm Men," as well as other information in the book.

Ragnar Ulstein, historian and author, many thanks for your time spent with us and wisdom shared.

Torleif Lyngstad, historian, you were a major contributor in helping us to understand the happenings regarding the Baalsrud affair in and around Kåfjord. Thank you for the hours spent with us.

Tore Hauge, author of *"De brente våre hjem,"* thank you for your interest and help.

Edvin Wikan, Tromsø policeman, thank you for sharing your personal knowledge and pictures.

Our appreciation goes to the Idrupsen family, our steady guides who recounted in detail the evidence of the dreadful day, March 30, 1943. Our thanks to Dagmar, Olaug (Idrupsen) Hågensen, Halvor and Idrup Idrupsen.

Peder Nilsen, your modest and tender spirit made the events at Løvli and Tyttebærvika and your involvement come alive for us.

Alvin Larsen, in 1943, you helped carry a wounded soldier up the Revdal mountains on a sled. Since 1995, you helped "carry" the story, as our enthusiastic confidant and guide from Furuflaten. We thank you for the countless hours of your time spent guiding us through Furuflaten.

Asbjørn Dalhaug, your unending enthusiasm for Jan Baalsrud and his benefactors helped us clear up details we had struggled with, and guided us into Lyngsdalen where Jan suffered the avalanche.

Peder Isaksen, your methodical description has helped to reveal the efforts the Manndalen people made to rescue Jan. You introduced us to the courage of the Manndalen people, and for that we are grateful. We have enjoyed many an hour in your home, sitting around a groaning table of delicacies prepared by your loving wife, Eliva.

We thank you, cousins Arvid and Viggo Heika from Kopparelv, who played in the snow as Jan peeked around your century-old farm building. You described for us Jan's visit to Kopparelv, an event discussed many times in your families.

At 92, Signe Hansen, you still remember the day Jan came over the mountains to your home in Karanes, as clearly as if it was yesterday, and his handsome smile. We appreciate your help.

Pete Taylor, many thanks for the innumerable hours you freely gave to this project.

Leif Erik Iversen, we are deeply indebted to you for your many pictures and for your help, chauffeuring, and guiding, for opening your home to us on several occasions, and for going the many extra miles.

Arvid Grønnslett, we thank you for unnumbered hours spent on our behalf and we are grateful for your guidance during the Baalsrud mountain-touring.

Annika Gustafson, your delicious meals and comfortable accommodations eased the physical strain of intense research.

Thorleif Henriksen, your deep interest and help with this project is greatly appreciated.

Else Aas, dear friend, thank you for your continual support of every project promoting Norway.

Jack Fjeldstad, we appreciate your generosity. Your friendship with Jan and your portrayal of him in the movie, *"Ni Liv,"* gave you insight into Jan's character, which you shared with us.

Jaye Compton, we thank you for the many long hours spent on a tight deadline to complete the final typesetting and prepare this manuscript for printing.

Thank you to all of you, too many to mention, who have for years sustained us with your faith and interest in this project, and for your willingness to help where needed.

We are profoundly thankful for our mates, Wenche Haug and Melvin Scott, Jr.; as you both know, this book would not exist had it not been for your support, encouragement and patience during the years we spent researching and writing.

We sincerely thank all of you as we share this piece of Norwegian history. Our lives have been enriched as we have been inspired by the courage and selflessness of Jan and his benefactors.

Tusen takk,
Astrid Karlsen Scott & Tore Haug

INTRODUCTION

WE TRAVELED to the Troms District in northern Norway to walk in Jan Baalsrud's footsteps and to meet with his benefactors who helped him escape from the Gestapo in the spring of 1943. We were educated! And we discovered that what we knew from earlier times about Jan's escape and those who helped him was much deficient, often inaccurate, and frequently fictitious.

Peder Isaksen, one of Jan's benefactors from Manndalen, expressed his feelings to the newspaper *Tromsø* in 1987. He said he had a deep wish that one day a book would come out that would tell the truth about what had happened in Manndalen in 1943 with regard to the Baalsrud affair. Peder continues, "Little or nothing has been told of what happened here, (in Manndalen) and what has been told is wrong. I am especially indignant over how badly the Samis have been portrayed."

We, the authors, have been received with the greatest kindness, and were given preferential treatment by all we associated with in the Troms District. Jan's benefactors from 1943, together with others who were indirectly involved and were drawn into the Baalsrud happenings, have reconstructed, explained, drawn maps and shared the dramatic details of those dangerous days in minute detail to us. Historians and reporters have generously shared their records and their knowledge.

Our research includes Jan Baalsrud's own report, documents from German war archives, reports, letters, interviews, and, from Jan's benefactors who have passed on, accounts which were previously unknown. All these things have helped us to put the facts in their proper places and given us a profound understanding of what took place.

It has taken five years and many trips to the Troms District to gather all the data. We hired a helicopter to fly us into the inaccessible areas (for most of us in the winter) of the Arctic Mountains where Jan trudged alone, wounded and hunted in freezing, stormy weather. We hired motorboats and crews to track down information and to understand the distances involved. And we hiked many a mile, visiting the Baalsrud cave in Skaidijonni and the Gentleman stone in the Revdal Mountains, and into Lyngsdalen where Jan was caught in the avalanche. We climbed precipitous mountains in our attempt to understand every fraction of this story. What you will read in this book will be new to many of you, but nothing is dramatized or fictitious. The story is filled with its own drama - it does not need any embellishments. All the details included are as we learned of them from the participants. Every boulder and small islet has been searched out, described and can be found on the maps we have included. Cross-checking of our sources, weather reports from the actual days in 1943 and the helpers' explanations have untied many a knot.

Even after all this, we struggled with some of the major happenings for five years. The reason is that the sources did not agree. Then, as we neared the end of our journey, small details led us in the right direction. Suddenly the puzzle pieces fit. Important, unexplained riddles were finally revealed to us.

The events of this story are all true; however, in the chapter "A Tragic Decision," we changed identifying names and relationships of people involved with the merchant in Bromnes so as not to bring unhappiness to their families.

Much of the dialogue presented in this book is actual conversation as recalled by the participants. Other conversation is based on the recollections of people still living. Where dialogue had to be re-created, we held fast to the facts.

Our foremost motive has been to honor not only Jan's courage, and that of the men of *Brattholm*, but also that of his selfless helpers, and to give an accurate and complete account of the whole Baalsrud affair. We believe we have accomplished this by searching out the many helpers who had never been mentioned before, either in books or films. Many of his helpers have passed on without being honored for their contributions. For them, our efforts are too late, but their self-sacrifice, toil and bold courage will continue to shine brightly for all of us.

The women's and the Samis' offerings have also been close to our hearts. The Baalsrud story would not be complete without mentioning the Sami brothers' contribution; Nils and Per Siri and Aslak and Per Thomas Baal are given a central place. The same goes for Hjalmar Steinnes and John Olav Ballovarre from Kåfjord and the brothers Leif and Rolf Bjørn in Birtavärre.

Jan's 11 friends from *M/K Brattholm* suffered a fate seldom brought to the forefront. We have written about their torment in our book, and though the horror of it might not suit itself to print, we have included it. By showing a glimpse of what they suffered for Norway, we hope to honor them.

When we first started to collect the background material for this book, we had no idea what a task we faced. It would have been an impossible undertaking without the willingness of all we approached. In our efforts to get to the truth, our innumerable questions, phone calls, letters and frequent interviews with many were always received with the greatest of courtesy and openness. Because of the help given us, the story of Jan Baalsrud and his benefactors will be an inspiration of selflessness and courage for many years to come. Our deepest thanks.

Astrid Karlsen Scott   Dr. Tore Haug
Olympia, Washington   Jessheim, Norway

GERMAN ATTACK AGAINST NORWAY LAST NIGHT
NORWAY AT WAR WITH GERMANY

Frightening newspaper headlines tell of the German invasion on Norway, April 9, 1940.

German soldiers march down Karl Johan's gate, Oslo's main street.

Reichskommissar Terboven and Minister President Quisling arrive at Akershus Castle.

AT ANCHOR IN SCALLOWAY

MARCH 22, 1943: "Well men, we are on our way home at last." Sigurd Eskeland, a tall slender man, broke the silence while with his fingers he made a small clearing on the train compartment's fogged up window.

"*Jaja,* and this time we are not leaving before we drive the devils out!" another chimed in. "If the Germans only knew what we have in store for them!" Jan Baalsrud flashed his handsome smile and with blue-gray eyes blazing, drew a finger across his throat.

"*Ja,* think about it. Our efforts might bring the war to a standstill in the north. That thought excites me!" The third man, Per Blindheim, straightened up and leaned toward his comrades. "Believe me – I'm eager to play a small part in liberating Norway."

The Norwegians returned to silence, each absorbed in his own thoughts, unaware of the train's rocking motion. The train sped from London through Scotland's lower Grampian Mountains en route to Aberdeen. Strong winds from the Atlantic Ocean brought dark clouds sloshing heavy rains against the windows, blurring their view of the Scottish Highlands.

The men were returning from a furlough in London. They had been selected for an extremely dangerous and top secret commando operation in northern Norway, in the Troms District. Though many military men felt this particular mission was suicidal, the saboteurs were anxious to be on their way.

March 23, 1943: A small fishing vessel took the Norwegians from Aberdeen to Scalloway in the Shetland Islands, a cluster of small islands off the northern tip of the Scottish coast, 210 miles west of southern Norway.

Scalloway Harbor where Brattholm *lay anchored*

During World War II, the Norwegian Resistance used the Shetland Islands as a base. They ferried refugees from Norway to Shetland in small fishing vessels and returned with supplies and trained resistance fighters.

Several boats bobbed at the quay in Scalloway including a 62-foot Norwegian fishing cutter, *M/K Brattholm*. The Norwegians spent the final day preparing for their upcoming journey, double-checking the ammunition, explosives and the other provisions and loading them into *Brattholm's* hull. In the early evening they were joined by the team's fourth saboteur, radiotelegrapher Gabriel Salvesen, who arrived by plane from London.

March 24, 1943: Evening shadows veiled *Brattholm* as she set forth from the quay heading for occupied Norway. Aboard, in addition to the four saboteurs and the seven-man crew, was Erik Reichelt, a man of vital importance to the operation codenamed *Martin*.

In the fall of 1942, Erik Reichelt had been sent as a courier to the Troms District by Consul Nielsen, chief of the S.O.E. branch at the British legation in Stockholm. Reichelt's assignment was to find men loyal to Norway and to get to know them and the Troms District. Reichelt was also to track down patriots willing to help saboteurs who would arrive later by boat. Reichelt had familiarized himself with the district and had come to know the resistance leaders in the area. The plan was that he would return to the Shetland Islands with the crew after he helped the saboteurs get established, and in contact with the incorruptible men in the Northland.

Brattholm's route across the north Atlantic, one of the most treacherous waterways in the world, was toward Senja, a large island 35 miles due south of the city of Tromsø, in northern Norway.

Brattholm, on her first voyage across the Atlantic, had left Norwegian waters under daring circumstances; her return passage, unquestionably, would be even more dramatic. A first-rate boat, she was heavily armed and well supplied with the best navigation equipment for crossing the high seas. Her beam was 18 feet, four inches wide and she had a nine-foot draw. A two-cylinder 60 horsepower Wichman motor enabled *Brattholm* to cruise at seven to eight knots.

Brattholm's skipper Sverre Odd Kvernhellen was much admired by the crew. Years of operating vessels in the Norwegian Sea and several Atlantic crossings had made Kvernhellen an exceptional navigator.

Machine guns hid in large fishing barrels on *Brattholm*'s deck, a camouflage to prove they were peaceful fishermen should they be approached by the enemy. Eight tons of dynamite, explosives, a hand radio transmitter, survival kits and other provisions filled *Brattholm*'s hull. All were necessary requirements for survival in the Arctic and had been carefully planned and chosen. She rode heavy in the water.

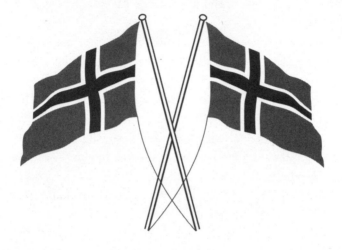

If there is anyone who still wonders why this war is being fought – let him look to Norway.

If there is anyone who has any delusions that this war could have been averted – let him look to Norway.

And, if there is anyone who doubts of the democratic will to win, again I say, let him look to Norway.

Franklin D. Roosevelt,
President of the United States of America,
September 16, 1942

M/K BRATTHOLM

SEPTEMBER 3, 1940: Leonard Larsen and his grandfather were enjoying a balmy Saturday evening on their Remøy Island farm when a man appeared. The stranger carried an unusual phonograph, and, without a word of explanation, started it up, but no sound emerged. In a heavy German accent, the man asked Leonard many questions. Leonard realized the conversation was being recorded and he became wary.

For the past several months, Leonard and his friend Alfred Remøy had worked for the Norwegian underground. The two young men and their friends Fritjof Remøy, John Remøy, Julius Remøy, Johan Remøy, and Lars Sævik, had helped many refugees escape occupied Norway across the Atlantic. All young bachelors, the men helped English and

M/K Brattholm *docked in Ålesund, Norway*

French soldiers as well as Norwegians.

After the stranger left, Leonard sought out Alfred Remøy and some of the other men who had helped the refugees. The mysterious man had been busy with his phonograph all across Remøy Island and the young men realized their peril.

"We must get away from Norway," Alfred urged. "If there is no room for us on any other fishing vessels, I will steal *Brattholm*." Alfred shared ownership of *M/K Brattholm* with two brothers, Petter and Arthur Sævik.

"It's pretty risky to take the vessel across the Atlantic," worried Leonard. "And it will be quite a blow to Petter and Arthur."

"*Ja*, but our lives are at stake," Alfred said. "This is war! If you men want to come along, we sail!"

The young men decided to make their escape while they could. A few nights later, as the dark autumn night blanketed the Norwegian coast and fear of the Nazis haunted every dwelling, *M/K Brattholm* lay moored near the Sæviks' home.

Taking care to muffle the sound of their oars, the seven resistance workers rowed a small boat toward *M/K Brattholm*. They had thoroughly planned their escape, but their nerves grew taut when the rowboat gently bumped up against *Brattholm*. In tense silence they attached a hawser to the fishing vessel and loosened the moorings.

They pulled the cutter 150 meters across the inlet to Skotholmen Islet.

The two strongest men pulled on each set of oars with all their might to get the 72-foot *Brattholm* to slide along the pier.

Oil was stored in barrels and tanks on Skotholmen. The young men broke into one of the tanks and filled *Brattholm's* bunker with fuel and lifted additional oil barrels onto *Brattholm*'s deck.

Another small dinghy, this one with an outboard motor, came forth from the darkness. A friend had agreed to tow *Brattholm* further out to sea. When the men felt sure that *Brattholm* could not be heard from the shore, they started her engine. By 5 a.m., the cutter was on the open sea.

A few hours later, Petter and Arthur Sævik were shaken when they discovered *Brattholm* missing.

"Arthur, *Brattholm* is gone!" Petter shrieked, looking through the window. "Call the police! The thieves can't have gone far. Have the police hunt them down!"

The woman who received the incoming call at the telephone exchange was an aunt of one of the young men aboard *Brattholm*.

"Unfortunately, there is no answer at the police station. I tried several times, but they must be out on a call. Please try later."

The aunt owned a small grocery store and she had helped the runaways with food for their voyage. She knew who had stolen the Sæviks' boat and she was determined to give them as long a head start as possible.

Furious, the Sævik brothers called back later, and finally reached the police. But *Brattholm* was now far out to sea, heading north. While planning the getaway, the young men expected that the theft would be reported immediately and they decided to set a course straight north, and later, northwest toward Iceland. That decision spared their discovery by German patrol planes sent out once the hijacking had been reported. The Germans assumed the runaways were heading west for the Shetland Islands, the destination point for most boats escaping from Norway.

The men aboard *Brattholm* heard the planes, but the thick Atlantic fog cloaked them in safety. The weather worsened with a heavy wind and high seas. The men moved the heavy oil barrels below deck to stop their constant rolling and to stabilize the vessel. *Brattholm* struggled against the storm. A beam tore loose and slammed into Fritjof's back. He was badly hurt and the men considered turning back to get him to a doctor, but Fritjof refused and they continued ahead.

The men's and *Brattholm's* relentless struggle ended when they reached Rejkjavik, Iceland's capital, five days later. They were welcomed by both Norwegian and English authorities, who had received advance notice of their arrival. The young men had planned to earn a living by fishing while in Iceland, but instead the boat was taken over by Nortraship and rented out to the British Navy Sea Transport. On November 18, the resistance workers were ordered to sail to Seydesfjord, on Iceland's east coast. For two years, the cutter carried English troops and supplies to and from the outposts in the Icelandic fjords.

In November 1942, *Brattholm* was recalled to Reykjavik. She and her crew were ordered to the Shetland Islands. Two armed whaleboats escorted them to Lerwich, in the Shetland Islands, without mishap. *Brattholm* was put into secret service between the Shetland Islands and Norway against the Germans. The seven Norwegian underground workers were sent on to London where some ended up in the Norwegian Merchant Marine and others in the Navy.

THE CONVOYS

FEBRUARY 2, 1942: A gruesome battle over Stalingrad in the Soviet Union took place between the Germans and the Russians. Germany lost the battle against the Russians but not before leaving the city in ashes. It would have been an impossible victory for the Soviet Union without the huge weapon supplies delivered from the United States and England.

When Denmark was attacked and invaded by the German Army in 1940, England occupied Iceland with the consensus of her people. Iceland was strategically located in the North Atlantic.

Convoys to the Soviet Union with war materials and other provisions were sent from the West via Iceland, the shortest and the safest route at the time. They sailed through the Arctic Ocean a few hundred nautical miles above the North Cape, the northern tip of Norway, and on to Murmansk and Archangel in the Soviet Union.

The plan worked well, with most ships bearing the desperately needed materials reaching their destination. The convoys only lost one ship, but after the first few months, the situation changed drastically.

Arctic pack ice forced the convoys within 300 nautical miles of the Norwegian coast.

To pinpoint the convoys' position, German reconnaissance planes were sent out from Bardufoss Airport in the Troms District, as well as seaplanes from Skatøyra seaplane-harbor close to the city of Tromsø, in the same district.

As summer had returned and the midnight sun did not set, it was easy for the German pilots to detect the convoys. The information from these sorties was forwarded to the German High Command.

Convoys were sent from the west via Iceland with war-materials. They sailed to Murmansk and Archangel in the Soviet Union through the Arctic Ocean above the northern tip of Norway.

June 27, 1942: Convoy P.Q.17 left Iceland for Archangel with 34 ships. German spy planes spotted them, and soon the German bombers and U-boats were on their way. They sank 23 ships and several hundred men went down.

Due to the terrible loss of lives and ships, the convoys were briefly halted. This caused large weapon supplies to accumulate in the West. In this serious situation the Allies had to find a way to stop German planes from flying out of northern Norway.

Early in the War, England had established an organization, Special Operations Executive (S.O.E.). Its purpose was to organize secret operations in countries occupied by the Germans. The Norwegian branch of the S.O.E. and the British had, for some time, planned sabotage activities against the German reconnaissance operations originating from the northern Norwegian airports. The military strategists felt these efforts, along with Russian participation in the defense of the convoys and strengthening Allied escorts, would make it reasonably safe for the convoys to resume.

The four saboteurs' assigned work placed them at the heart of the war. The importance of the men's success was beyond measure. A successful outcome of their actions could possibly shorten the war - though their lives were at risk.

Their most daring assignments, and crucial to the mission's success, was to detonate the air tower at Bardufoss Airport located 50 miles southeast of the city of Tromsø and to sink the seaplanes at the seaplane harbor in Tromsø. Jan Baalsrud, an expert swimmer, was charged with the perilous responsibility of affixing the explosives to the seaplanes' pontoons beneath the water.

The expedition leaders in England had high hopes for, and much confidence in, the operation planned so carefully in top secret meetings.

Martin Linge

THE LINGE COMPANY

WHEN HITLER'S war machine brutally attacked Norway on April 9, 1940, in reality, the battle was over within two months. But not everyone gave up. Many Norwegian youths wished to continue the fight; they had not capitulated morally. They wanted another chance against their powerful enemy. An inner moral strength, idealism, eagerness to fight and a deep love and patriotism for their country kept them going and were the motives behind their optimism.

After a while, many a Norwegian youth had to escape from Norway, and some were able to work their way over to England.

There they contacted the Norwegian division of S.O.E., where they received a short period of training before they were sent back to Norway on secret missions as early as the summer of 1940.

One man, Captain Martin Linge, participated in the battle at Åndalsnes. He was wounded, and came to England in September 1940. This idealistic man refused to give up the fight for Norway until she was liberated. He realized that the Germans were vulnerable, and that they could be thwarted as long as the right method was chosen.

He understood that specially trained Norwegian commando soldiers, who knew the Norwegian nature, climate, geography and the Norwegian temperament, could cause havoc for the enemy. Soon, Martin Linge was given the responsibility for representing the Norwegian Government in S.O.E. An office was established in London, and from there, Norwegian fugitives who arrived in London were recruited for these well-planned assignments. Linge personally selected the men.

In March of 1941, British forces together with Norwegian soldiers from England carried out a raid against Svolvær in Stamsund in the

Lofoten Islands in northern Norway. Linge led the Norwegian soldiers. The raid was successful; they did not lose one man.

Because of the success, they made the decision to further develop a Norwegian military company, about 200 men. In the end, the whole company was transferred to the Scottish Highlands, a place which was chosen with great care. The terrain was excellent for the type of training necessary for commando soldiers. The group was divided between three buildings, Glenmore Lodge, Forest Lodge and Drumintoul Lodge. Company Linge was given their own division within the Norwegian High Command in July 1941.

Company Linge participated in two separate raids against occupied Norway during Christmas of 1941, one raid against Reine in Lofoten and the other against Måløy. Again Captain Linge led the Norwegian forces. The Germans fought bravely, but in the end had to fall back. Captain Linge ran in front leading his men, and he reached his goal, but was felled by a bullet.

The Company had lost a great leader, and it was a heavy loss. But new leaders took over, and the assignments never stopped. That same year, plans were laid for sabotage work to begin along the Norwegian coast to be carried out by the Linge men.

FEARLESS MEN

THE FOUR saboteurs were members of the Linge Company, a group of selected Norwegian men who were part of the Special Operations Executive, S.O.E., and who received sabotage training in Scotland. They all lived for the opportunity to return to Norway to fight the Germans.

The Linge men were chosen for the special sabotage services because of their abilities. They were men from all walks of life, farmers and office workers, students and fishermen. For some, it was their first contact with the military. Others were veterans from the Winter War in Finland and in Norway.

Lieutenant Sigurd Eskeland was chosen as the *Brattholm* expedition's leader. Sigurd's slender build masked his physical strength. His wisdom and maturity qualified him for the job. He was 41 years old, born in Gjerstad by Risør in southern Norway.

Though several years senior to most of the men in Company Linge, Sigurd participated in the same training as the younger men without showing any sign of fatigue or lack of will.

Lt. Sigurd Eskeland

Aboard *Brattholm* he was the only man who knew the whole story and all the demanding tasks assigned the saboteurs once they reached Norway.

As a young man, he'd served for a time as a postal official in northern Norway. While there, he made many friends among the stalwart Norwegians in the Troms District and had become familiar with the city of Tromsø and the geography of the surrounding islands.

Later, Sigurd immigrated to Argentina where he became a successful mink farmer. Not long after he had established a comfortable future in Argentina, Germany attacked Norway. The news of the April 9, 1940 attack caused him great anguish. He left the comforts of his home and set out for Europe, arriving in England in May of 1941.

Second in command was 25-year-old Second Lieutenant Jan Baalsrud. He grew up in the city-center of Oslo, Norway's capital. Jan attended ILA School. When he was sixteen years old, his mother perished in a car accident. The oldest of three siblings, Jan shared with his father the

responsibility for taking care of his 12-year-old brother, Nils Ivar, and his eight-year-old sister, Bitten, fell to him.

Jan enjoyed sports - soccer was his favorite. He was a rough-and-ready guy with a tender heart and a high tolerance for pain.

Coal-black hair and dark brows framed Jan's resolute blue-gray eyes. Strikingly good-looking with an athletic build, he was 182 cm tall. In 1938, following a stint in the military, he traveled to Hannover, Germany where he studied cartography at Wetzlar. In

2nd Lt. Jan Baalsrud

1939, he received his certificate for apprenticeship as a land surveyor and instrument maker.

Two days before the Germans invaded Norway, Jan returned home from Junior Officer School in Fredrikstad. On April 9, he reported for service in the Norwegian Army. Later he saw combat at Østfold, south of Oslo near the Swedish border. His unit put up a gallant fight, but the Germans outmaneuvered and outnumbered them with their superior strength and war materials. Soon the Norwegians were surrounded.

Jan escaped to Sweden. Here, almost chaotic conditions existed because of the great influx of escapees coming across the borders. He was interned in Gothenberg; however, his former commander came to his defense and within three weeks he was freed.

The Swedes wanted to make use of his talent as an instrument maker, but Jan wanted to use his energies to help Norway. The Norwegian Embassy in Stockholm advised him to contact the British Embassy, who recruited him as a secret agent. In that capacity he made three trips to Norway from Sweden. During the hours of darkness Jan slipped across the border, and hid during the days. When able, he visited Gardemoen Airport and made rough drawings of the German fortifications and their ongoing construction, which he forwarded to England.

On Jan's third return trip to Sweden, the Swedish police arrested him. Tried in a Stockholm court, Jan was charged with espionage for a foreign country against a foreign country, and received a six-month jail term. After three months he was transferred to Varmland where his cellmate was the son of a ship owner. While in prison, his cellmate learned he had inherited a great deal of money from an aunt. The prison officials' attitudes changed toward the rich ship owner and his friend, and soon they were set free. They were ordered out of Sweden – a difficult situation for Jan, who was condemned to die by the Germans in Norway, and now had but two weeks to leave Sweden.

A few years earlier Madam Kollantay, a close friend of Stalin, had served as the Russian Ambassador to Norway. While serving in that position, she had become a warm friend of the Norwegian people. Presently she was the Russian Ambassador to Sweden, and she learned of Jan Baalsrud's plight. She arranged a visa for him enabling him to travel to Leningrad in the Soviet Union and continue on to Odessa on the Black Sea.

From Odessa, Jan traveled via Turkey on to Bombay, India. During his two-month stay in Bombay he met another Norwegian fugitive, Per Blindheim, and the two young men developed a deep friendship.

They traveled on to Aden, Mozambique, Durban, Cape Town, Brazil, Trinidad, the USA and Canada, and eventually London. In the spring of 1942, their six-month long journey ended when they arrived in Scotland and joined the Linge Company.

Sergeant Per Revold Blindheim came from Ålesund, and was the same age as Jan. Per was the son of a master baker who owned a bakery

located at Kirkegaten 8 in Ålesund, and he learned much of the trade from his father. Per finished middle school and business school and then followed in his father's footsteps, training as a baker.

When the Soviet Union launched an unprovoked attack on Finland on November 30, 1939, Per was angered at the injustice and volunteered to fight with Finland. At the war's end on March 8, 1940 Per returned home.

Sgt. Per Blindheim

Within weeks, his homeland was at war. He was mobilized into the Norwegian Army and fought at the battles of Romsdalen and Gudbrandsdalen Valleys.

Subsequent to Norway's capitulation, Per worked in an office in Ålesund, and later in Tromsø. Near the end of 1942 he escaped to Sweden with the hope of reaching England. Like Jan Baalsrud, he traveled nearly the world around to get there.

Per wanted a second chance to fight off the Nazi grip. He was an outdoorsman, and a loyal friend with a happy outlook, strong and yet compassionate. Without hesitation, Per fought for what to him was priceless, Norway's freedom.

The fourth saboteur, Sergeant Gabriel Salvesen, came from Farsund. He was among the many patriotic youths who raged against the Nazi occupation of Norway and had determined to fight against the tyranny. Like many other Norwegians, he escaped Norway and sailed across the Atlantic in a fishing vessel. He arrived in England in August 1941. The following spring he joined the Linge Company.

Salvesen was an experienced seafarer with great technical insight. He excelled in all his training, and became an excellent wireless

Sgt. Gabriel Salvesen

telegrapher. Within the Linge Company he was highly respected by his leaders and teammates. It came as no surprise when he was one of the four men chosen to participate in the perilous top secret mission to northern Norway. His mastery of wireless telegraphy was vital to the establishment of a radio communication system between occupied northern Norway and England.

Strong of mind and will, the four saboteurs were well trained for their mission, having spent months in England and Scotland preparing for this assignment. They'd learned every weapon skill and military drill known. The men climbed ropes up precipitous mountains and ran for hours through obstacle courses in difficult terrain. When near exhaustion, they swam raging rivers. They learned compass and map reading, and learned to deviate from true north because of the Earth's magnetic field. They studied Morse code and became proficient at receiving long messages by signals and lamps.

Quick to learn about fuses, detonators and explosives, they were given actual assignments to plan and execute, demolishing railways, oil refineries, and large construction sites. As the saboteurs gained confidence, their assignments grew in difficulty.

Highly qualified, with unique talents and strengths, these saboteurs from Company Linge, the Norwegian branch of the British Special Operation Executive (S.O.E.,) were among the best men Norway had to offer in the fight against Hitler.

Upon their arrival in Norway, their first task was to find a safe hiding place ashore for the explosives and the other provisions. The most daring assignment of their mission was to detonate the air tower at the Bardufoss Airport in the district of Troms. In addition they were to destroy German communication lines, disrupt anything they could, and blow up ferries. They were to slow down and halt, if possible, German troop movements. Lastly, they would organize

Erik Reichelt

and train small units of Norwegians in all types of sabotage work.

The expedition leaders at the headquarters in London had chosen early spring for this mission to increase the chances of the saboteurs' survival in the Arctic. The North Atlantic was frequently calmer at this time of the year, which made navigation easier for a small boat.

With the four saboteurs aboard *Brattholm* was another man, 25-year-old mate Erik Reichelt, from Kragerø. Erik had important work to perform once they landed in Norway. He was graduated from Middle school and Mate school. In 1941 Erik married Kari Rønning in Tønsberg. They had one child.

Since the beginning of the war, Erik had been heavily involved in intelligence work and in the transport of fugitives in Tønsberg and the Oslo area. He left Norway in 1942 but returned several times on secret missions.

His father, Captain Gerhard Reichelt, lost his life on December 21, 1941 when his ship, *D/S Annovare,* was torpedoed in the Atlantic Ocean. His brother, Borti, was shot in 1944.

CROSSING THE ATLANTIC

MARCH 24, 1943: *Brattholm* made good headway as she left the Shetland Islands heading northeast toward the Norwegian coast. The weather was pleasant and the seas calm. Some five hours after they had left Scalloway, with more than 200 miles to go, the engine acted up. It coughed, muttered, and sputtered until it gave out. The boat floated with the current, rolling and bobbing sideways on the swells. The cook turned green with seasickness from the motion and he retired below deck.

The rest of the men worked feverishly on the motor, their skipper joining in, but to no avail. The hours dragged on. It seemed an impossible task. Every test known was made. They continued work for the better part of the day, drifting helplessly in the North Atlantic. Eight hours after the motor stopped, they found the cause: a small metal piece in the oil conduit had stopped the flow of fuel to the motor. The piece was removed and the motor started easily.

Following the mishap, the motor functioned smoothly. With its steady thumping, and a speed of seven knots, the men sailed on.

The cook stayed below for most of the crossing, unable to attend to his duties. Per took over the cooking. His experience in his father's bakery in Ålesund made the men happy with the change - his cooking was a vast improvement over the food the cook had served.

March 26, 1943: The day dawned with a light cloud-cover and with some blue patches shining through. It looked to be another day with fairly good weather, and it gave the men more time to ensure the equipment was in top condition, to mentally contemplate their training in Scotland and to rehearse their challenge ahead. Each man aboard *Brattholm* knew

Machine guns were concealed in fishing barrels.

his assignment and was busy throughout the voyage.

Three German planes broke the calm productivity. One, a large four-engine bomber, flew low, heading straight for them.

"Action stations!" shouted captain Kvernhellen.

The men rushed to their positions by the fishing barrels with the concealed machine guns. The bomber circled the vessel a couple of times, and then, to everyone's surprise, turned and disappeared over the horizon. On other days the men spotted two warships. Since they paid *Brattholm* no mind, her crew assumed they were allies.

March 28, 1943: The Norwegians expected to reach their home waters this day. All peered toward the east, but Norway still hid on the horizon. The Germans kept close control of the Norwegian coastline. As *Brattholm* neared the coast, her passengers expected a German patrol to emerge at any moment. The saboteurs had to be prepared for all eventualities; hand grenades were readied and preparations to demolish *Brattholm,* should it be necessary, were taken. Under no circumstances could *Brattholm* be confiscated with all her papers, maps, ammunition and other provisions aboard.

A vague outline of the Norwegian coast came into view in the late afternoon. A deeply personal experience for these young men, the sight of their homeland brought a shine to their eyes. A cry went up, *"Alt for Norge,"* All for Norway!

"We're home at last!"

"Jaja, we'll give what it takes!"

"Nothing can stop us now."

"We'll make the Germans wish they had never come." The lively conversation broke loose in the midst of back slapping, hand clasping and hugs.

"Jaja. Now it is our turn!"

All were forced to leave Norway because of the war. Their lives had turned to chaos. Some had lost friends and family, but now they were back with a vengeance. Several of them had journeyed around the world before they landed in England and signed up with the Linge Company. Now the circle was complete: the Norwegian coast was close at hand.

Brattholm reached the Norwegian fishing limits and sailed within its boundary. German patrol planes paid no attention to the innocent looking cutter, shielding eight tons of explosives in her hull and plowing her way northward. The men, however, took note of the many German planes flying above them. All headed northward, no doubt toward the Arctic Ocean in search of the Allied convoys headed for Russia.

Salvesen looked up toward the sky. "We will soon put a stop to that!"

March 29, 1943: *Brattholm* and her twelve men arrived safely at their goal, the majestic island of Senja some 320 miles above the Arctic Circle. Occasionally, the prevailing winds enclose the island in a veil of low-hanging clouds; at other times fog completely blocks her beauty. But today, Norway's second largest island stood proud and tall. Linked together, a chain of boldfaced jagged granite mountains ranging from 200 to some 1800 feet high constituted Senja. Granite walls surrounded the island's narrow strips of land while the ocean skirted the frontage of the clustered, quaint homes. Small boats of every variety crowded the docks, some secured to the buoys. This was Norway! It felt good to be home.

The instructions were, when they reached Senja, to draw as near the mouth of Malangenfjord as possible. From there, Lieutenant Eskeland and Reichelt were to take the cutter's small boat and row up Malangenfjord 18 miles to Tromsø. The plan was thwarted when a German patrol boat shooed *Brattholm* away from the entrance to the fjord (the Germans did not wish to be disturbed during their pursuit of a Norwegian suspected of illegally listening to a radio). Eskeland and Captain Kvernhellen decided to go further north rather than risk contact. Happy to leave unscathed, the men were puzzled at the presence of the patrol boat. They had not been forewarned to expect any German patrols in this particular area, although information from northern Norway to England was scarcer than that from southern Norway.

As they journeyed north, Captain Kvernhellen and Eskeland pored over the maps. Archipelagos break up the sea-lanes in the Troms District and underwater boulders made it a treacherous journey.

They cruised north, now more than 300 miles above the Arctic Circle, on the outer side of Kvaløya Island; this area is called Sagaland, with many traces of the Viking period.

Some 32 miles north of Tromsø, *Brattholm* made her way between Sør Fugløy (Bird Island) and Sandøy Island. The blue-black cliffs of Fugløy heave themselves more than 1500 feet straight up from the water's surface, providing a home for more than 50 species of birds.

The vessel passed through Grøtøy Sound. With Grøtøy Island to the north, *Brattholm* swung around the tip of Rebbenes Island, past the headland of Toftefjordnes, and sailed on into a landlocked fjord on the north side of Rebbenes – the peaceful Toftefjord.

Around 4 p.m., *Brattholm* anchored safely off a small rockbound island, a calm undisturbed place. The islands protected *Brattholm* from open view. Here in the innermost area, the fjord was less than 2000 feet wide. When Captain Kvernhellen stopped the engine, a hush fell over the men. Arctic peace filled them with serenity. High mountain ridges, their ascent scattered with the dwarfed Arctic birches and other deciduous bushes and large boulders, shielded them to the south, east, and west. To the north where the fjord emptied out into the open sea, numerous small islands gave good coverage.

They had found the perfect hiding place.

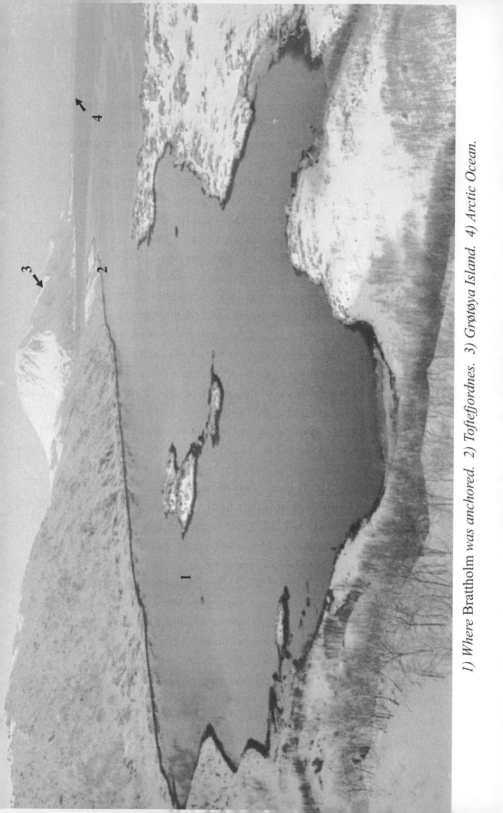

1) Where Brattholm *was anchored. 2) Toftefjordnes. 3) Grøtøya Island. 4) Arctic Ocean.*

I WON'T TELL A SOUL

MARCH 30, 1943: The map had not shown any buildings, so the men were surprised to discover a modest yellow cottage with a small barn partially hidden on the east side of the fjord. Soon after they secured the fishing vessel, Eskeland and Kvernhellen lowered *Brattholm's* motor dinghy and rowed to the shore to investigate.

They pulled the dinghy up among the rocks then trudged through the deep snow to the solitary cottage.

From the window, Haldis Idrupsen saw the two men approach her house. Her children saw them too and became curious. Haldis tensed. She was home alone with four of her five children, ranging in age from seven to seventeen. Her husband Hans was away at the Lofoten fishing grounds, with their oldest son Idrup. Lofoten, a 40-mile stretch of islands, lies 125 miles south of Toftefjord and is the richest cod-fishing field in the world. The two were not expected home for several weeks.

Haldis opened the door and greeted the strangers. The men told their fabricated story.

"Hallo. I'm Eskeland, this is my partner Kvernhellen."

Haldis nodded. "What are you doing in these parts?" She was still a little nervous.

"We are fishermen and have had a bit of bad luck - motor trouble."

"We need to get to Tromsø to buy some spare parts," Kvernhellen broke in.

Haldis caught a glimpse of a uniform collar protruding out from underneath one of the men's coveralls and wondered if the men were genuine. They seemed to be in earnest though and she dismissed it.

Haldis Idrupsen

The men wore Navy uniforms underneath their coveralls. The uniforms were issued to them before leaving the Shetland Islands for Norway. It was the hope of the English authorities that it would serve as a protection to them in case of capture.

"My husband is away fishing. I am afraid there is no one here who can help you."

Peder, her seventeen-year-old son, watched closely and listened intently to their story. He had

Idrupsen home in Toftefjord

been surprised when the fishing cutter with the Norwegian split flag flying high came in from the sea. But maybe it was not surprising considering that down the fjord a bit there was a fish-processing plant. He and the other children were used to seeing countless fishing vessels come and go. There seemed to be something unique, almost mystical, about this large fishing vessel anchored in sight of their home.

"You wouldn't know of anyone who could give us a lift to Tromsø, would you?" Eskeland queried Haldis.

"I know of two half-brothers on Grøtøy Island," Peter interrupted. "Since you are new to this district, I'll be happy to guide you over there."

"Thanks, but we're exhausted and worn out from the long hours of fishing the last few days. Think we'll turn in first."

They began to leave. Eskeland turned abruptly. "You don't have a telephone do you?"

"No. I wish we did, but such luxuries are not available in Toftefjord," laughed Haldis.

"It's so peaceful around here. Are you the only family in this area?"

"Oh no. Families are scattered around the islands. The nearest one is only about a mile away."

Eskeland raised his cap and nodded.

"So long then."

"Thanks for your help," Kvernhellen smiled and also started to leave, but he turned back to Haldis. "Oh, have you seen many Germans around here?"

"No, we haven't seen a German soldier in Toftefjord since the war began three years ago," Haldis answered.

"May they stay away the rest of the war. Thanks again." Eskeland concluded the conversation. He and Kvernhellen started for the boat.

"*Ha det bra,*" take care of yourselves, called Haldis.

The men were happy with the information they had learned, especially that the nearest neighbor lived about a mile or so away, and that the family did not have a telephone.

On leaving the Shetland Islands, the plan had been to contact a person in southern Troms, known to be quite reliable, and in whom the expedition leaders in England had great faith. Even so, when in their attempt to dock on the island of Senja they were forced out to sea by the German patrol boat, they had chosen Toftefjord because of its remote location, and the convenience of being fairly close to several other trustworthy contacts.

The next person they hoped to reach after their frustrated attempt at Senja was a merchant in Mikkelvik, a few miles from where they had anchored. Subsequent to their visit with the merchant, they intended to visit underground leaders Kaare Moursund and Tore Knudsen in Tromsø.

After the visit with the Idrupsens, Eskeland felt compelled to get the provisions hidden ashore and to be on their way. Under the cover of darkness, Eskeland, Kvernhellen and Blindheim took leave of the other men and set out into the fjord in their small boat. Second Lieutenant Baalsrud was left in charge of *Brattholm* and her men.

The boat chugged along on its three-mile-long journey out of Toftefjord into Vargsundet Sound and around the top of the island until it reached the sparsely populated area of Mikkelvik on Ringvassøy Island. The men looked up the merchant; his name was Peder Nilsen, but due to the late hour he had retired. Nilsen was a fur merchant and the young man who worked for him and who opened the door explained that there was another merchant in Bromnes, and that it was possibly him they were looking for. He had a Mikkelvik mailing address but his shop was in Bromnes. Returning to their boat, they continued on a northwesterly course toward Bromnes on Rebbenes Island.

On the southeast end of Rebbenes, one of the many smaller islands encircling the larger Ringvassøy Island, lay the tiny hamlet of Bromnes with a few closely built houses, and one general store, resembling a *fiskebu,* a fishermen's shelter. A couple of fishing dories lay moored at the dock, and the three *Brattholm* men engaged the men aboard in conversation.

"Getting ready to go out?"

"*Ja,* we're just about ready."

"We hear there is plenty of herring this season."

"That depends on how soon one gets to the fishing grounds. And if the weather holds."

Eskeland recounted his fabricated story. "We have had problems with our motor on this fishing trip. Somehow we've got to get to Tromsø for a spare part."

"That's quite a ways."

"What are the chances that you could give one of our men a lift to Tromsø to get help? We'll pay you well."

"No, I'm afraid not. We want to get to the fishing grounds while the herring is still plentiful," said one.

"I have a good friend," said Pål Olsen. "He runs the general store here in Bromnes. He could possibly be of help with transport, seeing that he owns his own boat."

Pål Olsen and Karl Johnsen, skipper of one of the boats, offered to take them to the friend's home, just a short walking distance away, close to the water. The house, like most homes in this area, was an unpretentious wood house – in this case a joint home/store combination. The general store supplied the islanders, as much as possible under the difficult wartime conditions, with many of their needs.

It was close to midnight when the proprietor was awakened from his sleep. He seemed befuddled by all the men waiting at his door at this unusual hour. PÅl introduced the three *Brattholm* men who repeated the story they'd told the fishermen earlier. "Could you help us get to Tromsø to pick up a spare part for the failing motor?" The proprietor shook his head; he was in the middle of taking inventory of all the livestock on Rebbenes, and this task would keep him too busy to make the 60-mile round trip to Tromsø by boat.

Eskeland knew the area well from his service as a postal official in the Troms District before the war. He had reliable information about the trustworthiness of the merchant of Bromnes, Anaton Pedersen, a man highly respected by all the islanders. Besides, there was only one merchant in the hamlet of Bromnes. But Anaton had passed away months earlier, and the news of his death was unknown to the saboteurs. The *Brattholm* men suggested they talk privately with the proprietor in the adjoining room.

"We're the men from England. We have a hull full of explosives, radio equipment and provisions. We were told you were willing and able to get men to help store such things."

The proprietor's eyes just widened. He looked at all three men, one at a time, and then nervously backed away, running trembling fingers through his disheveled hair. "What do you mean?" He asked, his voice cracking.

"We'll pay you well. 5000 *kroner.* And we'll throw in some white flour and tobacco."

"It's just a small thank you for your help." Kvernhellen smiled cheerily.

"We know flour and tobacco are in short supply and it's our way to help make life a little more pleasant for those of you who risk so much by aiding us," added Eskeland.

As the men talked, the proprietor's demeanor darkened and he became extremely anxious. Rubbing his hands together, he paced back and forth in the tight quarters, weighing the odds in his mind. Should he be caught in the act, or reported by one of the Nazi sympathizers who seemed to have eyes and ears everywhere, it would mean sure death for him and possibly his wife. The Gestapo's lack of mercy on those who aided the "enemy" was well known to all Norwegians.

Haakon Sørensen

"No, no. No!" He shook his head. "I can't help you! I have too many responsibilities."

As the conversation continued, the *Brattholm* men learned that the man with whom they were conversing was not the man they had come to see, Anaton Pedersen. In his stead was his assistant, Haakon Sørensen, a 38-year-old married man without any children. He took over as proprietor since Anaton's children were too young to take on the responsibility of running the store.

By the time Eskeland realized his mistake, that Haakon was not the man they had come to see, and that the man they had expected to see was dead, it was already too late.

"Check out Jernberg Kristiansen, and his half brother, Sedolf Andreassen on Grøtøy Island." Haakon appeared worried. "I'm sure Kristiansen will be happy to help you with transport to Tromsø." He made an attempt to sound encouraging.

"We've not had this conversation, you understand?" Eskeland stared at Haakon. "Don't breathe a word or it might mean trouble."

"Oh, I won't tell a soul. What good could come of that?" Haakon sighed with relief when the men prepared to go.

The unfortunate incident added further doubt and gloom to the men's spirits; the pressure to get the explosives safely ashore was mounting.

A TRAGIC DECISION

BROMNES, MARCH 30, 1943: Haakon Sørensen crawled back in bed a little after 1 a.m. His mind in turmoil, he was unable to sleep. He rehashed every word he had exchanged with the three mysterious men. "Who were they really? Were they Norwegian saboteurs as they claimed, or German provocateurs?" He tossed and turned.

Within the hour he tensed at another knock on the door. It was his friends returning. Pål and Karl had become a little suspicious and came to inquire what had happened. Haakon's wife also got up and joined them.

Extremely disturbed, Haakon forgot all about his promise and poured out all that Eskeland had told him.

He begged for advice on how to handle the situation. "What am I to do? Do you believe the story they told me about coming from England?" His friends just listened.

"If they really came from England, it would be a terrible misdeed to report them," Pål said.

"What about all the ammunition they brought? Are they telling the truth? How am I to know?" Haakon was at a loss for what to do.

"I smell a rat here. Maybe you should call the sheriff," his friend suggested.

"What if they are who they say they are, Norwegians fighting the Germans?" The merchant did not even hear his friend's suggestion, and rattled on in his agitated state. "If they are Norwegians, a telephone call to the sheriff would be disastrous!"

"*Ja*, but what if they are German provocateurs? Don't be an idiot, Haakon. Make the call!" prodded Pål.

Haakon glanced at his wife. "If I don't call and they were Germans sent to test us, we will both be imprisoned or shot." His friend urged him again to make the call and then he and Karl left. Haakon felt defeated. No matter which choice he made, he would be condemned.

Sleep escaped the merchant for the duration of the night. "Don't be an idiot Haakon!" reverberated through his mind. The visit from the *Brattholm* men bewildered him and he lay awake weighing his options. By the time the morning sunrays brightened the mountain ridges, he had made his decision.

The Bromnes store is in the building to the left. Haakon Sørensen made the call to Sheriff Hoel from Anaton Pederson's house on top of the hill.

The Sørensens did not have a telephone. Haakon threw on his pants, yesterday's shirt and added his heavy jacket. As he hurried up to the Pedersens' large white house on top of the hill, the wind was bitter cold.

When the Pedersens' door opened, Haakon was shivering – but not from the cold. The Pedersens were accustomed to Haakon using their phone. He was glad when the kitchen door closed and he was left alone in the hallway with the wooden wall phone. He hesitated. Still arguing with himself, he finally grabbed the earpiece. His hand jerked violently and the phone leaped from his hand. He had not realized how frightened he was. As the mouthpiece bounced off the wall, Haakon scrambled to grab it. He held it tightly in his left hand and with his right he cranked up the phone. Upon hearing the exchange operator's cheerful greeting, Haakon requested the sheriff; she told him it would just be a moment. It was a dreadfully long moment for Haakon.

The first ring! He rapidly drummed his fingers on the telephone writing rack, waiting for Sheriff Hoel on Karlsøy Island to pick up the telephone.

"Hello."

"Uh - uh, Sheriff Hoel?"

"*Jaja*, good morning!"

"This is merchant Sørensen at Bromnes."

"*Ja*, Sørensen, I recognize your voice." A painful silence followed.

"What can I do for you, Haakon?"

"I was away inventorying the cattle further in on the island yesterday."

"Yes, yes?"

"Well, something happened last night that I feel I should tell you about."

"Yes?"

The merchant spilled out every detail, all that he had learned from the three mysterious *Brattholm* men the night before. He told the sheriff of the fishing vessel docked at Toftefjord, and how the men aboard were in need of assistance to take a man to Tromsø for a badly needed spare part. He also volunteered that before they visited him they had already been to Mikkelvik.

"I will check into it. Thanks for the call." The telephone clicked.

Sheriff Hoel

In 1941 Sheriff Hoel joined the *National Samling,* (NS), National Unification Party, a political party founded in Norway in 1933 to support the Nazi movement. He joined as a result of a directive that had gone out from the ministry. All government workers had been warned that unless they joined NS, their jobs would be terminated. The cost of joining was 76 *kroner*, approximately $10 by today's exchange. In 1943 Sheriff Hoel had held the position as sheriff of Karlsøy municipality for 17 years. He was 56 years old.

Haakon Sørensen's early morning phone call and the story of the three men and their fishing cutter puzzled Hoel. He wondered why they would offer 5000 *kroner* for a 30-mile boat ride to Tromsø to pick up a spare part. Though he wasn't a Nazi, Hoel was terrified of the reprisal the Germans would inflict on him for not doing his job as sheriff. He immediately called the police station in Tromsø.

Edwin Wikan

Police officers Edwin Wikan and Einar Kjeldsen were on watch that evening between March 30 - 31, 1943. It was early morning when Sheriff Hoel came on the line. He instructed Wikan to call the Gestapo and to let him know the results.

Edwin Wikan was a police officer who refused to conform to Nazi orders. He tried to sabotage the call from Sheriff Hoel by not sending the message out. He hoped that by doing so, should the men in Toftefjord be patriots, they would have time to get away.

Some two hours later Hoel called back, and wanted to know what was happening. Police Officer Wikan took the call and said it had been delayed because of another important case that had come up, but that they soon would be able to call the Gestapo. He was asked to report the incident to the German Security Police at once, and he realized that this time there was no way around it - he had to call police president Fiane and relate what Hoel had reported.

At that point, Wikan did not know it, but Hoel himself had already called Hagen in the Norwegian State Police and Grau in the Gestapo Security Police.

Hagen, a friend of Hoel's, warned him to handle the happenings at Rebbenes Island with care, because German provocateurs might be the instigators. He suggested Hoel take the sheriff's boat out to Toftefjord for a closer look at the situation. Before leaving, Sheriff Hoel called merchant Nilsen in Mikkelvik and asked him to be on the lookout for further developments.

Next, Sheriff Hoel called his assistant Valdemar Figenchau, who lived at Vannskammen and asked him to take the boat ride out to Rebbenes

Island. No sooner had Hoel hung up the phone than Merchant Nilsen from Mikkelvik called and confirmed that an unknown vessel was docked in Toftefjord. Hoel then rescinded the command that sheriff assistant Figenchau go out to Rebbenes.

Karl Grau, Jr., a German translator, said the Gestapo would dispatch a boat with about 20 or 30 men aboard and that Hoel himself was to be on board to pilot them.

Obersturmbandführer Stage was in charge of the operation. He sent the largest and fastest boat available in Tromsø, a high-speed minesweeper from five minesweeper flotillas. Aboard were Adwehr soldiers, sailors and Gestapo folk (SIPO). Grau was also aboard and they picked up Sheriff Hoel en route.

Police station in Tromso where Edwin Wikan worked

ANYONE WHO...

4. PURSUES PROPAGANDA ACTIVITIES FOR AN ENEMY COUNTRY OR OTHERWISE REPRESENTS, OR OBTAINS OR SPREADS INFORMATION OR OTHER THINGS WHICH ARE DETRIMENTAL TO GERMAN INTERESTS, OR

5. LISTEN TO ANYONE OTHER THAN GERMAN OR GERMAN CONTROLLED OR STATIONARY RADIO TRANSMITTERS, OR...

....

WILL BE PUNISHED BY DEATH....

....

Oslo, October 12, 1942
Reichskommissar Für die
besetzten norwegischen
Gebiete Terboven.

BATTLE IN TOFTEFJORD

MARCH 30, 1943: Jan and the crew were anxious for the others to return. The relief on their faces was apparent when, shortly after midnight, the silhouette of the dinghy emerged from the shadows. Eskeland, Kvernhellen and Blindheim told the men aboard *Brattholm* about the disappointing conversation with the merchant Haakon Sørensen.

Together they discussed the many variables that could occur because of this twist in their plans. In the end, the decision was made to look up the fishermen recommended by the merchant. Soon after, Eskeland, Kvernhellen and Blindheim pushed off in their little dinghy and set out of the fjord northward toward Grøtøy Island.

They were glad for the cover of darkness and that only a moderate wind was blowing, though it was piercing. On arrival at Grøtøy, after introducing themselves and explaining their mission, Jernberg Kristiansen and his half-brother, Sedolf Andreassen, warmly welcomed the men. Eskeland did not mention that they had come from the Shetland Islands. Rather, he told them they had brought a fishing vessel up from southern Norway loaded with provisions of various kinds: explosives, weapons, ammunition and food. They were in desperate need of assistance to get the goods hidden ashore.

Happy to help with the mission, Jernberg and Sedolf immediately offered their assistance. They knew of a safe hiding place on the west side of Toftefjordnes, just under two miles from where *Brattholm* was docked, and they agreed to come and guide the cutter. The brothers arranged to meet them in Toftefjord the following day at 4 p.m.

They shook hands; both fishermen were elated to play a small part in helping to free Norway.

After their all-night excursion, the three men arrived, exhausted, back at the fishing vessel around eight in the morning. The weather was still holding, and they felt satisfied and somewhat encouraged with the help offered them by the half-brothers. All the same, an uneasy feeling tugged at Eskeland. He was not at all sure he could trust the merchant at Bromnes, who had promised to keep silent. They had to be prepared for all eventualities.

While Eskeland and the others searched for help, Jan examined the ammunition and weapons, making sure all things were in order. Charges with one-minute and seven-minute fuses were prepared. The intent was that the seven-minute fuse would ignite the eight tons of provisions, and the one-minute fuse was to be used in case of a surprise attack should they have to abandon the fishing vessel.

They placed the lists of people to contact with matches and a gasoline bottle. In case of an emergency, whoever was closest was to pour the gasoline over the papers and set a match to them.

As time passed, the men felt more at ease, and concluded that if the merchant had reported them, the Germans would have had plenty of time to have come from Tromsø by now. All twelve men were aboard, and they began thinking in terms of relaxing. The men from Grøtøy were expected at 4 p.m. and the *Brattholm* men had made all necessary preparations to have the provisions brought ashore at Toftefjordnes.

At noon they heard the monotonous drone of planes in the distance. Since they were far away, no precautions were taken. Now and then they heard a few shots fired at the approach to the fjord. The *Brattholm* men assumed they were German patrol planes carrying out their assignments. (Later, it was learned the Germans had been patrolling the entrance to the fjord to prevent *Brattholm* from leaving, should she attempt to do so. The shootings the men heard were warnings to fishing vessels to force them back into the fjord.)

The saboteurs looked forward to 4 p.m. when they could rid the boat of all evidence and see the crew safely on their way back to the Shetland Islands. The saboteurs were eager to finish their mission. They went below to take a well-earned rest. Sleep came easy to the weary men.

A short while later their peace was shattered.

"Germans! The Germans are here!" The shrill sound of the lookout's cry rang out on the deck; it bounced from bow to stern and penetrated the very guts of the fishing vessel. The men jumped from their berths. All signs of fatigue vanished. Their well-trained minds and bodies responded immediately to the alert. Was this not what they had trained for?

In the tight quarters below, they crashed into each other as they grabbed for their boots and hand weapons. They scrambled up the steep, narrow ladder, through the hatch, and onto the deck. Jan, on the way up, grabbed a Sten gun and his pistol. He bolted through the hatch onto the deck in time to see the top of the mast of a German warship above the rocky ledges of the islet. The thumping motor became noisier as the ship steadily approached them from behind the rock-bound isle, their protection from discovery. The ship cut off all possibilities of retreat.

Half of the fishing vessel was hidden by the elevated part of the isle where they had anchored. The distance from the Germans had narrowed to some 400 feet, and when *Brattholm* became fully visible to the warship, the Germans fired. *Brattholm*'s machine guns were dismantled, but the men instantly saw they could not win this fight taking the warship with frontal attack. *Brattholm* had to be blown up.

The deck was in total turmoil as the men tried to avoid the line of fire while carrying out their duties.

"Men! Abandon ship!" Kvernhellen yelled to the crew. "Leave all codes and compromising papers behind." The seven-man crew swiftly lowered one of the rowboats and jumped in one by one.

"Row!"

"It's too risky! They'll kill us!" Priceless moments were lost because the cook felt it too chancy to row away from *Brattholm*. The men switched back and forth and another of the crew took to the oars. They pushed away from the vessel and rowed rapidly toward the west side of the fjord, warning shots flying over their heads and the soldiers in fast pursuit.

The saboteurs stayed behind to wrap up their assignments. Eskeland and Blindheim scrambled down into the hold, lit the seven-minute fuse, and placed the radio equipment on top of the charge. Salvesen and Baalsrud poured the gasoline on the name list and lit it. Erik Reichelt held the second rowboat up close against *Brattholm* on the far side from the Germans, where they could not see him. He was to wait there until the other four had finished their work aboard the boat.

The warship rapidly neared *Brattholm*. Eskeland yelled at Jan to shoot at them with whatever he had. Jan aimed at the bridge and opened fire with his Sten gun. His gun was a mere toy against the Germans' powerful cannons, but it had the effect they hoped for. The warship momentarily stopped, which gave the four men an opportunity to almost complete their duties before it once more continued toward *Brattholm*.

The warship's intense fire persisted as the saboteurs finished their work. Most of the shots whistled above their heads and rammed into the mountain on the other side of the fjord. As soon as their tasks were completed, all four crouched and darted toward the rowboat. They vaulted over the railing and down into the boat Reichelt held waiting. Eskeland misjudged and splashed into the water; the others hauled him in.

Brattholm was deserted. The sputtering fuse and its small vapor of smoke were the only movements on deck. The men stayed low in the rowboat in *Brattholm's* shadow. The few short minutes they sat there and clung to the side of the boat felt like infinity. Across the fjord, the crew who had escaped in the first rowboat had reached the rocky beach on the west side of the fjord, only 500 feet away. Two of them were standing in the boat with their hands in the air; three others were ashore and in the process of giving up. One man, rendered incapacitated, probably shot, was sprawled across a rock a little further in; it looked to be the machinist. Captain Kvernhellen was the only one who had managed to head for cover.

Eskeland stared intently at his watch until the fuse had been burning five and a half minutes. To the second, the five had to push away from *Brattholm*. With all their strength, they rowed rapidly, taking advantage of *Brattholm*'s cover. It was only seconds before they became visible to the Germans a short distance away. Nothing but a little water separated them from the warship.

The moment they were seen, the Germans fired. At the same time, they lowered two rowboats with four soldiers in each. Both boats were rowed at high speed toward the west side of the fjord. The four Lingemen and Reichelt also rowed hard, heading for the east side of the beach.

The warship pulled up close to *Brattholm*. At the same moment, the seven-minute fuse went off. The men heard a muffled sound, and realized, to their horror, that it had failed. Only a small fire was burning. The Germans also had heard the noise, and saw the flames, and knew the danger brewing. In spite of the narrow and shallow strait, the Germans quickly reversed the warship and maneuvered a short distance away from the fishing cutter, all the while continuing the vigorous firing towards the little rowboat on its way to the shore.

Machine gun bullets whipped up the water around them, and the rowboat's wooden planks shattered, sending splinters flying through the air. The men heard the bullets slam into the rowboat on one side, boring themselves out the other. Amidst the panic, they shouted frantically to each other "Row on! Keep rowing!"

Blindheim, in a somewhat subdued, melancholy voice, turned to his friend Jan and said, "*Jaja* Jan, we were given a few good years together."

The boat had received too many hits. As if by a miracle, none of the men were hit. Tree-white splinters protruded all around the gaping holes left by the bullets and the water gushed in. It engulfed their feet and in the moment's bewilderment, left them paralyzed, unable to move.

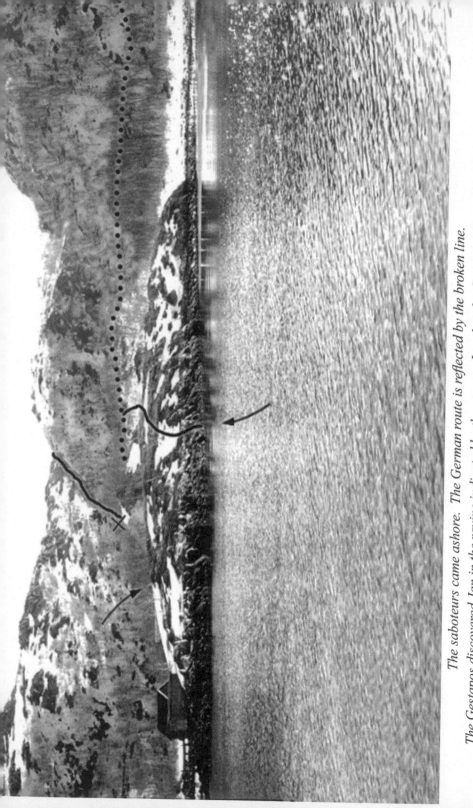

The saboteurs came ashore. The German route is reflected by the broken line.

The Gestapos discovered Jan in the ravine indicated by the arrow. Jan shot the Gestapo officer at the X.

EXPLOSION

MARCH 30, 1943: A thunderous boom filled the fjord. People from neighboring islands stopped their labors and turned toward Rebbenes Island as the roar reached them. The men in the sinking dory were hurled backwards and thrown on top of each other.

The eight tons of explosives in *Brattholm's* hull had ignited. Voluminous masses of water surrounding the cutter were thrust aside, and a huge forty-foot crater formed at the bottom of the fjord. Seconds later, the water plunged into the hole and out gushed a colossal tidal wave that rolled on to the shore. *Brattholm*'s masts were broken into short stubs, and whirled through the air like matchsticks. Pieces of engine, wheelhouse, lantern glass, metal and hatch covers flew over the five men. Burning oil barrels cut through the air, like torches and with big thuds, crashed into granite boulders far up the mountainside behind them.

In an instant, *Brattholm* was extinct. At the time the sea enclosed *Brattholm's* debris, a document case fell out of the sky and splashed onto the water's surface. It bobbed along on the huge waves like a life jacket. Aboard the *Schnell* boat an officer signaled to some soldiers to lower a rowboat. With shrill screams and frenzied gestures he pointed toward the document case. The rowboat splashed into the waves and moments later, their lucky discovery was brought back to the ship.

The bullet-ridden dory began sinking beneath the five men. Their only choice was to swim. At the moment Jan delivered himself to the glacial waters, the sock and rubber boot on his right foot got caught in the splintered boat and went down with the dinghy.

The frozen waters instantly permeated their uniforms and underclothes. The piercing cold jolted their flesh while the ice floes barred them from the shore. In their efforts to thrust floes aside with their bare hands, the ice forced the men backwards away from the shoreline. It was quicker to swim around the ice than it was to pass through it.

The hundred yards or so to the rocky seaside seemed so far. No one thought of surrendering, but the frigid water sapped their strength. Bullets crashed near them, cracking the ice; a miracle was needed.

A rowboat with four German soldiers worked its way around to the head of the fjord on the west side; simultaneously they kept a close eye on the five men swimming. The Germans' plan was to cut them off before they reached the rock-bound shore.

Baalsrud, Salvesen, Blindheim and Reichelt reached the bank followed by Eskeland a few feet back. All were utterly spent. Jan mustered his strength and crawled up the steep slope by the waterfront. He managed to crouch on a hillock behind a rock some yards higher up. Jan's right foot was bare, and yet the hardened snow did not appear to be any colder than the water. His uniform, heavy with saltwater, soon become rigid and creaked each time he moved; he was being encased in ice.

The rock was his only refuge from the dangers around him. He struggled to get in a position where he could look down toward his friends without being discovered by the Germans. All of them still lay exhausted by the water's edge. Per Blindheim dragged himself toward a rock, but a bullet penetrated the back of his head and he fell backwards halfway into the water. Dead. A sickening feeling engulfed Jan as he watched his good friend killed. Repeatedly he called for his other friends to follow him. Stillness was his only answer.

The warship continued its bombardment. The bullets rammed into the snow and the hillside down by the water. The German soldiers landed, but dared not stay too close to the edge for fear of being hit. Rather, they scrambled up the hillside away from where Jan was hiding. The snow up the slope was deeper than the snow down by the shoreline. With each laborious step the soldiers sank deeply, hampering their chase. Jan watched their movement between the gnarled black and white trunks of the dwarfed birch trees. He saw no way of escaping.

As fate would have it, the Germans suddenly noticed where he crouched. Tumbling down the hill towards him, they opened fire 150 feet away.

The saboteurs came ashore where author Tore Haug is sitting.

When Toftefjord is calm, part of M/K Brattholm's *twisted skeleton is visible on the bottom.*

Surprisingly, they ran past him towards the Idrupsens' house further down on the eastside, then towards the water's edge, blocking him from using that way as an escape route. To the left Jan now had four pursuers, behind him the warship and the water, and to the right, a path which led straight toward the Germans who had subjugated the crew. Momentarily Jan thought maybe the cold would win out. He felt as if the bitter chill would take his life. Only a few feet from him lay his dead friends.

Jan, a good sportsman and in top physical condition, had become a commando soldier through his training with the Linge Company in the Scottish Highlands. He let his instincts take over at the right moments. His overwhelming desire to live crushed the possibility of surrendering. Jan's iron will triumphed over the frigid Arctic, his exhaustion and bare foot, and the test of wits between him and his chasers. In a dire situation such as this, most men might sink into the deep snow, bow their heads, and plead for mercy. But like his Viking ancestors, admired for their bravery, fighting spirit, and extraordinary courage, Jan determined to take up the fight against the insurmountable odds. He had to act. Stooped over, almost to a crawling position, he bolted forward into the snow.

The four German soldiers who scrambled down the hillside had crossed a long deep furrow behind the hillock where Jan was hiding. In doing so, they disappeared from Jan's sight. He was not sure where they would come out, but he grabbed his only chance of escaping, and dashed straight toward the mountainside. Jan ran away from the water's edge, and headed for the Germans' newly made tracks; he crossed them, and pressed on directly toward a shallow ravine which swept upwards from the fjord, and which he had noticed between the birch trunks while he was observing the soldiers' movements.

This ravine was a little to the left of his hiding place and toward the Idrupsens' house, where the four Germans had disappeared over the ridge. Jan reasoned that in the ravine ahead, he would be hidden from the ship's barrage of death, and could possibly reach the top of the mountain that way. The four soldiers were still out of sight and he pushed onward.

Rushing through the deep snow, the Germans discovered him. Most likely they had intended to creep toward Jan at the water's edge and subdue him where he had hidden behind the rock. Astonished to see him 120 feet behind them on the way up the steep incline, they quickly turned and rushed toward him, demanding that he stop and surrender. Jan kept running. Filled with Viking spirit, no thought of relinquishing the fight ever entered his mind. Summoning his last strength, he tumbled through the deep snow. When Jan reached the ravine, he began clawing his way up the nearly vertical mountain, but the powdery snow had no favorites. Using the heavily intertwined underbrush, Jan pulled himself up a few feet, only to slip backwards and start anew. Jan's struggle weakened him, but he refused to give up. Only a few feet away, and yet so far, a large rock jutted out above him. With his indomitable will, he determined he *would* make it! Exerting all his strength, Jan threw himself behind the stone and pulled out his pistol.

The energy and vigor he had enjoyed earlier in the day had deserted him. The chill Arctic air hurt to inhale and he was cold, so very cold. Two choices were left open to him: he could continue the useless climb and die, or he could stay and fight. Jan cocked his pistol.

"*Halt! Halt! Ubergeben*!" Stop! Stop! Surrender! The Germans, hastening ever closer, called out for him to stop. The shots from their guns churned the snow around Jan like a foaming river.

Swiftly he popped his head out from behind the rock, aimed at the soldiers, and pulled the trigger. Nothing happened. He pulled the trigger again, and again and again. The pistol that had been at his side during the swim remained silent, crammed full of ice. The shouts from the German soldiers grew louder as they approached Jan's hiding place. With fingers blue and clumsy from cold, he feverishly dislodged the magazine and removed the first two cartridges.

Should the pistol not work this time, his life would end. Anew he swiftly popped his head out and fired. Relieved, Jan heard the pistol go off. The nearest soldier, a lieutenant in Gestapo uniform, received two hits. His arms shot heavenward and he fell backward into the snow. The soldier following him was wounded, but not mortally. The last two soldiers turned around in panic. They alternately ran and rolled down the steep slope toward the water and disappeared from sight.

COURAGE THAT DEFIED DEATH

MARCH 30, 1943: The snow clung to Jan's frozen uniform. Teeth chattering uncontrollably, Jan shivered in the merciless cold. He struggled with cramped, frozen fingers to force the pistol back in his pocket.

As the echoes of the final shots dissipated into the mountains, he took comfort in the sudden respite from the guns, and momentarily felt safe. An eerie stillness settled over the mountain slope broken only by Jan's breathing and movements.

From his vantage point behind the protruding rock he scanned the mountainside all the way up to the plateau nearly 200 feet above his head. It would be a strenuous climb. All the same, he had already climbed more than 100 feet. Compared with the view below, the snow above him was untouched, and spread itself like a huge, soft white blanket, beckoning him upward. The snow below was a patchwork of footprints, scattered spots of crimson blood and one dead Gestapo officer.

The ravine was Jan's only hope. Beginning in the marshes down by the fjord, the ravine cut deeply into the mountainside all the way up to the plateau. Here in the lower part of the ravine, he was concealed from the warship.

From across the fjord Jan heard screams, some quiet, others more piercing and sharp. There did not seem to be any complete sentences or clear instructions issued, just short yells. Between the shouts were long periods of quiet. During those moments, a tense stillness returned to the ravine on the mountainside. Jan knew what was taking place on the other side of the fjord: the yells were from his *Brattholm* friends, caught and mishandled by the Gestapo.

The arrow points to the mountain crest that shielded Jan from the warship.

Each shout reminded him of the urgent need to climb. Every muscle tensed as he struggled upward. Jan fought for a foothold. His frozen foot was an encumbrance but he grasped for small rocks, shrubs or birch tree trunks to cling to. He inched his way upward, continually slipping and sliding backward and starting all over again. The only thought in his mind was "climb!"

At the upper part of the ravine, the steep precipice on the south side no longer provided protection from the warship. Jan feared the moment he came into the Germans' view, their bullets would penetrate his body and he would roll down this mountain he had fought so hard to conquer. Memories flashed through his mind. He saw his former peaceful life: the family gatherings, his parents, and the hikes in the mountains with his father and younger brother Nils Ivar, his dear sister Bitten. In split seconds he relived the preparations for this mission, and he saw his friends, the men of *Brattholm*. Fear gripped him; he felt totally alone and unnerved. Yet, Jan possessed a natural determination; it unlocked his will. Jan's resolve to live surged up from deep within him and mingled with his iron will. He knew his chances were slim, but giving up and sacrificing himself to the Germans' baseness would accomplish nothing. He kept climbing.

The Germans sighted him and the guns roared out. The bullets lashed the snow into white waves that frothed around him. Pain. The snow turned red. Jan coiled up. A bullet had torn off the bottom part of his large right toe. "Will the next bullet end my life? I'm so close to the top. I must try." The cold snow and the freezing temperature prevented the wound from bleeding heavily. All the same, Jan's injury was extremely painful and made it almost impossible to climb. He managed to drag himself uphill a few more feet. He could hardly see in the stirred-up snow but crawling and scratching, he reached the plateau. The whole way up he fully expected that one last bullet would end it all.

The texture of the snow on the plateau was coarse. The sharp grains of the crusty snow felt like a grater scratching against his wound. He limped doubled over for a few steps, slipped and fell, pulled himself up again, then clawed and scratched his way inland and out of sight of the Germans. At last their bullets could not reach him anymore.

Enervated, Jan sank into a pile, and for a few seconds, lay still, gasping for breath. For the first time since he'd defended himself against and shot the Gestapo lieutenant, he could rest. Once more he noticed the fjord's silence. After lingering a few moments, he mustered strength and courage to crawl back to the brink of the mountain to see what was happening. With bated breath he looked down upon the blue-gray Toftefjord below. The German warship was quite visible. The deck was a scurry of activity.

Jan spotted his friends – the four men who had swum with him and the crew on the opposite side of the fjord. None of them were moving and he presumed they were all dead. He also spotted some of the widely-spread debris from *Brattholm*. German soldiers swarmed about; some had gone ashore on some of the smaller islets. "How could it all have gone so wrong?"

Jan scrutinized his chances, and was left feeling desperate. On this arctic mountain plateau with nothing but snowclad mountains and freezing water as far as he could see, loneliness and fear gnawed at him. He was in a place totally unknown to him. He was comforted by his knowledge of cartography, his good sense of direction and his memory. Seemingly he had lost his friends. He yearned to help them but he was powerless. The Germans would surely follow in his tracks soon. His wet clothes had long since frozen to ice and for the most part, his large toe on the bare foot was gone. Though death seemed imminent, he determined he would fight until the last pittance of strength left him. His courage defied death.

Jan knew he had to keep as warm as possible. He flapped his arms and limped about. Somehow he had to escape this forsaken place. On the east side of the mountain plateau, the snow was shallower; in places there were only patches. He tried to leap from one bare plot to the other as much as possible. In this way he hoped to baffle the Germans if they came up to the plateau hunting him. Sometimes he walked backwards in the snow to confuse his pursuers further.

For a long time Jan continued toward the southwest part of Rebbenes Island. He reached the periphery of the mountain. There were too many houses below to attempt that direction. Later people down in Leirstrand reported they had seen a man up on the mountain ridge. They had heard the roar from Toftefjord and they were on the lookout, but they puzzled over this stranger who disappeared seconds after he had appeared.

Jan turned eastward. He was unable to reckon time anymore but he had reached the end of the plateau and looked down on the little settlement of Bromnes. He looked over the scattered rooftops and yearned for help. Because of its nearness to Toftefjord, Jan realized this would be one of the first places the Germans would search.

The craggy, treacherous descent toward the shore was strenuous. Jan hung on to the scattered underbrush where it was not covered by snow. Clinging to jagged, protruding rocks, he slowly worked his way down toward the beach. He ended up some 300 feet from the little dock in Bromnes where the three men had come in to seek help the night before.

Jan was aware that the Germans would soon catch him unless he could find a way to fool them. Once he reached the shore, instead of going toward Bromnes and the built-up part of the village, he turned in the opposite direction and went northward. He went away from the people. Desperate, hungry, and suffering, Jan almost turned back toward Bromnes. He knew he'd find comfort in the village. In place of satisfying his urgent needs, he let his instinct rule and forced himself to take the opposite direction.

Along the shoreline there was no snow, which eliminated his worry of leaving tracks. There was a wide belt of slippery, icy seaweed that hid the sharp uneven beach rocks. It was nearly impossible to move forward. Jan slid in every direction and fell every-which-way each time he tried. It took all his concentration and progress was slow. He continued northward. A few feet on the inside of the seaweed, he found it wasn't slippery, but there were huge craggy rocks, boulders and clefts which he had to pass through or over.

Jan hurried as fast he was able; his only hope was to get away before the Germans arrived on top of the ridge. In his wild escape it was difficult to see where he was treading. Sometimes his wounded foot hit upon sharp rocks, which smarted. He was grateful when his foot hit even surfaces.

The craggy, treacherous descent down to Bromnes.

The blood had begun to seep out again. With his life at stake he would not let pain stop him.

After he had crossed the SmÅtrollneset he continued northward some distance. About 30 feet from the shore he spotted a small islet, about nine feet high and 45 feet wide. Maybe his pursuers would not see him if he was on the islet. To cross the wide belt of seaweed, Jan had to crawl. Even then he slipped and

*Jan waded out to the little island (indicated
by an arrow) when the tide was low.*

fell sideways, his arms and legs shooting out in every direction. Seaweed
and rocks hit his stomach and hips, but there wasn't time to be careful.
Jan repeatedly turned to search for Germans on the mountain ridge. He
knew he was a sitting duck for them. He reached the water and waded
in. His Navy uniform filled with ice water once more. Soon he had to
swim again.

For some time Jan had felt he was close to freezing to death. Should he
die here in the Arctic, his family would never know. For the rest of their
lives they would wonder what had happened to him. He did not want to
cause them that pain. It was the love of his family and his refusal to die
by himself that forced him to suffer this added cold. His body quivered
and his muscles stopped responding. His consciousness had slipped into
a strange emptiness filled only with a bizarre scenario of horror, pain,
aloneness, grief and utter despair. Yet he pushed himself forward. He
did not know where he was, nor where he wanted to go. But the calm
voice within always prompted him to go further, someplace away from
the nightmare he was living.

VÅRØYA ISLAND

MARCH 30, 1943: Small waves coursed around the islet as Jan grasped the wet beach rocks. Iced up and slippery, Jan attempted to hold on but lost his grip and slid backwards into the water. Moving to the left a few feet, it was easier and he was able to get a foothold.

Jan dragged himself up onto the islet and lay exhausted on his back. His uniform, soaked, was heavy and he hoped some of the water would run off before it froze. Jan's clothes soon creaked ominously anyway.

On top of the islet was a square deep hole. Jan exerted all his efforts to pull himself out of the water up over the edge and let himself fall in the hollow with a thump. He believed the Germans would reach the mountain ridges of Rebbenes shortly, but he hoped his enemy would not look for him on the islet.

His right foot was nearly numb. Covered with frozen blood and grime, part of the foot had turned a corpse white. A slow trickle of blood oozed out. His running, climbing and swerving had effectively kept the wound gaping. The pain had subsided somewhat, but he was aware that he had frostbite.

Jan sat up and tugged at his only boot. Full of water, it gurgled when he pulled and adhered to his foot. Wrenching on the boot sapped his stamina, but at last the boot gave way. The wet sock came off with the boot. He jerked it out and wrung it as best he could. With trembling fingers, Jan stretched the neck of the sock and bunched it up with his thumbs and fingers all the way down to the tip of the toe. It amazed him that such a simple thing could take so long a time and require such concentration. With infinite care he pulled it over his wounded toe, grimacing when it stuck to the wound or other rough parts of his foot. Once on, the sock felt comforting, almost warm. He slipped his bare left foot back into the soaked boot. Having both feet covered, though sparsely and wet, gave him solace.

Numbness brought on by the freezing cold gradually crept through his body. It was almost overwhelming. For two hours Jan tried to stay active. He lay on his back in the hollow and flapped his arms, but it was not enough. He crawled out and rolled back and forth on the 45-foot islet, keeping a steady eye on the mountain ridges across the fjord. He wondered if it really mattered. He felt sure if he stopped to rest, death would result. Though he feared the Germans, they were no longer his worst enemy. The bitter, all-encompassing cold was.

In the late afternoon he had clung to the rock for two hours when he heard voices and he saw several flashlights in the dim light. The Germans had arrived and they were hunting him. They searched carefully behind each rock and boulder and they signaled each other. Jan crawled back down in the hollow feeling confident they would never find him there. He watched the soldiers: they were rather unsystematic, almost as if they were frightened. After all, one Gestapo officer was dead and another wounded, and they were not sure they were safe.

Slowly they moved back over the grassy, rocky hillside, their voices

Jan's second swim was to the rock indicated by an arrow —
his third swim was to VÅrøya Island on the left.

became distant until he couldn't hear them any more nor see their flashlights. It became evident to Jan that the Germans knew he was alive. They still thought him to be on Rebbenes Island and were determined to hunt him down.

He had to get away from this little islet. It was too close to Rebbenes. Another 150 feet away he noticed a smaller rock about ten or 15 feet across and it only protruded above the water about three feet from what he could see. He waded into the water. The bottom here was even and at first it reached only up to his waist. But as he waded toward the rock, the bottom slanted sharply downward and Jan had to swim once again.

Frozen through, Jan pulled himself up on the outside of the rock. He was further away from the Germans here and felt safer. As long as he was lying down, no one could see him.

Jan had swum out to the little rock when the tide was out. Now he noticed the tide was returning. He continually had to crawl higher up on the rock. Soon only the top was visible above the water's surface. The rock would soon be covered completely and Jan had to take to the icy waters for the third time.

He only had two possibilities – he could return to Rebbenes where the Germans were or continue further out in a northerly direction towards the next island. Jan estimated the distance to be around 300 feet. The current looked strong but he knew he was a good swimmer. On the other hand, Rebbenes was much closer and maybe the Germans had given up hunting him by now. He reasoned he could work his way south toward the hamlet of Bromnes as soon as his pursuers had left Rebbenes.

He began to swim back toward the little round island. The strong current helped push him along.

He was about half way back to Rebbenes when he again heard German voices up in the hillside. Though dusk was approaching, he realized that to return to Rebbenes would be to sign his own death warrant. Jan turned. Now he was fighting the current, much stronger than he had realized. He hoped to find the rock he had left earlier, but the water completely covered it. Jan needed to rest and he was freezing, but he could not find the rock.

His only hope now was to reach the larger island, VÅrøya. Jan believed it was the island straight ahead, if he remembered the map right. If he was unable to reach it, the current would force him down to Bromnes and toward Ringvassøy Island, which would mean certain death. He would rather drown than fall into German hands.

As he realized how slowly he was moving, he tried to swim faster and harder, but his strokes became shorter and quicker. He was surrounded with black water; the current churned around him and formed large eddies which floated past him in the opposite direction. In spite of Jan's expert swimming ability, he was in the midst of his life's most grueling scuffle. He was about 25 feet from shore when his strength gave out. His muscles refused to function; they were stiff and they would not obey his strong mind. "Is this is how it will all end?" he asked himself.

Jan became aware that he was still alive when his whole body went into spasms as he lay partially in the water with the upper part of his body over a low rock. He did not remember how he got there. The spasms seized him and the unbearable pain forced him to move up into a crawling position. He moaned and twisted and moved as fast as he could. Finally he forced himself to limp along and after a while, the spasms weakened. Jan flopped back down on the uneven rocks, but was only able to stay down for a couple of minutes. The cold was getting the upper hand. He forced himself to move again.

Jan clutched the long dried up, ice-covered grasses and painstakingly pulled himself up again. VÅrøya Island was one of the smaller islands, midpoint in the sound between Rebbenes Island and Hersøya Island further east. VÅrøya's low rolling hills were bare of trees and most other vegetation, and were uninhabited. The terrain was low, reaching only a height of about 150 feet. Jan hid himself in the hollows to stay out of the Germans' sight. Though water streamed off his weary body, it wasn't long before his uniform stiffened again as it froze.

Jan forced his mind to concentrate, to think, and lay new plans. He ended up toward the east side of the island. Here he discovered yet another bay and another island toward the east. This surprised him. From his vantage point on the mountain plateau of Rebbenes Island it

*VÅrøya Island. Arrow shows where Jan was picked up
by Olaug and Dina.*

all looked like one large island. This bay was about 450 feet across, and he again noticed a strong current. The island ahead was much larger than the one he was on. In a cove he saw a compact two-story wooden house built on a slope and surrounded by a small field, not too far from the water's edge. He remembered he had seen this house from the plateau in Rebbenes.

While he was taking it all in, a small rowboat came from the south on its way into the sound. Two people were aboard. Jan tensed. Coming from the south as it was, the boat surely could not be Germans looking for him. Yet Jan felt safest hiding. The boat glided past through Vargsundet Sound.

Jan's situation had deteriorated and seemed utterly irreversible. His hope of finding some help here on the island had been dashed. There was nothing for any human being here. Darkness was slowly but steadily moving in. Alone here on this island at the mouth of the Arctic Ocean, without any hope of warmth or shelter, it would be impossible to withstand the cold for many more hours. In spite of all the suffering he had experienced in the hours since the Germans overwhelmed them in Toftefjord, Jan knew what he had to do. He had to leave this island also - but how? Only frigid water with a strong current surrounded him.

In the oncoming dusk, across the water, the Germans' torches flickered back and forth, signaling each other. He wondered how much longer they would hunt him tonight – or did they even realize one man had escaped? While watching them, he felt the temperature drop by several degrees. Time was running out.

Jan limped back and forth as best he could. He looked toward the newly-discovered island and the house. The current looked swift, but he had no choice. Warm rays of light cast their glow on the snow beneath the little windows and smoke had been visible from the chimney before the twilight shadows blocked the view. How comforting it would be to be dry and warm again. He had to act now! Slowly he crept over icy, slippery rocks and headed straight for the water's edge.

Suddenly Jan became aware of children playing close to the house, and he momentarily stopped and watched them. They were veiled in mist but their voices reached him. Yes! It was children's voices. Deep emotion gripped him as he heard their playful sounds. A new thought formed in his mind. Maybe it would work?

He had to be careful not to be seen or heard on Rebbenes Island behind him.

"Ho, ho. Ho, ho!"

"Ho, ho. Ho, ho!"

One of the children heard him. She grabbed the arm of another. The playing stopped. All the children turned and looked toward him, or was he imagining? It was getting so dark it was difficult to see. But then the most delightful sounds reached him.

"Ho-ho, Ho-ho!"

It was nearly seven in the evening. Olaug and her cousin Dina thought it was Peder, Olaug's brother who had returned from fishing, though they did not quite understand why he was over on VÅrøya Island. They left the other children, jumped into the rowboat, and headed out to pick him up.

"Peder!" they called as they neared the island.

"Ho -ho," came the answer.

They had almost reached the shore before they discovered that it was not Peder. The girls began to turn the boat around. They relaxed a little when the man spoke Norwegian.

"Come back! I am not dangerous." The stranger spoke with a southern dialect. They rowed to the shore and picked him up.

Jan did not know it was possible to be so cold for this long and still live. His whole body shook violently as he crawled in the boat. His body began to cramp again and he massaged his arms and legs while the girls started to row. Jan took out his pistol and said, "Remember, if we are discovered before we reach the shore, it was I who forced you to row me across." He patted his pistol and the teenage girls understood.

From left, Olaug Idrupsen, Dina Pedersen, and Dagmar Idrupsen

*I venture to say no war
can be long carried on
against the will of the people.*

— Edmund Berke

THE GESTAPO BRINGS TERROR

MARCH 30, 1943: Amidst the fresh and transparent purity of the Arctic solitude on this idyllic spring afternoon in late March, the two youngest Idrupsen children, without knowing, used the splendor of the day to its fullest. They frolicked in the deep snow outside their home in Toftefjord. The fun the rosy-cheeked siblings shared eclipsed the chill of the wind brought in from the frigid iced-up fjord.

The peaceful surroundings were disturbed only by the delighted squeals coming from seven-year old Halvor and his 12-year old sister Dagmar. Inside, close to the kitchen's cozy-warm black wood stove, big sister Olaug was helping her mother with the dinner dishes; it gave them a chance to visit without interruptions from the younger children.

The previous day, two men from the fishing vessel *Brattholm*, still anchored by the solitary island in the narrow fjord, had been ashore and visited them. *Brattholm* added to the tranquility of the day as it rolled in the gentle whitecaps. Chunks of broken off ice floated close up to the boat.

The children playing on the lower hillside could easily see the movements on the deck and found it exciting to have this large fishing vessel so close at hand, and all to themselves.

"Halvor, would it not be fun if the men returned and let us visit them on the boat?"

"I am first," Halvor demanded.

Suddenly the humming of an engine from the fjord behind the headland reached the children. They leaped for joy; it was a boat and obviously it had to be Papa and their brother Idrup, the children believed, returning from the fishing grounds early. Papa always, on his return from his trips, brought a surprise package for the children, which made his returns even more exciting.

The boat came into view, but it was not Papa's. Rather, it was a huge, dark and threatening boat unknown to the children, outfitted with bulky cannons, and soldiers with rifles on the deck. Dagmar supposed something was terribly wrong. The murky boat and the soldiers with their pointed rifles gave her an ominous feeling. She called for Halvor to come, grabbed his wrist and the two darted towards the house. She tore the kitchen door open, and they rushed in to the safety of their family.

"Did you see your papa?" her mother asked, peering through the tiny kitchen window panes without really looking, at the same time pointing out at an angle toward the mouth of the fjord.

"But Mama, can't you see?" Dagmar's frightened eyes and gestures startled her.

The mother looked and saw - a German warship! She suddenly understood the connection between the fishing vessel and the warship and froze in place. She hardly had time to react before the shooting began.

"They're going to kill everyone!" the mother cried out in horror.

The Idrupsens fled up the hillside behind their home.

The family heard the cracking guns and shouts from terror-stricken men aboard the fishing vessel. Whining projectiles flew about. Haldis made a quick decision; they were leaving their home. Swiftly they grabbed only the most necessary clothes to ward off the cold. The children clustered about her as she fumbled to lock the door behind them.

The family scattered and rushed, struggling up the craggy snow- covered hillside behind their house. Upward they climbed toward the plateau.

The Idrupsens had only reached about halfway up the slope when a deafening explosion rolled over them coming from the fjord; the mountains, unable to hold the noise, sent it back out again over the fjord. The leafless birches all around them and up the other mountainsides encircling the fjord laid down flat as if a strong hurricane was blowing grass and lanky stemmed flowers that could not withstand the force. Burning oil barrels flew through the air like tiny toys, landing up in the mountain outcrops. Black smoke rose from where the fishing vessel had been anchored. It was gone! Several rowboats were in the water. Yells and shooting vibrated around the fjord that had stood undisturbed for thousands of years but now, in a flash, had been transformed into a burning combat zone. War had come to their tranquil Toftefjord.

Halvor and Dagmar ran in front up the hillside. Olaug stayed back a little, and waited for her mother, fraught with fear and exhaustion. Once the roar eased and the echo silenced, they still heard thuds of wreckage fall to the earth. All the way up on the plateau some of the pieces fell.

Haldis was breathless. Coming to a standstill, she sank down on a rock almost hysterical.

"They have no consideration for others," she cried. "We might as well give up, we're all going to die!" Dagmar ran back down to her mother, trying with Olaug, to comfort her as best a 12-year old could. They steadied her between them and brought her, still sobbing now and then, up to the plateau.

On the plateau, it was nearly flat and there were only patches of snow. They were able to hurry along. The family headed for the steep slope on the east side of Rebbenes. Across the Vargsund Sound, on the island of Hersøy, they had family. Aunt Anna Pedersen and her children lived there in a dark green wooden house.

From the water's edge, they could see Aunt Anna's house on the other island. They jumped about, shouted, and waved their arms in hopes that somebody on Hersøy, a half mile away, would notice.

Home with Anna Pedersen were her three children Ingvald, Ragnar and Dina. Her husband Hans, like most of the men around these islands, was away fishing in the Lofoten Islands. Anna and her family had heard the explosion and were extremely anxious to know how their family on Ringvassøy was. They kept looking out across the sound, hoping that somehow Haldis and the children would come into view. Joy surged through them when they did see their family waving from the other shore. Ragnar and Ingvald quickly ran down to the dock, scrambled into the rowboat and rowed to pick them up.

Between sobs, Haldis and the children told of the happenings in Toftefjord. Anna Pedersen sickened as the story unfolded. Such horror was not known here among these peaceful islands. Though they were aware a war was raging in their country, up to now they had mostly been left untouched by it. Ingvald became anxious to get the whole story and rowed over to Bromnes to learn about the happenings of the last few days. He tied his boat to the dock in Bromnes. There he learned the fishermen aboard *Brattholm* had been betrayed by the merchant in Bromnes and reported to the sheriff at Karlsøy. Ivanna Pedersen, Anaton Pedersen's widow, the man the saboteurs were supposed to have met up with, was furious. She said that had she known that these men would be informed on, she would have cut the telephone wire for Haakon Sørensen.

The two women sat by the little kitchen table and over a cup of coffee spoke of the events that had just happened. They both felt comforted being together. Suddenly their lives had turned about, changing from serenity to fear and insecurity. If only their husbands had been home they could have drawn from their strength. Anna's son, Ingvald, was still away at Bromnes, while the other cousins played together outside.

"It's amazing how children are able to regain their composure so quickly," sighed Anna.

They kept a lookout for Peder, Haldis' son. He had been fishing, supposedly close to Rebbenes, when the fighting began in Toftefjord. No one knew where he could be found.

A SICKENING FEAR

MARCH 30, 1943: Small fishing vessels dotted Grøtsund Sound just outside of Toftefjord. Peder Idrupsen, Haldis' son, was on one of them. The fishermen enjoyed the peaceful afternoon until two approaching German fighter planes and a bomber shattered the tranquility. Warning shots were fired at the fishermen at the mouth of the sound, driving them back into the fjord. Then the planes turned, headed into the inner fjord, and swooped down close to Peder. His nose filled with the exhaust and hurriedly he pulled his lines in and started rowing homeward. The planes flew away.

Peder Idrupsen

When Peder reached the outcrop between Andammen Island and Toftefjord, he heard a loud, steady drone coming from the direction of BÅrdset Sound among the outer islands. A German Schnell-boat headed for Toftefjord! He felt sure there was a connection between the fishermen anchored close to his home and the warship. Soon shooting began and shortly afterwards, a deafening explosion. The racket echoed across the water and black smoke billowed skyward. It settled over Godstrandtinden Peak in the distance.

Concerned about his family, Peder rapidly rowed homeward. But a young girl from the only family living at Toftefjordnes came running down to the edge of the water, and screamed "Don't go any further!"

Peder set ashore. Borrowing binoculars, he ran to the nearest hilltop. All he could see in Toftefjord was the warship. *Brattholm* was gone!

Several rowboats were in the fjord and it looked like the Germans had taken prisoners and were bringing them aboard the Schnell-boat. The fishing cutter had vanished. Peder stood and watched the warship leave Toftefjord.

Soon after, he rowed home. Toftefjord and the beach, even the tree branches were littered with *Brattholm*'s wreckage. Myriads of cigarettes floated among the debris along the shoreline. Peder pulled his rowboat up on the rocky beach and sprinted toward his little home. On the way he saw several razors, pieces of wood and iron rods. All the windows were blown out in both his home and the nearby barn where the animals bleated their terror. The front door to the house was locked! They had never locked the door before. Peder ran around the house to the back. The back door was open, swinging on its hinges.

Rushing into the house, Peder called for his family.

"Mother! Olaug! I'm home! I'm home!" No answer. The only sound was the wind, still chill under winter's grasp, rustling the curtains through the broken windows. The kitchen was in disarray and leftover dinner was scattered among broken dishes on the counter and the floor and kitchen chairs were turned over.

Panic gripped Peder. "Where are my siblings and mother? Have the Germans taken them prisoner?"

Everything had happened so quickly. There was no time to think or reason; he did not know where to turn. "Maybe they had been able to escape? But where can I find them?"

He pondered these questions as he walked among the wreckage scattered across their beach lot. The fjord was still filled with floating rubble. Now Peder noticed that even the surrounding mountains held scattered debris.

A man came skiing down the mountainside, a friend from Leirstrand who was concerned about the family's well being. Peder did not know what had happened to them but he had decided to row out to his aunt Anna Pedersen on Hersøy Island. The friend accompanied him.

A WARM WELCOME ON HERSØY ISLAND

Hersøy, March 30, 1943: Jan helped the girls secure the boat. "You're so wet and cold. You've got to come home with us!" Dina pointed to the house Jan had seen from VÅrøya Island. "That's my home."

Anna Pedersen and Haldis Idrupsen were horrified when they saw who the girls brought home.

There were no questions. The women immediately knew where this man had come from. Like mothers know so well to do, they saw a need and went to work. A kettle of water was put on the stove to heat. Off came Jan's navy uniform and the underwear. On went warm wool undergarments belonging to Anna's husband. While Haldis rinsed Jan's clothes out in water

Anna Pedersen

to get rid of the salt, Anna stoked the range with wood the children had brought. Soon the little kitchen heated up until it was nearly impossible to remain inside. The women massaged Jan's arms and legs to start circulation, and then they cleaned and bandaged his foot.

The women gave Jan a blanket to wrap around himself and hung his clothes to dry over the range. Jan recovered quickly and a spirited conversation ensued. He explained the fate of his comrades and the subsequent events. Children and adults listened horror-struck. The event could not be hidden from the children; they had heard the explosion and their cousins' and aunt Haldis' explanation.

Anna Pedersen's home on Hersøy

All found Jan's good disposition following such a disaster amazing. He was able to both tease and laugh, and showed no sign of fear. "I'll be back in London celebrating in two weeks," he joked. His upbeat mood was a completely natural occurrence. Known as psychological euphoria, it sometimes happens after a devastating experience such as Jan had suffered. But Jan felt the weight of the tragedy as well.

His main concern was for this caring family. He told them exactly what to say when the Germans came searching. Jan had no doubt they would come around, because of the Pedersens' vicinity to Toftefjord. "And remember, I threatened you with my pistol to do as I commanded," Jan said as he pointed to the pistol lying close by him on the kitchen table.

Anna's son Ingvald returned from his row-trip to Bromnes. He gave the details of what he had learned and Jan understood why the Germans had launched the surprise attack against *Brattholm.*

Jan planned to leave as soon as his clothes dried. He had to protect this beautiful family even if they had no thought for themselves. Two of the older girls stood watch outside. Should someone approach they were to come in and give warning. Two boats arrived and docked. The girls ran in to warn Jan and he rushed outside and hid behind some large boulders. The first boat held friends of the family wanting to know if the Pedersen family was all right after the huge explosion. The second boat held Peder Idrupsen and his friend.

Peder left the man in the boat while he went to check on his aunt and her family. On the way up to his aunt's house, his cousin Ingvald ran to meet him.

"Who is the man in the boat?"

"Just a friend from Leirstrand."

"Hurry! Take him away. We have one of the escapees from *Brattholm* here!"

Just then Peder saw Jan pop his head out behind one of the rocks. Peder hurried back to the dock.

"Thank goodness Mother and all the others are here. They are just fine. I'll take you back to Leirstrand." Peder untied the boat stepped in and rowed off.

Once Jan was back inside, Anna found him a pair of socks and an old seaman's boot that fit his wounded right foot. Jan kept the military boot; it would not be as slippery.

He discussed with Ingvald and Ragnar how to best continue his escape. They decided that Ingvald would row Jan the nearly two miles to Mikkelvik on Ringvassøy Island. The family sketched out a map for him and gave him information about people they knew along the chosen route. They told Jan who was trustworthy, where the Nazis lived, and the built-up areas he should avoid. Jan memorized the map and burned it. Around 1 a.m. he left with Ingvald.

"*Tusen, tusen takk,*" thousands and thousands of thanks. "No words can express my deep gratitude for all you have done for me. I promise you, I'll never be caught. You have nothing to worry about."

"Be careful, Jan. Remember who to stay away from."

"So long."

Ingvald and Jan slipped down to the dock and set out into the fjord in silence. There was no place to hide out on the open water. The thump of the oars echoed across the channel. This late in the year, even at the hour they had chosen, the Arctic night was only murky gray when the sky was fairly clear as it was tonight. If the Germans were still out hunting an escapee, their chances of success were good this evening.

Toftefjord, March 31, 1943: In the wee hours of the morning, Haldis Idrupsen and her children left for home shortly after Ingvald left with

Jan. Haldis was appalled at the sight of her home. With all the windows broken, the cottage was ice cold and in total chaos. Their home was wrecked, but under the circumstances they had so much to be grateful for. They still had each other.

The night was a sleepless and uncomfortable one for the Idrupsen family. Early in the morning they heard a large boat. They woke each other and rushed to the glassless windows.

"German soldiers! They are returning!"

The terror-stricken children began to cry. The horrors of yesterday were still too vivid in their innocent minds. They watched the soldiers lower a small skiff and approach the house. Soon they banged on the door with a gun butt.

"*Guten morgen!*"

"Come in." Haldis replied. Her offer was rejected – the family was ordered outside. Peder placed himself close to his mother to protect her. The Germans had brought a translator and began their interrogation. They wanted to know all the family knew.

"Are you aware that one man from *Brattholm* escaped?

"No."

"When is the next boat from England expected in Toftefjord?"

"We don't know anything," answered Haldis.

"I don't know of any boats. Don't you think *one* is more than enough?" interrupted Peder. The officer in charge gave him an icy stare. He left no doubt that such a rash remark was received with disdain. Haldis nudged her son. Both shuddered unnoticed.

The soldiers searched the house and the barn. Behind the door in the cow barn Haldis' husband Hans kept his rifle and a shotgun. The soldiers did not discover it.

The family breathed a sigh of relief when the Germans returned to the warship.

Peder was frightened at the thought of their return. The following day he took his father's guns, rowed far out into the fjord, and threw them overboard. They could not take any chances.

TROMSØ HAPPENINGS

THE NORWEGIAN Navy had worked to build up intelligence services along the coast in northern Norway as early as the summer of 1940. Editor Oscar Larsen in the newspaper *Tromsø* had heard rumors about this. He realized the importance of building an intelligence service before the Gestapo was able to infiltrate the population.

One day in the late summer of 1940, Larsen gathered several prominent persons in Tromsø to a secret meeting in his home. Eight men were present including Larsen, editorial secretary Tor Knudsen and department head Kaare Moursund. The men discussed how to build a resistance group and what they could do.

Knudsen and Moursund became two of the most actively involved people in building up the resistance movement. Before long, they had organized several smaller resistance groups throughout the Troms District. Knudsen and Moursund were responsible for collecting funds for needed activities, including the printing and distribution of underground newspapers, the installation of clandestine radio transmitters, and the establishment of lines of communication in the Tromsø region.

In the spring of 1941 a radio transmitter was opened in the attic of the office building of the *Tromsø* newspaper. Telegrapher Egil Lindberg attended the station. Later it was moved to the attic at Tromsø Merchant Bank. The bank was located about 20 feet from the Gestapo headquarters in Bankgaten 13. The problem was that the street lamps flickered each time the telegraph keys clicked. The transmitter was again moved, this time to the tower at the Tromsø Hospital.

One evening in the late fall of 1942, a man rang Kaare Moursund's doorbell. The man introduced himself as Erik Reichelt. He said he had just arrived from London. Moursund's wife and medical student Sverre Sandmo were present at the time, and Tor Knudsen had dropped in for a cup of coffee.

Reichelt was originally from the Skien district, and he had come to Tromsø to gather information. He was interested in what the people in the area felt about the occupation authorities, and what the mood was among the Norwegians in the Troms District. He was particularly interested in learning about the mine fields in Kvalsund, Langsund and Malangen. These were the most important gateways to Tromsø. Moursund promised Reichelt he'd contact the pilots aboard the local boats to learn more about the mine fields. The discussions lasted about two hours before everyone went his own way. Reichelt never mentioned a word about the planned *Brattholm* expedition that would arrive only four months later.

FATE OF THE BRATTHOLM MEN

TROMSØ, MARCH 30, 1943: Per Blindheim was killed at Toftefjord. Skipper Kvernhellen had been able to hide for some time, but was eventually captured before the warship sailed out of the fjord.

When the *Schnell* boat arrived in Toftefjord and the shooting battle began, Sheriff Hoel had become quite disturbed and retired below deck. He was still aboard as the warship made its way up the fjord to the Tromsø docks with the men captured from the ill-fated mission in Toftefjord.

The city of Tromsø lies three hundred and fifty miles north of the Arctic Circle; heavy snows of several feet cover the city during winter each year. Tromsø is sometimes called the capital of northern Norway; it is also known as the Gateway to the Arctic.

Today, seagulls squawked and played in the air beneath the somber clouds, then hung suspended as if this was an ordinary day. A few nervous but curious people watched from a distance as the Schnell boat docked, and the longshoremen, noticing something unusual happening, paused in their work.

Two ambulances slowly rolled down the cobblestone streets and stopped on the dock. Near the ambulances, a German Gestapo officer stepped out from a black car adorned with swastika flags flying from short poles mounted on each front fender. Dressed in mossy green vestment, officer's cap with black brim and the German eagle, a double-breasted long wool coat, shiny black high boots and leather gloves, he paced back and forth. Stopping at intervals, he tapped the leather gloves in his right hand over his left wrist, carefully watching the happenings.

A few German soldiers carried two stretchers up the lowered gangplank. They returned with Eskeland and Reichelt fastened to each stretcher with heavy straps. The instant the doors of the waiting ambulances slammed shut with the stretchers and their cargo, they sped off to St. Elizabeth's Hospital. The Gestapo officer rushed back to his car and ordered the driver to follow them.

Eight disheveled prisoners chained together and under heavy guard appeared at the head of the gangplank. Ordered down to the dock, they

were loaded into the waiting canvas-covered truck and taken to Gestapo headquarters at Bankgaten 13. Gestapo agents were waiting for them.

Numerous Gestapo agents worked at the headquarters in Tromsø. Men and women imprisoned by the

Gestapo Headquarters in Tromsø

Gestapo agonized about their upcoming treatment, knowing full well the Gestapo's lack of pity for prisoners. Before interrogation, they rehearsed the answers to the assumed questions in their mind, and could but hope they would be believed.

Two of the Gestapo agents at the headquarters were more feared and detested than all the rest. One, a short, slight man named Kneiser, was known to be extremely cunning in his interrogation of the prisoners, constantly laying shrewd traps.

The other Gestapo agent's name was Adam Schmidt. A man of a totally different sort, stocky and only about five feet tall, Schmidt's lopsided flat face was framed by thick dark blond hair. Some said his face reminded them of a flounder. He was an uncouth boor who took pleasure in torturing prisoners. No method was too grisly for Schmidt, the most hated of all Gestapo agents in Tromsø.

The men from *Brattholm* were interrogated individually. Crewmember Sjur TrovÅg was the first. Three grim-looking agents were stationed around the room. Schmidt, with his crooked false smile, bid him welcome as he strutted around his desk and pointed for him to sit down in the chair held out for him. Schmidt offered Sjur some candy. The Norwegian shook his head. Schmidt's face turned red; with his eyes flashing, he clenched his fist and lunged out toward Sjur, jamming his fist into his face. The young man flew backward out of the chair and slammed into the wall behind him. The three other Gestapos in the room pounced on him, kicking and beating until Sjur was nearly unconscious. They grabbed him by his arms and legs and dragged him through the door and down the narrow steps into the dingy basement. Unbolting the cell door they threw him like a potato sack into the over-crowded cell that held most of the other *Brattholm* men. No one mistook the Gestapo's intent; they wanted the other men to know what was in store for them upstairs. Sjur's swollen face and hoarse moaning filled his cellmates with dread.

St. Elizabeth's Hospital, March 30, 1943: Followed by the Gestapo car, the two ambulances delivered Erik Reichelt and Sigurd Eskeland to St. Elizabeth's Hospital. Sigurd had been shot in the thigh. Erik, with grenade fragments in his stomach and a broken finger, was so seriously ill that his doctor, a courageous man, refused Gestapo agent Adam Schmidt and his cohorts permission to interrogate him. Schmidt and his men left in a huff, but made it very plain they would return soon, no matter how sick Reichelt was. The wounded saboteurs were placed on the second floor of the hospital and soldiers with automatic weapons were stationed in front of their rooms.

The Gestapo had knowledge of Erik Reichelt's contacts with the resistance leaders on his earlier trips to Tromsø. Because of this, his treatment was more vicious than what the other *Brattholm* men received. The Gestapo agents put him through barbarous torture hoping he would reveal secrets to them.

Tromsø, March 31, 1943: The day following the battle in Toftefjord, Haakon Sørensen and Sheriff Hoel were summoned to appear at Gestapo Headquarters in Tromsø. They gave a complete report and Sørensen also explained that the men from *Brattholm* were referred to the two half-brothers at Grøtøy. These two were quickly arrested and brought to Gestapo Headquarters.

After Sørensen and Sheriff Hoel explained the happenings to the Gestapo, they were told they were to stay until the following day. The Gestapo summoned them once again. As a reward for work well done, each one was given a large crate of food, 30 packages of cigarettes, cured sausages, coffee, butter and ten bottles of hard liquor. In addition, Sheriff Hoel received 500 *kroner* and Sørensen was rewarded with 5000 *kroner*.

Sørensen felt uneasy about taking the gifts. He was told that refusal would be understood as a demonstration. He took the gifts.

Both men returned to Sheriff Hoel's home on Karlsøy after leaving the Gestapo headquarters. Sørensen remained until the following day because the weather was too stormy to return to Bromnes. In the evening they tasted some of the liquor.

St. Elizabeth Hospital, Tromsø, April 1, 1943: Schmidt and his men returned to the hospital. A terrified hush filled the hospital corridors as personnel and guards were rushed off the floor. The Gestapo interrogated Sigurd in the bathroom, but Erik, too ill to be moved, was interrogated in bed. A short, suspense-filled time passed, then Erik's spine-chilling screams pierced through bone and marrow of all who heard them. He had nothing to tell the Gestapo despite their inhumane torture.

Reichelt's heart-wrenching outcry and suffering meant nothing to Schmidt and his agents as they tormented him for several hours without compassion. They had only one mission: gathering information. Since the Germans had for some time been convinced that the Allied invasion would happen in northern Norway, Adam Schmidt believed that the *Brattholm* men might hold the key that would unlock some of the enemy's ambitions. Therefore, no punishment was too brutal or too drawn out - no sacrifice too exacting to get the information he desired.

When the Gestapo agents left the hospital, the nurses rushed to Erik's side. They found him, lying on bed linens soaked with blood. His face was swollen and misshapen. He had received several blows to his face and thick needles had been forced underneath his fingernails, leaving deep bloody grooves that had turned purplish-black.

Erik was in a daze, and no doubt realized that his life was coming to a close. Turning to one of the nurses, he whispered, "please send greetings to everyone at home."

Tromsø, Evening, April 1, 1943: Moursund and Knudsen, the resistance leaders Reichelt had met with a few months earlier in Tromsø, were rounded up in their homes. Schmidt and Kneiser interrogated both. The two prisoners had agreed beforehand, to concede to the Germans all the information they knew they already had, if they were taken prisoner. Moursund and Knudsen knew everything and everyone involved with the resistance movement in Tromsø and the surrounding area. Their hope was to pacify the Germans so as to escape torture and not be forced to reveal other secret information that would put many other lives at stake. Most likely the Gestapo agents became perplexed over their responsiveness because the men were not tortured.

Tromsø, April 2, 1943: Early in the morning, 20 Norwegian prisoners who were incarcerated at Krøkkebærsletta, a German internment camp in Tromsø, were summoned for a special assignment. They were ferried across Tromsøy Sound, herded into a canvas-covered truck and driven to the Gestapo headquarters in downtown Tromsø. Ordered inside, they each were given a long-handled shovel. Led back outside, they were rounded up and pushed back into the truck, which set off for the Njord factory on the outer edge of Tromsø.

As the truck came to an abrupt stop, the prisoners were ordered out. Soldiers with machine guns stood ready. The officer yelled for them to head in the direction of the rifle range at GrønnÅsen, several hundred yards away. Dressed in rags, the prisoners sank into the wet snow and labored to advance uphill lifting, and sometimes dragging, their spades along with them.

Situated on a steep hill, the rifle range was covered in part by marshland with numerous dwarfed deciduous trees, mainly birch. From here, one could view Tromsøy Sound and the lofty mountain ranges across the fjord. At the foot of the mountains in Tromsdalen Valley, the closely-built wooden homes came into view among the evergreens and the white snow. It was a majestic panorama, but not one the prisoners paid attention to.

The twenty prisoners struggled to keep their composure. When ordered to dig a large grave, to a man they thought it was for them. The strong tried in their way to encourage the weaker.

"Don't worry, they have no reason to kill us."

"And if they do, let's not give them the satisfaction of seeing our fear."

"If they kill us, I guess that's our fate," another chimed in.

When told that the grave had to fit eight bodies, the prisoners were both bewildered and relieved. One prisoner then recalled a conversation overheard when the spades were handed out.

"*Hei,* I remember hearing some talk about eight men from the fishing vessel *Brattholm* at the Gestapo headquarters," he said just loud enough for the other prisoners to hear.

"But those men were in the service. They wouldn't execute them."

"Oh, wouldn't they? When did the Gestapo ever follow the laws of society?"

"I pity those men. *MÅ Gud bevare dem,"* may God protect them, a rough, trembling voice added.

"Ruhe!" Silence! A Gestapo officer cocked his gun and came closer.

The strenuous work of digging the large grave continued in silence. The deep snow was shoveled away to enable them to break up the heavy marsh soil. The frost lay shallow because of the heavy snow, and yet it took real strength to hack with their spades at the intertwined roots. The Gestapo and their loaded machine guns made the prisoners uneasy. One could never be too sure of what would set the soldiers off. The prisoners' conversation had made them more alert.

Once the gaping hole had been readied, the prisoners removed the snow from one edge of the grave. The Gestapo wanted it cleared twenty-five feet back to where the executioners would stand to give them a full view of the edge of the grave. The soldiers did some trial shooting and found all to be satisfactory. The shots unnerved several of the younger prisoners. Some tensed, others grabbed hold of a comrade's arm, while others who turned pale had to be steadied by their buddies.

"Take it easy, we'll be all right!" encouraged an emaciated, tall prisoner.

Earlier in the day the Gestapo had instructed the men that they were to remain until after the execution to cover up the corpses. Instead, when the grave had been dug in the late afternoon, the Gestapo hustled them down the hill and back into the truck that had brought them to GrønnÅsen. The temperate April spring day sent sporadic rays of sunshine through the back of the truck. Nearing the center, the streets filled with run-off from the melted snows and brief sun breaks warmed the day.

When they reached Skippergata in downtown Tromsø, another truck with a tarpaulin cover fastened to the iron frame covering the truck bed approached. The eight Brattholm men and their executioners sat inside. Silence fell over the prisoners who had been forced to dig their graves.

Earlier in the day the eight *Brattholm* prisoners had been brought up from the basement in Bankgaten 13, Gestapo headquarters. Police officer Edvin Wikan watched, heavy-hearted, a short distance away. Gestapo soldiers ordered the cluster of men into the waiting truck. Wikan had watched such happenings before and surmised something dreadful was about to take place, though he did not know what. The prisoners were chained together two by two, some with cow chains, and others with thick cords.

The *Brattholm* men had been ordered to walk barefoot. At the last moment the Gestapo changed their directives. The truck with the prisoners would be parked a good distance away from the rifle range, and most likely they would encounter passersby on the long walk. The Gestapo did not want to appear cruel. The prisoners' wrists were linked together, the right arm of one to the left of the next. Because of the torture inflicted on them during the last 48 hours, some had difficulty walking. Their comrades helped them along.

It was nearing 8 p.m. by the time the prisoners began their walk to the rifle range. The soldiers threw their capes over the prisoners so the chains would not be visible to other pedestrians. Harassed and fatigued by their treatment, the prisoners trudged through the spring thaw. They carried their private burdens heroically. All knew death was imminent. What they did not know was what had befallen their other four friends. They would have gloried in knowing that one had escaped, Jan Baalsrud.

At the Tromsø rifle range, the Gestapo ordered the *Brattholm* men lined up in a row with their backs to the open grave. One Gestapo officer felt they moved too slowly.

"*Schnell! Schnell!*" Quick! Quick!, he pushed a prisoner with his rifle butt.

Some twenty-five feet in front of them the executioners lined up and readied their rifles. They took aim and fired a few rounds. The cracking shots resounded several times among the nearby hills.

Ordered by the Gestapo to be present, Sheriff Hoel observed the execution. As the sheriff watched his countrymen fall, he agonized over the telephone call he'd made only a couple of days earlier – the call which took so many lives.

Most of the men were shot in the abdomen and doubled up with pain as the bullets hit their mark. Those who fell pulled the others down with them, chained together as they were. Those who did not fall down into the grave were kicked over the edge, dead or not. The agony remained on their frozen faces as they laid helter skelter in the large black cavity prepared for them in the marshes. A load of Russian prisoners was brought in to cover their tortured bodies with the black soil.

The *Brattholm* men gave all for Norway and freedom. All had eagerly returned to Norway to take part in her fight for freedom. There were no flower-strewn caskets or platted wreaths or garlands for these young men. Instead, their sacrifice was dignified and majestic. There had been no whimpering or self-pity among them. They had chosen their work, and they knew the odds. To them a free Norway was worth even life itself, and in the end that is what they gave.

St. Elizabeth Hospital, Tromsø, April 2, 1943*:* By mid-morning the day following his arrest, Moursund was yanked from his cell and taken by car down the hilly snow-covered streets of Tromsø. All too fast, the colorful, individually constructed wooden row homes, some still with snow piled high in front, passed by them as the car sped up and down the winding streets. The sound of the tire chains hitting the car frame brought back many happy wintertime memories to Moursund. White-clad, snow-bedecked mountains surrounded the city he loved.

The black car he rode in turned a corner and rumbled down Strandgaten. Moursund's blood chilled. They were heading down the cobblestone street leading to the Tromsø hospital, where a transmitter had been installed in the hospital's tower. Moursund assumed the Germans had located it. To his amazement, the car did not stop, but continued some distance and turned in to St. Elizabeth Hospital. When he was ushered from the car up the cement steps leading to the hospital, bewilderment swept over him like a sudden wind gust. He could not have known Kneiser was setting one of his shrewd traps. The Gestapo led Moursund down pale green hospital corridors into a dimly lit small room of the same color. The room held only one bed.

Kneiser pushed Moursund forward and he was brought face to face with the patient in the bed. The man had an extremely deformed face and a deathlike pallor, making it difficult to tell his age. The patient, it was obvious, had been through a harrowing experience. He just lay there and moaned. Moursund wondered why he was brought here. To be shown what was in store for him and Knudsen? The patient's face seemed to lighten as if he recognized Moursund. His cheekbones were a dark bluish-green, and he had difficulty seeing through his swollen eyelids. His slurred speech made it difficult for Moursund to understand his words.

Abruptly, as Moursund scrutinized the man, he came to the ghastly realization that he knew this beaten, mishandled being. Four months had passed since he last saw his face, but this had to be him. It was Erik Reichelt!

Reichelt tried to speak but could not be understood. He was offered some water through a straw, and he tried again. He motioned to Moursund to come closer to him. Kneiser moved in at the same time. The swollen lips began to move as Reichelt exerted all his efforts to share these last important words with his friend.

"It was not I who betrayed you, Kaare," he groaned and closed his swollen eyes.

Kneiser's trap had worked. He now had the proof that Reichelt and Moursund knew each other. Moursund was taken back to prison. Reichelt died the following day, April 3, 1943.

Tromsø, April 5, 1943: The Gestapo tortured a prisoner at their headquarters in Bankgaten 13, a prisoner who had illegally listened to a radio transmission from London. He had received blows to the face and kicks to the groin from the man with the flounder face. He ended up in one of the cells in the basement. The cell door suddenly was kicked open, and two men were tossed on the dirt floor and the cell door slammed shut. The new prisoners were half-brothers Jernberg Kristiansen and Sedolf Andreassen who had offered to hide *Brattholm*'s provisions. Haakon Sørensen gave their names to the *Brattholm* men and then to the Gestapo.

A few minutes passed and their cellar door flung open with a clang once again. The soldiers cocked their machine guns and pointed them straight at the two, as if they were going to shoot. The half brothers struggled to their feet as best they could and huddled together in their corner. The other prisoner grew angry at such inhumane treatment, and he pulled at the half-brothers' clothes in his effort to calm these bewildered men.

"If they shoot you men, they will have to kill all of us," he shouted.

The soldiers grabbed the door and pulled it shut behind them. These two resolute fishermen had been torn away from their peaceful existence and thrown into the lion's den. They endured bestial torture and several hours of interrogation. Following Schmidt's treatment, all they revealed was that they had been offered 3000 *kroner* and some coffee in return for helping the men of *Brattholm*.

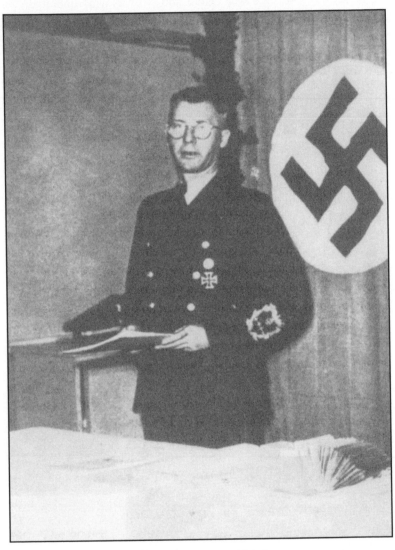

Reichskommissar Josef Terboven

On May 8, 1945, the war ended and Norway was liberated. The Gestapo officers in Tromsø were taken prisoner, and in the late summer of 1945, they were ordered to GrønnÅsen Rifle Range to unearth the executed *Brattholm* men. When they neared the victims as they dug, the Gestapo officers were forced to lay down their shovels and use their bare hands so as not to damage the bodies. Before the Norwegians were placed in their caskets, they were cleaned by the Gestapos.

Left: Graves are opened

Right: The Gestapo was ordered to excavate the graves

Left: A view of the mass graves

Left: Two men linked together with cow chains

Right: Their suffering was still evident

Left: The bodies are removed by the Gestapo

Right: The bodies were washed and readied, and placed in their caskets by the Gestapo

FALLEN
Per Blindheim, Ålesund, Norway
Killed at Toftefjord, March 30, 1943.

EXECUTED AT TROMSØ RIFLE RANGE APRIL 1, 1943
Bjørn Norman Bolstad, Solbergfoss pr. Askim, Norway

Gabriel Salvesen, Farsund, Norway

Magnus Johan Kvalvik, Husøy i Solund, Norway

Sverre Odd Kvernhellen, Husøy i Solund, Norway

Harald Peter Ratvik, Borgund pr.Ålesund, Norway

Frithjof M. Haugland, Norway

Sjur Ludvigsen Trovaag, Kalgras i Ytre Sogn, Norway

Alfred A. Vik, Øystesø, Kvam i Hordaland, Norway

DIED AT ST. ELIZABETH'S HOSPITAL
FROM GUNSHOT WOUNDS AND TORTURE
Sigurd Eskeland, Risør, Norway

Erik Reichelt, Tønsberg, Norway

A TRIUMPHANT FIND

TOFTEFJORD, MARCH 30, 1943: The attack on *Brattholm* in Toftefjord was an extraordinary coup for the Germans. That is why they rewarded the informers with both food and spirits. In addition, the killing of one of the commandos, Per Blindheim, and the capture of ten prisoners made the triumph especially sweet.

Brattholm's explosion tossed wreckage in every direction. The only thing remaining intact was the attaché case with the top-secret material. The attaché case was the one thing the saboteurs were to keep out of German hands at all costs. When the Germans saw it splash undamaged back down into the fjord, they quickly lowered a small rowboat off the warship and rowed out to recover it from the water. At that time even the Germans did not know how very successful their assault had been.

From the German Archives we learned that the attaché case contained numerous documents with secret information. The Germans had the *Brattholm* documents translated and scrutinized thoroughly. Analyses and reports were sent to several sources within two days. In addition to the recovered attaché case, the Gestapo interrogated and tortured eight of the *Brattholm* prisoners at the Gestapo headquarters in Tromsø. Two others were wounded and had been admitted to St. Elizabeth Hospital. They were also tortured. The Gestapo used every method available in their efforts to understand all that was happening around them.

Tromsø, April 1, 1943: A report was sent out. The exact translation follows:

SECRET COMMANDO WORK.

From GENERAL COMMANDER IN TROMSØ TO A.O.K.Ic:
"Evaluation of sabotage-fishing vessel in Toftesund, Toftefjord Sound:

12 men were aboard, all Norwegian under the leadership of Lieutenant Eskeland from Risør, (southern Norway), among them five seamen, all had a six-month training at sabotage school, including training as paratroopers.

Additionally four fishing vessels headed south from Tromsø in the direction of Bergen, among them were probably the fishing vessel *Trondheim* that was discovered empty in Trondheimsfjord March 22.

All the fishing vessels came from Shetland.

Assignment: To build up sabotage organizations that would take actions against military bases, battery positions, billets, chief of staff quarters, and bridges. Following a three months period of accomplishments, executing-on-command, and at the same time carrying out planned sabotage activities.

Arrangement to stockpile the sabotage supplies were made.

A few addresses of Norwegians willing to offer assistance were found. In that connection necessary steps are being taken.

Ten maps with military bases were noted. Five planned military camps with transcript or photos will follow via air with the quartermaster. Evaluation has already begun.

Further information show planned arson, sabotage actions, silent executions and the use of chemicals to attain temperature fluctuations. The Gestapo's initiatives will continue. Much more information is likely.

Preliminary information also to be found at Bds. and Ast.

Own interpretation: A full scale invasion in Norway is not likely within the next three months, thereafter waves of sabotage actions, and attacks are possible."

General Commander LXXI.X.K.
Ic nr. 69/43 g. Kdos.

The Germans feared a surprise full-scale invasion in northern Norway. They had obtained the names and addresses of Kaare Moursund and Tor Knudsen, the resistance leaders in Tromsø. Moursund and Knudsen were picked up in their homes during the evening of April 1. Erik Reichelt was tortured the following afternoon, proving he spoke the truth when he groaned, "It was not I that betrayed you, Kaare."

The same sender in the German General Commando squad sent an additional report to the same addressee:

Evaluation sabotage vessel, Toftesund:
26 maps confiscated and eleven situation reports, whereof five have sketched outlines, nine maps from Geographical Section Staff Nr. 4090 1: 00000, conveying Norwegian county charts 1:200000. Primarily maps of established territory reported, and some summary maps of Sweden, the latter probably because of the escape routes to Sweden.

General Commander LKKI.A.K.
Ic Nr. 148/43 III. Ang.

Tromsø, April 6, 1943: A third report was sent out:

SECRET
To the leader of the Air Force North/East.
Concerning sabotage vessel Toftesund.
Conf.: Tlf.-conversation Captain Treppe/Lieutenant
Colonel Langbein v.6.4

1: Following a report from a Norwegian an enemy vessel
was seized by own minesweeper in Toftefjord 30.3 around
5 p.m. As it neared, the vessel was blown up. The crew
was seized, and overpowered following a shooting battle.

Of the 12 men, two killed, ten taken prisoner, of which
two were wounded.

2: The Norwegian Navy sent the vessel out from
Scalloway. Armaments two machine guns, two machine
guns hidden in barrel, in addition four machine guns, six
machine pistols, four cases of egg-hand grenades, 1000
kilos explosives, one small hand radio-transmitter. The
leader aboard the vessel was a Norwegian Lieutenant.

3: The purpose was to build an organization for sabotage
actions against military bases, battery positions, military
staff and troop quarters, and bridges. The Administration
was in London.

Build up of the organization over a 2-3 month period.
Stockpiling the sabotage material was planned. The seized
maps presumably showed the operation territory for the
troops between Porsanger and Narvik. In this area certain
sketches showed diverse German Military bases and road
and railway junctions on the mainland, VesterÅlen and
Lofoten Islands. Four other vessels with saboteurs aboard
are supposed to land between Tromsø and Bergen.

The General Commander stated that ten men were taken prisoners, two of these were wounded, Reichelt and Eskeland. They knew that there had been 12 men aboard *Brattholm*, and that one was dead, Per Blindheim. They were not quite sure of the last man, was he dead or had he been able to escape? After all, this man had killed a German officer up in the ravine.

In another document, the Germans presented another version of the twelfth man:

> General Commander LXXI.A.K.A.
> Dept. Ic Ax: BV/2
> Nr.143/43 Secret.
> Conc. Sabotage vessel Toftesund.
> To the Army High Command Norway/Ic
> Oslo.

> —The escape of the crew from the fishing vessel was prevented by machine gun fire and hand rifles. One man was killed, one man seriously wounded and another man more lightly wounded. One member was killed in the explosion. The Gestapo took prisoners all together ten Norwegians, among them two wounded—

> —The mine sweeper brought the survivors back to Tromsø, and were taken into custody by the Gestapo. Another search on 31 March did not reveal any additional enemy positions and contacts between the Norwegians on the islands of Rebbenesøy and Hersøy and the saboteurs.–

According to this report, the twelfth man had blown himself up together with *Brattholm*. And Per Blindheim was dead. The ten survivors were brought to Tromsø, and with this explanation the German High Command had been able to account for all the men aboard *Brattholm*.

The Germans took the information revealed from the attaché case quite seriously. From another report we read:

> SECRET.
> To Admiral of the Polar Coast **(?)**
> Chief of the Air Force Lofoten
> Commander Airfield Territory Moen
> 1: Concerning the Sabotage vessel Toftesund:
> Establishment of five vessels between Tromsø and Bergen to build comprehensive sabotage groups under the direction of the best possibly educated men, modern equipment and large quantities of explosives and hand grenades. Administrated from England. The saboteurs are seeking to make contacts with willing Norwegians patriots.
>
> The enemy has the most accurate information about the military units in Storsteinnes, Setermoen, Finsnes, Kvernmones, Harstad, from Bardufoss Airport extremely good documents regarding their own work.
>
> Continuous vigilance, critical evaluation of sabotage defense, all military quarters, stations and important communication centers and continual education of the troops concerning sabotage Io Nr. 143/43 geh.II. Dangers and sabotage defense is necessary.
>
> Commanding Officer in the Polar Territory.

THE HELPFUL MIDWIFE

MIKKELVIK, EARLY morning, March 31, 1943: A small rowboat moved quietly toward the glazed, frost-covered rocks by the water's edge at Mikkelvik on Ringvassøy Island.

"That house over there in the middle of the field is where the Jensens live." Ingvald pointed to the wooden house. "I'll introduce you to the Jensen family," offered the 17-year old.

"Thanks, but no. I'll be just fine."

"It'll just take a minute. We know them well."

"No! You have risked too much on my behalf already." Jan was firm. "I do not want anyone to see you with me. Row back home and comfort your mother and family. They need you," he directed.

Jacoba Jensen's home in Mikkelvik.

The discussion ended; Jan climbed out of the boat. The men shook hands and said their goodbyes. Ingvald rowed homeward and Jan headed straight for the house some 200 feet from the shore. In the darkness the house stood out like a large boulder; no bushes or trees surrounded it, and Jan hoped he could get inside unseen.

The women on Hersøy Island had told Jan that Jacoba Jensen, the midwife on Ringvassøy, lived in that little house. They felt sure her husband Alfred could give him a lift to Tromsø. Because of the birthing mothers on the second floor, Jan hesitated to disturb the household in the middle of the night. His choices were few though, as his life was at stake.

Jan half-limped up to the entrance door rather optimistically. When Jacoba Jensen, the midwife, opened the door at that hour of the night he was somewhat taken aback. He explained his untimely arrival. Disappointment showed on Jan's face when he learned that Jensen had left for Tromsø a few hours earlier with his boat, *Vesle Tor.*

Jacoba opened the door wide, stepped aside and bid him enter. She tried to make up for his dashed hopes and showed him the same warmth and friendliness the women on Hersøy had earlier. The first floor of the little home had only a kitchen and living room. Jan was ushered toward the small wooden kitchen table, which soon was set with food Jacoba had on hand. He was hungry and the food comforted him.

Jacoba had a couple of women upstairs ready to give birth but this didn't stop her from wanting to help this brave patriot.

"Stay until my husband returns tomorrow."

"Nei, nei, it is too risky."

"I have an idea. We can dress you up as a birthing mother, and tie a scarf around your head."

"No, no this is foolishness," Jan chuckled.

"Being a midwife, I'll come along and care for you," Jacoba offered. "The Germans will not suspect a thing."

"I will not hear of it! You have already done so much. It's too dangerous for you and your family, and the birthing women upstairs."

"At least stay the night and rest up after your ordeal," she coaxed him.

"I cannot take advantage of your kindness. The Gestapo could flock in anytime. The worst scenario would be that I might have to kill myself. I cannot inflict such a drama on you women."

Jacoba waved her hand as if to say, "Nonsense." She realized she could not change Jan's mind. The midwife offered suggestions on where he could safely go, and who to avoid.

"A thousand thanks for all your help," Jan reached his hand out and shook hers firmly. He left without telling her in which direction he was heading.

Upstairs on the second floor, in addition to the birthing mothers, slept the Jensen's 14-year old daughter, Gunnvor. She awoke when she heard her mother talking with a man down in the kitchen. "Strange," she thought. "With Dad out of town. Could it be?... No! I don't believe it!"

She crawled out of bed and laid her ear to the floor. But the voices were muffled and she could not make out what they said. The next morning Gunnvor decided to get the story straight.

"Mother, who visited with you last night?"

"Oh that. It was only Søren from Fagerfjord. He just wanted to know if Dad was going to make a trip to Tromsø, because he wanted to come along."

That was all her mother would say and Gunnvor did not have the courage to ask any more questions. When her father came home the next day and her mother hustled him into the living room and closed the door, she was really puzzled. This was very unusual.

Gunnvor was unable to forget the incident, and when her brother Oddmund came home, she took him aside and told him about the mysterious visit. He understood the gravity of it all.

"You are to shut up about this," he cautioned her sternly. "If this should get out we might lose both father and mother."

Not another word was mentioned about this incident in the Jensen house until Norway's Liberation on May 8, 1945; then Jacoba Jensen told her daughter the whole story.

Outside in the darkness Jan's feelings tugged at him. Once more, without a moment's hesitation, he had been received with abundant kindness. The honorable woman who had helped him never expressed any fear for her own safety, though she knew it meant her death if she was discovered. Across the sound he saw the outline of Rebbenes Island where he had left his other newfound friends. He could only wish them the best.

Jan headed west, though his plan was to go east. His training in Scotland had taught him, and his own instinct was, to mislead. If someone was on the way to a barn, or watched from a window somewhere, he wanted them to see a stranger walking toward the west.

After several hundred meters he made a sharp turn southward and disappeared between some small round knolls. He then changed direction anew, toward the east. His chosen path took him around the few houses in Mikkelvik. Jan then headed for the water, and followed the rocky beach toward Fagerfjord. He stopped at a house at the end of the fjord, which Jacoba had suggested he do.

Engenes, March 31, 1943: About seven in the morning, Jan arrived at Engenes farm, home of Nelle and Leonhard Johansen, siblings. A friendly pair, the brother and sister welcomed him. Jan told them his story, the same story he had related to the midwife, without revealing any names. After a nice meal, they prepared a comfortable bed for him with several sheepskins in the summer-barn. Jan's concern was always for his helpers first and he had refused to sleep in the house.

Worn from hours of limping and trudging through deep snow and climbing over slippery rocks, Jan gratefully accepted their offerings, but not before he warned them about the Germans. He instructed them on what to say should the Germans come asking questions. Jan fell into a deep sleep that lasted the whole day through and into the late afternoon.

Around 7 p.m. Jan was again on his way, this time to a small hamlet called Karanes. In spite of his wounded foot, he felt refreshed and confident. He chuckled as he looked down on his feet with one rubber boot and one seaman's boot. He had studied and memorized maps of the area and felt sure, even with his footwear, he could scale the mountain that loomed ahead of him.

The mountain abruptly rose and was awkward to climb. Several times he thought he had reached the top only to discover another precipitous climb ahead, more difficult and higher than the last. In the distance, yet another wall rose up before him. Jan fought his way upward, making detours to reach the next cliff. The knitted Selbu mittens given to him by Ingvald were soaked, his fingers frozen. The snow was unduly deep and he sank to his waist often. When he fought to get out, his rubber boot filled with snow and with each step the snow packed itself firmly around his freezing legs. Sometimes the rubber boot came off and Jan turned it upside down and shook it to empty it of the snow.

Toward midnight the Arctic darkness deepened. Yet he could still make out the contour of ridges and gaps of precipices. Some four hours into the climb the ashen-gray clouds merged above. Large fluffy snowflakes began falling. Suddenly the wind increased and the snowfall thickened. Within minutes Jan was in the midst of a gale. In the darkness the wind tore at him and whipped the blinding snow around him, lashing his face and making it impossible to see but a few feet ahead. He pushed upward but soon realized it was futile to continue. Jan knew the fickleness of the Arctic winters; he had to get back to lower ground.

On his way up he had caught sight of a small sheepcote built on a hillside; he needed to reach it. The descent was agonizing and slow but as he neared the empty shed, his distress faded. The wind blew the slat door from his hands and he breathlessly stumbled in and brushed himself off. Farm implements lay scattered around the floor between the piles of hay. Jan gathered enough hay to make a mattress. The wet snowstorm left him soaked and frozen. Ice bits clung to his hair and eyebrows making them frosty white. He removed his boots packed with snow and massaged his feet and legs, trying to bring feeling back into them.

The cracks in the timber along the walls blew the snow straight through, filling corners and other areas with snow, but at least he had cover overhead. Inadequate as it was, Jan was grateful for this shelter from the raging storm. It did shield him from the powerful wind gusts and snow squalls. He buried himself deep into the hay but the night was a cold and sleepless one.

April 1, 1943: The following morning at 6:00 the storm ceased as abruptly as it had begun. Jan left his little shelter and took up his battle with the mountain afresh. Within a few hours a penetrating wind with a thick obscuring mist overshadowed him. The visibility diminished, but this time Jan felt it imperative to reach his goal if he was to survive. Every step he forced himself to take gave him a sense of victory. After several hours, the storm subsided, but heavy storm clouds hovered over him. He reached the ridge of the mountain plateau and far below he saw Veggefjord. (*Vegg* means wall, an appropriate name for this fjord bordered on two sides by mountains jutting straight up from the water.) As soon as he descended the steep mountain, Jan found that he next needed to traverse a white-shrouded marshland covered with shrubs and dwarfed birch trees. The marshland led to a cove at the head of the fjord; after crossing the rocky beach, Jan needed only to climb up the mountain wall on the other side; then he should be able to see Karanes close-up.

The Norwegian soldier expected the large rocks along the beach to be easier to cross than plodding through the deep snow in the marshland, but he found them to be cumbersome and slippery. When he came to the end of the beach where the mountain met the water, he realized the impossibility of scaling it. Should he slip, he would end up in the fjord. Instead, Jan turned inland several dozen yards where the mountains were not quite as treacherous. The snow was deeper, but there was less chance of falling. Once on top, Jan headed back toward Karanes. Thirteen hours he had struggled against the elements, but when he reached the tip of this mountain plateau looking down on the small forest below the tree line, he saw that it bordered a field running down to the shore. Toward the bottom of the field stood the house he had been longing to reach. He was in Karanes. Before him the silver-gray DÅfjord stretched long and wide and at the head laid the little village of DÅfjord, his next goal.

Caught up in his own struggle, Jan did not know that the storm he had been grappling with was the same storm which detained merchant Sørensen from Bromnes at Sheriff Hoel's home following their visit with the Gestapo in Tromsø.

KARANES

KARANES, APRIL 1-2, 1943: Karanes protrudes at the end of the northeast point of Ringvassøy Island, between Veggefjord and DÅfjord. The Hansens were the only people living at Karanes, accessible only by boat. Eighteen miles in a northeast direction lay the island of Vanna. Past Vanna was the Arctic Ocean.

Jan worked his way down the mountainside and through the forest, arriving at the farm of Ragnhild and Morten Hansen around one in the afternoon. In the clearing he spotted a young girl playing by herself in the snow. The little house he had noticed from the plateau looked warm and inviting. At the lower end of the sloped field was a small barn. A little boathouse stood near the breakwater where a rowboat lay tied up.

"Hello, little lady. I came to see your parents. Are they home?"

"*Ja da.* Come with me."

Ragnhild Hansen opened the door as they approached. Working at the kitchen sink, she had seen Jan coming down from the mountains and watched him greet Margareth, their daughter.

Unexpected visitors seldom came to isolated Karanes, and if they did, they always came by sea. Ragnhild wondered who this man was, handsome and terribly frozen.

"Please come in," she said as she stepped back for Jan to enter. "My husband is just firing up the wood stove. Sit down." Ragnhild offered him a chair close to the fire.

Morten Hansen looked a little surprised at their guest, but he was friendly and made Jan feel welcome.

At first the Hansens had a difficult time believing Jan because he refused to tell them where he had come from. Jan's earnest appeal for help won

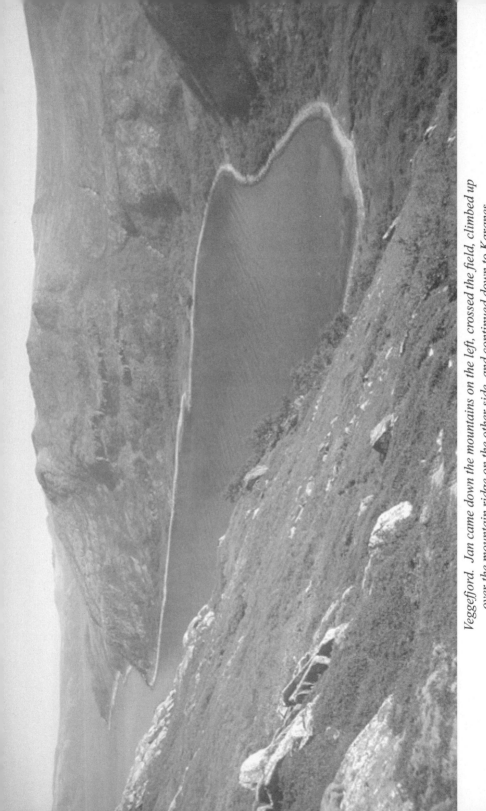

Veggefjord. Jan came down the mountains on the left, crossed the field, climbed up over the mountain ridge on the other side, and continued down to Karanes.

them over. The Hansens found him easy to talk to and were convinced when the commando revealed his Norwegian Navy uniform and pulled his boot off to show them his wounded foot. Shocked at his condition, they never pressed him for further information. The couple was convinced the stranger was telling the truth, and they were filled with amazement and admiration for him. They realized how much he had suffered, both emotionally and physically, and that he had to be totally spent.

The news of Toftefjord had preceded Jan. The Hansens believed his story in spite of the account that all the men of *Brattholm* had been killed. Seeing his sad condition, they offered to share all they had. If they worried about the Germans and the personal risk they were taking, they never let Jan know. Their concern was for this brave Norwegian soldier and how best they could help him to safety.

Jan was calm, but always on guard with his pistol nearby. He was anxious to get away from Ringvassøy Island as quickly as possible and on to Sweden.

The Hansens cleaned and bandaged Jan's wounded foot. They hung his clothes to dry on a line over the wood stove, and they shared with him the best food they had. Both Ragnhild and Morten enjoyed visiting with Jan and hearing his stories of England and his travels. Jan appreciated their kindness.

"I'm eager to see a map of the Troms District. Do you happen to have one?" asked Jan.

"I'm sorry, but we only have a local map. Let me show you your next best bet."

From a kitchen drawer across the room Morten pulled out a map and spread it out on the kitchen table. He brought a piece of notepaper and drew another map which he thought would be of help. Morten's plan was to row Jan to DÅfjord the following day, after he had rested. Jan asked some questions about the map and studied it intently. After a while he tore it up and burned it. "I keep it all up here," Jan said, pointing to his head.

"You're quite a guy," commented Morten. "You seem calm, yet I notice you are always on guard."

"I've got to be; one never knows when the Germans will show." Jan patted his pistol.

"Jan, we'd like for you to stay through the night. I'll make up a bed for you," offered Ragnhild.

"A thousand thanks, but that is too risky for you. Would you mind if I slept in the barn?"

"All right then," Morten said. "Mama, we'll have to make him a comfortable bed of hay."

Before retiring, Jan planned a possible escape route. Even in this remote area, he did not feel safe from the Germans. If they sent a patrol plane, it would be easy to follow his tracks in the snow; they were wide and deep and would lead straight to this house. There was no way to know if the Germans were still searching for him, but they were known to pop up in the strangest places at any hour of the day or night. Jan was not only grateful to the people who had been so generous and willing to sacrifice all for him, he was concerned for their safety; and always, with that concern, was the guilt of leaving his comrades behind.

Later that evening, after retiring and relaxing in his comfortable bed of hay Jan realized how exhausted he was. The last two evenings had not afforded him sound sleep. Fighting his way twelve miles through deep snow over wild mountain plateaus in dreadful storms had robbed him of his strength. He fell into a restless sleep but did not awaken fully until late the next day.

Karanes, April 2, 1943: Jan rested and visited with the Hansens during the remainder of the day until early evening. Though the stabbing pains running through his legs concerned him, Jan still felt good. Being with people and having someone to talk with minimized his discomfort.

During the day the Hansens left Jan alone for a while with their two girls, Margareth and Gerd, while they rowed out to sea to set the long line. "Hopefully the fish will take the bite today," said Morten as he and his wife made ready to leave.

Jan worried when they left. He asked the Hansens' daughters how far it was to a telephone; Jan was concerned the Hansens might report him. He needn't have worried. The Hansens were solid patriotic people and they never said a word about Jan to anyone until after the war.

"In Bjørnskar there lives a man, Einar Sørensen. He is one dependable Norwegian. I know him well. I've been fishing with him several times. You need to go to him, Jan," said Morten just before he was ready to leave.

"Do you think he'd able to help get me closer to Sweden?" Jan questioned.

"He'll not only be able to, but he'll be glad to help. He's probably your best bet to get to the mainland."

"Thanks. I'll not tell him who sent me."

Jan's Karanes visit was encouraging, but he felt pressed to hurry onward; there still were so many miles to cover. Straight south, another eight and a half miles into DÅfjord Sound, lay the sleepy village of DÅfjordbotn, his next goal. From the Hansens' window earlier in the day Jan observed the forested mountains rising to the rear of the village with homes scattered up the slopes. As the day wore on, it started snowing and soon turned to heavy snowdrifts. The north wind roared and stirred up the sea. Huge waves pounded the coast and made it impossible for Morten to take Jan to DÅfjord.

It was close to 8 p.m. when Jan said goodbye to the Hansens.

Thirty-five miles away at GrønnÅsen Rifle Range in Tromsø, precisely at 8 p.m., machine gun volleys ripped through the air. Linked together with cow chains, eight courageous freedom-loving men plunged headlong into a dark, dug out marshy tract. Jan's duty was to reach freedom and to tell their story of courage.

Jan worked his way uphill through the snowbound field into the bordering forest. He continued onward into the mountains so as to be hidden from possible onlookers. The Arctic spring added several minutes of light daily and he felt it too chancy to begin his trek on the beach. Jan didn't know it, but the Hansens stood in the window and watched him until the snowdrifts enveloped him and he vanished from their sight.

The wounded commando pressed forward. Enmeshed in his private emotional struggles and physical exertions against the elements, he was spared the knowledge of the fate of his friends from *Brattholm*.

The snow eased after a few hours and Jan headed south toward the rockbound shore. He would make better time there; the snow dwindled along the waters' edge.

Often the steep mountainsides plunged headlong into the sea. Not realizing how steep it was, Jan started his climb, only to be forced back down by the jagged impenetrable masses. His appreciation grew for the many tough weeklong mountain hikes he had endured in Scotland with a heavy backpack. His endurance level had increased, and he was convinced of his own ability to survive this ordeal. He tackled his way back down, and forced a path further inland. Back up on the mountain plateau, Jan worked his way around seemingly impassable places. Repeatedly his crossing took him up, down, forward, and back up again. The pain in his legs haunted him. Exhaustion came sooner this time than it had on his first hike after he had left the sheepcote. The Norwegian's iron will enabled him to push his body through more hours of struggle. Just after five in the morning Jan reached the village of DÅfjordbotn.

DÅFJORD

APRIL 3, 1943: Jan quickly found the little yellow house bordering the river, just like the Hansen family in Karanes had told him. It stood where the river cascaded over the rocky hillside and flowed straight down into the inlet. It was the only house pressed up against the hillside. But it was too early to wake up strangers. He dug himself down into the snow and lay quietly waiting for smoke to rise from the brick chimney. The forceful north wind blew in a northwesterly direction. Jan waited patiently.

THE HOUSE was bitter cold after the long freezing night. Artur Olsen, up first this morning, wrapped his robe around him snugly and went downstairs to stoke up the wood stove on the first floor. Sleepily he reached over for the aluminum coffee kettle, added the substitute coffee grains, the only kind available during the war, and water. With the lid lifter he removed the center griddle plate and placed the kettle over the heat. It always took time before the warmth spread through the house and it was reassuring to know a cup of coffee was brewing.

Upstairs Harald, six years old, and his elder brother slept in a separate room from their parents. The young boys liked taking their time getting up, always waiting until after the wood stove had been fired up. The cozy warm down covers kept them warm while the floor remained very cold. Unusual for Harald, this morning he awoke to the sound of his father stoking the wood stove on the first floor. The sound of the crackling fire clearly reached him upstairs.

Harald's morning thoughts were interrupted by a knock on the front door downstairs. The outer-door creaked as his father opened it and Harald heard a stranger's voice. He nudged his brother, and both became quite curious; the suspense made it impossible to stay in bed. They hurriedly dressed and went down to see who this stranger was.

Jan found that convincing Artur Olsen to help was not an easy task. The man was quite nervous and reserved. He had already heard rumors about an escapee from the Brattholm disaster. He also knew that the State Police was hunting people with illegal radios, and this he connected with the frozen man on his doorstep. What if he was a German provocateur?

Olsen finally took pity on Jan because of the freezing weather, and though still uncertain as to the stranger's identity, he invited him in.

"You can't stay long, but you need to come out of this weather for awhile."

"Choice weather for me," Jan smiled and kicked the snow off his boots. "My tracks are covered."

Unsure of what to believe, Olsen took a chance. "You can rest here for a couple of hours." He nodded for Jan to move closer to the stove. The crackling wood stove brought Jan's body temperature back up, and his clothes began to steam dry as he snuggled close to the stove. Olsen got his wife Jermine up, and she soon served him coffee and good food.

Jan's optimistic outlook impressed the Olsens. He rubbed his hand over his pistol and told them, "The Germans will never catch me, dead or alive."

Artur liked Jan. He began to believe his story and felt more at ease with him. He shared what he had heard about the Toftefjord incident.

"There was a rumor among the people that one man had escaped. But since we did not hear any more, we thought the man had succumbed. Besides, we did not believe anyone could make it in this frigid weather."

"Well, now you know they can."

"We also heard that the rest of the men were either killed in Toftefjord or taken prisoner and brought to Tromsø."

Jan leaned forward. He became edgy.

"Do you have any news of what happened to the men in Tromsø?"

Artur hesitated as he studied Jan's face. "I did hear that those who were captured were taken to Tromsø and…and executed." It seemed cruel to pass such news on to this man who had already been through so much.

Jan's demeanor fell. "I can't help but wonder what went wrong? It is a question I ask myself over and over again."

Olsen changed the conversation to less weighty topics. He drew Jan a map. Jan memorized this map also. While Olsen and Jan were visiting around the coffee table, the boys had to leave for school and their parents said they were not to mention this visit to anyone. Some provisions for Jan's lunch were prepared, and the boys gathered that he would also soon leave. When the boys returned that afternoon, the stranger was gone.

"Boys," Olsen said on their return, "I want to share with you the soldier's last words to me. They were, 'I have not been here. And you, forget that I have been here.' We must heed his wishes. It might make the difference between life and death for all of us. We will never speak of this incident again." Olsen's stern warning not to tell a soul was heeded. The family never mentioned a word about the soldier until after the war.

Again, Jan chose a mountain path hoping to reach Bjørnskar on the south end of Langsund Sound. Accessible by boat, Bjørnskar, nineteen miles south, was in a good location. Maybe he could find someone willing to take him further. He was totally dependent on the willingness of his countrymen to assist him, yet he was acutely disturbed, because to help him they risked life itself.

Langsund divides Ringvassøy Island from Reinøy Island toward the east. Reinøy lies in the main passageway toward Tromsø. On the south promontory of Reinøy Island lies Finnkroken, a heavily fortified German battery installation in the Troms District. Straight west across the fjord on the opposite side of Langsund lies Bjørnskar on the island of Ringvassøy.

Jan wanted to avoid Hansnes and the heavily populated coastal areas of Langsund. It was too risky to walk the shoreline in daylight through populated areas. Germans were stationed all around and the danger of being caught was imminent. He felt safest in the mountains.

Leaving the Olsens' home in Dåfjord, Jan climbed straight up the hillside along the river. When he reached the top of the elongated hill, he turned around in the direction of the cold, steel gray fjord for one last look. The haze partially hid the fjord from his view. Jan then headed for and followed the river path in toward the source, Solvatnet Lake. The snow on these vast mountain plateaus was deeper than he had experienced up to now. He felt like the wet, white mountain masses stood ready to swallow him up. With each step he fell in up to his knees. Often he sank in up to his waist and armpits. He struggled to free himself from the snow's vise-like grip. And when he was able to free his leg, time and again, his one slippery rubber boot would be left in the snow, and he had to dive for it. Step by step, hour after hour, by pure will, Jan forced himself onward against the strong wind and mist that surrounded him. The boots hurt him, and his toes throbbed.

Four days had passed since Jan fled barefoot through the snow around Toftefjord. He knew frostbite had already caused serious damage. Nothing could stop the process once begun. Jan remembered learning about the dangers of frostbite and gangrene from his scouting days. Surely this could not turn out that bad. Jan was uneasy but refused to let fear get the upper hand.

He forced himself onward.

From Solvatnet Lake, Jan set his course over Grønnliskaret Pass, around Soltindene Summit, and down towards Langsundet Sound on the south side. Suddenly the fog evaporated and gave him a glance of the fjord far below. He saw a few scattered houses. It encouraged him onward. His skirmish with the mountains had lasted 28 hours except for the two hours rest he had enjoyed at Dåfjordbotn.

From the fateful moment Jan crawled ashore at Toftefjord, he had put behind him nearly fifty miles on foot. Not very far during normal circumstances perhaps, but Jan had forced his way through long distances in treacherous conditions. Up steep mountains he'd gone, across deserted, frozen tundra and slippery rock-strewn beaches while suffering excruciating pain. His footwear and clothing were inappropriate for Arctic weather conditions. Both his feet had frostbite, and his right foot had a gunshot wound. Hostile weather, fear and loneliness added to his difficulties. No one could help or comfort him nor tell him if he was heading in the right direction. The heaviest burden Jan carried

Solvatnet Lake. In the background is Soltindaksla Mountain.

was not knowing the fate of his friends from Brattholm. It gnawed at him continually. "Had they really been executed? Maybe it was just a rumor." His instincts and education, his iron will and ability to endure pain had helped him through. Even so, the soldier nearing Langsund was a wounded man, mentally broken, and close to physical collapse.

DOWN FROM THE MOUNTAINS

APRIL 3, 1943: Jan's first goal in his journey toward freedom was to reach Bjørnskar, but Artur Olsen had suggested he look up Håkon Heika at Kopparelv by Langsund Sound. From the outer ridges of the mountain plateau, Jan looked down upon the few scattered houses by the fjord down below but was unsure if it was Kopparelv or Bjørnskar. The mountainside sloped steeply at first, and ended in a slanted field toward the fjord.

Jan felt good about the tempo he had been able to keep most of the way from Dåfjordbotn, even throughout his six hour struggle against the deep snow and thick fog. In the course of the day he had put more than nine miles behind him. It was three in the afternoon when Jan moved down through the field with the few dwarfed Arctic birches and crawled through the wire fence put up to contain the cattle in their summertime pastures. He didn't realize he was just above the Heika family farm in Kopparelv.

Kopparelv lies on the rainy side of Langsund Sound, skirting the beach. Håkon and his brother Marineus Heika shared the homestead but lived in opposite ends of the house from each other. Both were married, Håkon to Magna, and Marineus to Alida.

As Jan worked his way through the deep snow close to the dilapidated, century-old log outbuilding, he stopped briefly and looked around the farm. He saw two young boys frolic in the snow in the farmyard. The two cousins Arvid and Viggo stopped and watched him closely at first.

From time to time the Heika family had visitors from Skogsfjord, several miles away. The children called in to the adults that they had a

Cousins Arvid and Viggo Heika with author Astrid Karlsen Scott in front of the old outbuilding. The Heikas played here as children in 1943 and greeted Jan upon his arrival from Dåfjord.

visitor from there and then turned to their play. Jan stood there hesitating for a moment, and the boys realized this was a stranger. He looked worn and exhausted, and his clothes were soaked up to his waist; his hair tousled and frosty white. This time the kids ran all the way up to the kitchen window and shouted, "There's a stranger here."

Magna Heika went out to meet Jan, who asked to speak to the man of the house. There was something urgent about his request and she realized this was not just a casual visit. She thought it best to get him indoors before some neighbor caught sight of him.

For Jan, this home was like all the other places he had been. He was showered with kindness and courtesy and concern for his welfare. The table was soon set and his wet clothes removed and placed around the wood stove to dry. Jan wiped his pistol carefully, patted it, and placed it near him on the table. Magna helped remove his boots and wet socks and was astonished to see his feet and legs. She massaged them, applied some healing salve, and bandaged his wounded foot as well as possible.

Jan was able to relax and regain his strength. He enjoyed these kind people. The Heika family was amazed that Jan was so well informed about their little settlement. He knew exactly who the Nazis were and where they lived. They noticed Jan always kept the pistol close by; even when he drank coffee it was next to him on the table.

"I am quite eager to reach the mainland as quickly as possible," Jan explained.

No matter where Jan was, he was continually planning his next trek, where to go and how best to get there. As with one voice, those he had visited recommended that Jan seek a man named Einar Sørensen in Bjørnskar. Håkon Heika and his wife Magna also spoke very highly of this man.

"Einar Sørensen in Bjørnskar is your best bet to help get you to the mainland," said Håkon. "He is a courageous and dependable man."

"Å ja, there is no one better in this area. You must go to him," urged Magna.

"I have heard many good things about Einar. I need to reach him quickly," said Jan.

"He lives about seven miles from here. The only way to reach him is to walk along the beach. There are no roads."

"The beach will be a lot easier than the mountains," replied Jan.

IN THEIR efforts to win the war, the Germans infiltrated and made close contact with several Norwegians in the Troms District. Abwehr, a German spy organization, hired about two hundred of them outright. The secret to Abwehr's success was that they gave each agent a cover name. Many operated so unobtrusively that even their family and neighbors had no idea of their involvement with the enemy. These spies were diligent and were a great help to the Germans. One of the key assignments for some of them on the outermost islands was to keep a close watch on all ship traffic in the ocean and to faithfully report all sightings of boats and convoys to the German Headquarters in Tromsø. This was an easy task, because many were fishermen and no suspicion was attached to them when their fishing vessels sailed out. They were equipped with two-way radios the Germans had given them and taught them to operate.

One such agent was paid 1000 kroner (about one hundred and fifteen dollars today) a month during busy periods when his fishing vessel was in service; in less busy seasons he was paid 800 kroner per month. It was a goodly sum of additional income for a young man fighting poverty in the Northland in the 1940's. This agent's reason for joining was the promise that his father's fishing vessel would not be confiscated.

This dangerous man lived less than a mile from the Heika family. Being a close neighbor, he knew them well and often dropped in on them unannounced. Kopparelv was sparsely populated and the few homes were spread out. All the same, people knew each other and were always ready to help when a need arose. Abwehr recruited this spy in February of 1942. Even though Abwehr spies worked in secret, knowledge, or at least suspicions of this spy's involvement with the enemy had come to light, and most everyone in the area was afraid of him. The word had quickly spread and a warning to beware of this man was sent out.

To their horror, the Heika family and Jan saw him walking briskly toward the house. Jan leaped to his feet, bolted up the staircase to the second floor and closed the door. The spy had been in Tromsø and the Germans had assigned him the task of inquiring round about in the hamlets and villages about anyone or anything suspicious.

Håkon opened the door. "Well, come on in."

"Thanks. I'm here to invite you to come along with me to collect driftwood around the islands." Large free-floating logs, known as driftwood, were occasionally gathered and used as building materials. The Abwehr spy used this activity as a cover to go ashore and talk to people.

"Oh I don't know. I have a lot of responsibilities right now. I'll pass," said Håkon.

"What do you mean you'll pass? I'm amazed at you, Håkon. There's good money in collecting driftwood as you know!"

"I know, but I've other things going."

"What's the matter with you? This isn't like you, Håkon," said the spy.

"Sorry. I told you this isn't a good time for me."

"Listen here. I don't appreciate being turned down. You'll come or else. This is war and you know things just happen. You know what I mean?" Håkon was not quite sure what the spy meant, but with a family, he didn't want to take any chances.

"Well, I guess I'll have to do my work later. I didn't realize how important it was to you that I'd come along." Håkon said he would come along whatever day he needed him.

Later the spy sent a report to the German headquarters in Tromsø with information he had gathered about the Brattholm affair. He made his co-workers on the wood-collecting jaunt, including Håkon Heika, sign the report. The spy expressed afterwards that he felt the Heikas had acted strange on that particular visit, but was unable to ascertain what caused this.

When the spy finally left the Heika family, they were concerned, and didn't know what to do about Jan. When he was brought down, it was all too clear to the Heikas and to Jan that he had to escape while he still had the chance.

Again Jan had been spared disaster. All were relieved that the second floor ceiling had not creaked while the informer was present, and that the children never said a word, nor made a slip about Jan's presence in the house. It was also a godsend that the spy left in the direction he had come without milling about the farm. He could have discovered Jan's tracks leading down from the mountains.

Jan spent a few more hours with the Heika family.

"We know you're anxious to leave Jan, but you have to wait until the snowdrifts start up again before you continue on to Bjørnskar," Marineus, Håkon's brother explained. "I will walk with you down to the beach," he offered.

"See, what happens here in this sector of Langsund, is that the snowdrifts, at this time of the year, begin instantly as if dropped from the sky." Håkon clarified. "The snow will only last ten or twenty minutes, then the horizon will suddenly clear, only to start up again within a short while." The Langsund Sound was fairly narrow around Kopparelv.

"Should someone across the fjord be looking out a window with binoculars, questions could arise about the strange man who left the Heika home with Marinius and headed down toward the beach," Magna laughed. "And soon the telephone wires would heat up."

In isolated areas like these, any exception to the daily routine raises the curiosity level, and particularly so during wartime. The questions might be innocent, without malice, but in the end they would have the same devastating result. Jan's flight would be in the open, and it would only be a matter of time until the Germans learned of it.

"As soon as you notice the snowdrift clearing, drop down and curl up behind a rock if possible, or prostrate yourself flat on the beach and do not move a muscle until the snow starts up again," warned Håkon.

"You've all been so wonderful. I hope you'll be safe. Many, many thanks."

"We wish you God's speed."

With a few sandwiches in his pockets, and directions on how to reach Bjørneskar, Jan was ready to leave the comforts and the warmth of the Heika family.

"Now is the time, Jan. Let's hurry! These snowdrifts will cover us." Marinius had watched for the weather change through the window. The men set off down toward the beach.

BJØRNSKAR

APRIL 3, 1943: Jan felt energized when he left the Heika house. Twilight and the driving snow gave him and Marinius Heika good cover on their way to the shore.

"Here we are. Just follow the water's edge and you will reach Bjørnskar before too many hours," said Marinius.

"Many thousands of thanks, I…"

"Nonsense. No problem, we were happy to help. Hurry while you have the snow cover, Jan. And all good luck to you." Marinius enfolded Jan's hand in his and shook it warmly.

"All good to you and yours, and again a thousand thanks." Jan turned toward Bjørnskar.

The weather, as Håkon had warned, changed between thick snowdrifts and sudden cessations. He took care to lie down quiet as soon as the thick snow let up, hoping to blend in with the rocks. The episode with the spy at the Heika home made him aware of how vulnerable he was. He was willing to take his time to get to Bjørnskar because he knew carelessness would carry a high price. Soon it would be dark and the seven miles along the shoreline to Bjørnskar seemed an easy undertaking compared with traversing the deep snow up and down mountainsides and over plateaus. The snowdrifts and large rocks were probably the best possible camouflage he could have until total darkness set in.

The southern end of the Langsund coastline where Bjørnskar was located, like Dåfjordbotn, had no connecting roads. Jan hurried along as far and fast as feasible while the snow showers hid him. The rubber boots were perilous on the large slippery rocks and boulders and he limped around them when he could. By the water's edge the snow was sparse, so he stayed as close to the water as possible; then again, sometimes the water licked the rocks far inland, making it impossible.

There were no homes along the stretch to Bjørnskar. Because Langsund was heavily mined, there was no traffic on the fjord except for the smaller boats that could maneuver inside the minefields close to the shoreline. Jan's chances of being discovered here in the dark were slim.

Jan had been fleeing four days. The exertions he suffered consumed the physical strength he had regained while resting in the Heika home. In spite of the generous help and rest granted him by all the strangers along the way, his strength ebbed quickly. Despite the nuisance of the rocks, the going was easier down here by the water, but his ability to keep a steady straightforward course had vanished. His arms and legs lacked vigor. Jan's feet moved ahead but his arms hung limp by his side, except when he steadied himself on a large rock. His tracks were those of someone intoxicated, wavering from side to side, but he counted each step as a victory. Jan's whole body ached, his feet the worst. In spite of it all, the word "impossible" was not part of Jan's vocabulary. He didn't know how to give in. In the past he had cheated death more than a few times, and now to reach Bjørnskar was just a question of enduring a few more hours. All he needed to do was to put one foot in front of the other, and not give in to the weight of the anxiety or the pain. In fact, walking seemed almost automatic by now; it had become a habit.

He had been told that there were no houses between Kopparelv and Bjørnskar. Bjørnskar consisted only of three houses belonging to the same family. In the southernmost house lived Bernhard Sørensen and his wife. Close by in the middle house lived his son, Einar Sørensen, and his family. Einar was the man so many had suggested that Jan should contact.

It was near nine in the evening on an unusually dark night for this time of the year. For some time Jan had kept his eyes open for three houses. Jubilation surged through him when he saw a small light coming from a house in the distance as he came around a bend on the shore. The remainder of the way was made quicker and easier with the hope of

The Sørensen's home in Bjørnskar.

warmth and friendly people close by. A German patrol boat was stationed just inside of Sjurnes, less than a mile from Bjørnskar. Jan tempered his excitement with caution.

Nearing the house, Jan made out the silhouettes of a man, a woman, and two young boys sitting around the kitchen table close to the window. He did not know Einar Sørensen and his family were discussing the gruesome tragedy in Toftefjord four days earlier. Einar related to his wife Elna and his two boys what he had heard during his visit to Tromsø. "The rumors are flying. People believe that one man did escape the Gestapo's claws."

"Then it will not be long before he will come visiting us," Mrs. Sørensen firmly resolved.

She was used to her husband's generosity toward escapees and his reputation among the underground. That moment, all noticed a dark shadow below the kitchen window. Einar took a closer look and saw a fatigued and somewhat wobbly form steadying itself by the south house-corner. The form stopped a few feet back from the steps leading to the kitchen door, and peeked

The Sørensen family. From left, Odd, Elna, Ragnhild, Einar and Svein in 1950.

through a window. Einar turned to his family and looked somewhat astounded. The four of them looked at each other and all thought, "He is here already!" Einar hurried to open the door and went out into the cold to meet the stranger, who asked for Einar Sørensen.

Jan was ushered into the warm kitchen, where he again told his story, that he had come from Toftefjord and as far as he knew he was the only survivor from the skirmish with the Germans and the warship.

"My situation is desperate. I need to escape across the border to Sweden as soon as possible."

Einar did not feel comfortable with Jan's story; it was difficult to believe that a wounded, hunted man could have survived the Arctic weather conditions for four days not knowing the area, and not properly outfitted.

"Tell me, if you can, how did you find Bjørnskar? And how did you know we were here? Who sent you?" Einar had to know.

It was obvious to Jan, from the many people who spoke highly of Einar, that he was a respected and trustworthy fellow. Jan knew he would be in a despairing position if he was turned down. He tried a bluff. "The reputation of your good deeds has reached London."

"You mean they arrived in London?" Sørensen asked, surprised. His answer revealed that he had helped others escape.

"I can't tell you for sure if those you helped reached London, or Sweden, but at least the report of your efforts has reached London." Jan felt a twinge of guilt for leading this good man on.

Subsequent to Jan's explanation, Einar was satisfied; it was not a question of him being willing to help, but rather how he could best help Jan get out of the difficulties that he was in. His wife was not so easily convinced. She wanted more answers and continued her questioning.

"Tell us how many other homes have you visited?"

"None."

"Who were the people you saw?"

"Yours is the first home I have stopped at."

"Who gave our names to you?" Elna ignored Jan's answers and kept pressing. Jan became a little irritated at this lady and somewhat indignant at her repeated questioning.

"Listen here. How many ways do I have to repeat the same answer? I've told you yours is the only home I have visited."

Jan firmly denied ever having been any other place. During his saboteur training with the Linge Company in Scotland it was strongly impressed upon the men never to reveal the name of anyone who had helped.

Elna backed down. "I'm sorry. We just have to be sure. You understand, don't you?"

"I understand and appreciate your concern. And I realize you have to be careful. I am also grateful you invited me in out of the weather."

Following the settling of this little controversy, all three enjoyed and were open toward one another. The Sørensens had Jan remove his wet clothes and hung them to dry, and they gladly shared with him what food they had available. Under such soothing conditions, Jan soon relaxed a bit and felt his body slowly recovering.

Considering his traumatic, demanding last few days, Einar noticed that this man was in incredibly good condition. However, he had a difficult time understanding how he had been able to survive the trek across the untamed mountains in the middle of the arctic winter storms with a wounded foot and no skis. Einar had great admiration for such a man, his courage and fortitude. Jan lightly dismissed it by saying, "I had good training in Scotland; I was in good shape, and I am the right age."

He took out his pistol, polished it and stroked it; a grateful smile brushed his face. "This gun saved my life when I shot the Gestapo chasing me up the ravine in Toftefjord."

At first, they did not talk much about the battle in Toftefjord. Instead they concentrated on the possibility of getting Jan to Sweden. He felt bad that he still did not know the true fate of the men from Brattholm.

"I just returned from Tromsø earlier today," said Einar.

"What can you tell me?" Jan leaned forward attentively.

"The people were in shock. Rumors were flying as the story of the battle in Toftefjord got out. The tragedy was on everyone's lips."

"What did the people know? Or was it just rumors that they'd heard?"

"It was rather chilling," Einar continued. "When the evening sky darkened they all stayed inside and pulled the blinds. They were frightened, and in spite of that, they could talk of nothing else. Terror spread of what reprisals the Germans would mete out on the populace. There was special concern for the resistance men and whether the movement would be unraveled. Everyone's nerves were raw."

"And the Germans? What did they do?"

"Oh…that was the astonishing part! It was not only the Norwegians who were scared; the Germans were unnerved as well. The Gestapo headquarters was buzzing and the German soldiers were called on an immediate alert. Throughout the city they were marching through the streets with loaded guns, breaking into homes, pushing people around, questioning and arresting some and hauling them into the patrol wagons. Patrol cars, with screeching sirens, sped off to the Gestapo headquarters with them. Many Germans wondered if the Brattholm affair would be the beginning of the suspected Allied invasion."

"And what did you learn about the Brattholm men?"

"The way I heard the story," Einar continued, "was that a fishing cutter had anchored in Toftefjord and that the boat had had trouble with its motor. But there were no fishermen aboard, only saboteurs from England."

"How did the Germans find us?"

"The story was that a merchant at Bromnes had betrayed the saboteurs. The Gestapo was called and a German warship, a Schnell boat, launched the surprise attack against them. The cutter had been blown up, and the remaining crew imprisoned."

Jan was totally absorbed in Einar's report. "And my comrades? What did you hear about my comrades?"

Einar hesitated, but he realized he couldn't keep anything from Jan. "It was believed that most of them were shot on the spot. Nonetheless when the warship returned to Tromsø the people had noticed that the Gestapo had three prisoners, two of them seriously wounded. The third man seemed older than the rest."

"That must have been Eskeland," Jan interrupted.

"It was also said," Einar was loath to pass on this piece of news, "that two of them were shot the following day, but that a third one was still alive either in the hospital or imprisoned."

Jan was helpless against the depression that settled over him when he learned the fate of his friends. The realization set in that he was indeed the only survivor. Guilt swept over him that he had been unable to help his comrades. It also occurred to him that the two contacts in Tromsø, Moursund and Knudsen, the underground leaders, had to be forewarned.

"This is a messy situation, Einar. With one, or possibly more of the Brattholm men still alive, there is no doubt the Gestapo will torture the men. It's obvious that in time, one or more will break," said Jan.

"It's humanly impossible not to," agreed Einar.

"We have to warn Moursund and Knudsen somehow. I would like to go and warn them myself." Jan was in earnest.

"That's unthinkable! You'll be arrested and executed."

"Einar, do you dare take the risk? It is a lot to ask."

"You know our identification cards are always checked going in and out of the city. And I have just come back," Einar was thoughtful. "The Germans have the uncanny ability to keep track of everyone and everything going on around them. Moreover, gas rationing is on and Tromsø is some 20 miles away."

"It's too much," Jan reflected. "It was a terrible thing of me to have asked."

"Give me some time, I'll find a way."

"Please be extremely cautious. You know the possibility remains that Knudsen and Moursund might already have been rounded up, or they at least might be shadowed."

"Yes. All things considered, Jan, it might not be safe to keep you here overnight."

Jan and Einar sat at the kitchen table and discussed Jan's continued flight.

"If we can get you to the mainland on the other side of Grøtsundet Sound, you will be closer to Sweden without risking your life going into Tromsø," said Einar. Both men were aware that Jan's flight was extremely dangerous both for his helpers and for himself.

They decided to leave around two in the morning, the darkest time of the night. Einar would take Jan across the fjord in his rowboat. Jan would be set ashore close to some friends of Einar's, a family where he knew Jan could safely get some rest.

Jan left his code name with the Sørensens in case he didn't reach his destination alive. The code was MARTIN 3. Elna wrote it down on the back of their kitchen calendar in the right hand corner, a simple square piece of cardboard. In the center of the front, a smaller block of 365 pieces of white paper was glued. Bold black numbers were printed in the center of the white paper, one for each day of the year. Holidays and Sundays were easy to distinguish and those numbers were printed in red. Each day a numbered piece of paper was torn off. On the back of the Sørensen calendar it now said, "MARTIN 3." Maybe this was not the safest place if the house was raided. In any case, they all hoped that Jan would reach Sweden in safety, eliminating the need to give his code name to the Norwegian authorities in the future.

EINAR AND BERNHARD

EINAR NEEDED someone to come with him to take Jan across the fjord. The choice was between his stoic, seventy-six year old father and his oldest son, Odd. Just fourteen years old, Einar's son was a good lad and strong; moreover he was anxious to come along and help his father. In truth, both Einar's sons would have liked to help.

There was a good chance that no one would return. Should this be their lot, his wife would lose both a husband and her oldest son, and Einar felt that was too much to ask of a woman. He chose his father Bernhard.

Bernhard had worked hard all his life and had even rowed the 125 miles to the Lofoten fishing grounds on occasion. He was still strong and vigorous despite his years. And, with his heart full of hatred for the Germans, he would relish the opportunity to snatch Jan away from under their noses. Einar went next door and discussed it with his father, who readily accepted the challenge. He and his father worked out the details of how to transport Jan further.

The Sørensens outfitted Jan with dry clothes. Jan wore the civilian clothes underneath his Navy uniform. Should the Germans be lucky enough to catch him, he wanted them to know he was a soldier above all, nothing but a Norwegian soldier.

Elna prepared some traditional open-face sandwiches for Jan, the only kind Norwegians made, with a little cured meat. She placed a small square piece of wax paper between each slice of bread, and then wrapped them all securely in a separate piece of wax paper. Jan put several of these packages in his pockets. He had learned how tough it was to be hungry in the mountains, but a knapsack he did not want to carry.

At long last, Jan's one military boot and the one sea boot were retired for real ski boots. The Sørensens even had a pair of skis with bindings that fit. The boots were quite snug for Jan's feet, but at least he could wear one pair of dry socks with them, and Jan felt it was quite an improvement over the rubber boots.

The old unmatched boots had been with Jan in so many places they had become part of his own pain and struggles. They reminded him so much of the generous ladies who had first given them to him, Haldis and Anna at Hersøy Island. He was reminded of the snowstorms, and of being numbed by cold, pain and frostbite. When he changed his boots at Einar's, Jan felt like he was leaving two friends behind.

Southeast of Bjørnskar across Grøtsundet Sound was the little settlement of Snarby, almost seven miles across the water. Jan had to get off Ringvassøy Island if he was to make any serious progress toward Sweden. On the southernmost point of Reinøy Island, on clear days, they could see Finnkroken from Bjørnskar. From here the powerful searchlights of the German batteries constantly skimmed the waves. A few hundred meters out from Finnkroken lay Finnøya and Nipøya Islands; between them was a narrow sound. This was Sørensen's route to Snarby.

There were three main gateways for ships to sail into the city of Tromsø. Kvalsundet Sound on the west side of Ringvassøy Island, Langesund Sound on the east, which was loaded with mines, and the third entrance, Grøtsundet Sound, which was guarded by a German patrol boat which went shuttle-wise back and forth twenty-four hours a day. It went as far north as Grøtnesodden and to the battery installations at Lattervika on the north side of the Ullsfjord. In the south, the patrol boat turned between the battery installations at Tønnes and the estuary at Kvalsundet Sound. From here it was open sea to Tromsø. Most ships or small boats on their way to Tromsø for the first time were ordered to stop for control at the battery installations at Tønnes.

It was unusual that boats were stopped, however, unless they arrived at unusual times or came from unusual directions. In that case, they would have to be prepared to stop. A rowboat on its way from Bjørnskar to Snarby in the early morning hours was definitely unusual as far as distance and time of day went. The challenge was to cross the wide fjord without being discovered by the patrol boat.

The route the patrol boat took southward gave them a little more time than the northern route. The Sørensens' plan was to cross the fjord to Finnøya and Nipøya Island, lie in hiding on the northern end of Nipøya, wait for the boat to pass them on its southern route, then start out again across Grøtsundet Sound toward Snarby.

A thick fog surrounded them when they left. The men were a little concerned about the unstable weather conditions. The wind blew a strong gale and they were surrounded by a thick whiteout. The Sørensens knew the rough seas would increase as they went further south, where the prevailing winds came screaming down the shipping lanes from the Arctic Ocean. There was a limit as to what a small rowboat with three men aboard could handle, but on the other hand, the Sørensen men were used to rough seas and wind, and they knew the seas had to be quite high before the rowboat would capsize. The thick snow reduced their visibility, so much so that all land vanished from sight, but they had learned to navigate by the directions of the waves. The blinding snow, though limiting, was also a good camouflage from the patrol boat.

The patrol boat chugged past Nipøya and the three men watched intently as the lanterns disappeared in the soupy gray-white mixture of heavy fog and snow. As soon as the boat vanished in the darkness, they started out on the remaining four miles across Grøtsundet Sound. With the wind to their back, they made good headway. Though Jan had rested, he did not have much strength left. He was still very tired, so much so that he was grateful when they did not ask him to row. If they had, he was sure they would have had a hard time believing he was a Navy man.

Often when the men dipped the oars into the white-capped waves and pulled them out again they were splashed with seawater, but beyond that, they reached the other shore safely without any major mishaps.

With warm handshakes and well wishes, Jan was put ashore just north of the headland at Lyngnes. From there it was only a few hundred yards to the nearest farm. The Sørensen men, Jan learned later, had an extremely

Jan was brought ashore just north of Lyngneset.

tough return trip. They fought a roaring northwesterly headwind and did not arrive home until the morning hours. Luckily no one had seen Jan, no one discovered that the men had been rowing most of the night – and no one knew they returned with one less man.

The family at Bjørnskar had outfitted Jan for the next segment of his escape. In spite of the difficult times, with shortages of commodities and food, a generous spirit of selflessness and compassion characterized all the people he met in the Troms District of northern Norway. They offered all they had to the wounded soldier, a stranger in need. At the same moment they placed their own lives and those of their families in danger. Jan was deeply touched by this. He knew and understood only too clearly what they had offered. The Germans had tacked copies of a public notice on telephone poles and bulletin boards across Norway with an unmistakable message. The notice read:

ANYONE CAUGHT HELPING
THE ENEMY WILL BE SHOT!

To the Germans, the "enemy" was anyone involved in opposing the Germans. Jan knew this, and it was this knowledge that continually made him shrink from placing more people in harm's way. Desperation forced him to seek help, but he was careful never to reveal where he came from or where he was going. He could never, on purpose, remember the names of any of his helpers when he was asked.

Einar kept Jan's boots hidden in the boathouse. One day, several weeks after Jan had left, the district doctor came by boat. His boat was rather large and he called for Einar to row out to meet him.

"These are for you to replace the ones you gave away," said the doctor, who winked at his friend as he handed him the package.

"I don't understand," said Einar.

"You will. I hope you'll get a chance to enjoy them."

Einar was astonished when he opened the package and beheld a new pair of ski boots. He didn't ask questions, but shook the doctor's hand warmly. Einar was still shaking his head when he left his boat.

Be convinced that
to be happy means to be free
and that to be free means to be brave.
Therefore do not take lightly
the perils of war.

— Thucydides

LØVLI

APRIL 4, 1943: The rugged Sørensen men rowed away as Jan picked up the skis and poles and placed them on his shoulder. He continued a few yards along the sandy beach. The Sørensens had pointed out the house where Jan should seek help. Directly ahead about 300 feet from the beach lay the houses belonging to the Løvli farm, owned by Alfred and Anatona Lockertsen. They had a grown daughter and a 12 year-old foster son, Alvin, who had come to live with them a year earlier.

Today was Sunday. Alfred and his wife's bedroom was a small side room on the first floor, close to the front entryway. The walls were not heavily insulated and Alfred awakened to a noise in the anteroom. It was inky-black, and he rolled over and glanced at the green-lighted figures on the alarm clock. Four in the morning! No one ever came visiting at this hour of the night, and especially not at this time of the year. A visitor now could only mean someone was in grave need of help or it was the Gestapo! Alfred reasoned the Gestapo would have made more of an uproar. Rolling out of bed, he dressed hastily and went to open the door. A dark-headed, frozen stranger faced him.

Jan greeted Mr. Lockertsen and at the same time apologized for the early hour. His presence, tall and handsome with the skis and poles at his side, exacted Alfred's close attention. He had come out of nowhere, and it was still night. When Jan explained to Alfred that he had escaped from the Germans following a battle in Toftefjord, Alfred just shook his head. He had a difficult time believing this man was who he said he was. Alfred had also heard about the happenings at the mouth of the fjord. The story he had heard was to a great extent similar to that of Einar's at Bjørnskar, but not quite. It was Alfred's understanding that all twelve men from Brattholm were taken as prisoners and executed. This caused him to be quite skeptical and cautious about Jan's story. If what Alfred had been told earlier was the truth and all twelve men had been caught and executed, then who was this man standing before him in the doorway? Was he a charlatan or was he telling the truth? Was he a bona fide Norwegian commando soldier or was he a provocateur, sent to trap him? His searching eyes observed the stranger was clean-shaven, but his cheeks and nose had a deep ruddy hue making him appear windblown and frozen. Alfred wanted to believe, but he was not persuaded that Jan was telling him the truth. On the other hand, he concluded that if he was telling the truth, he desperately needed his help. Jan was invited in, and was told to lie down on the large sheepskin in front of the kitchen stove to get some rest. Lockertsen wanted to steal a couple of more hours of sleep before getting up, but sleep escaped him; he lay on his bed staring up at the dark ceiling, pondering and being anxious.

The man lying on his kitchen floor, was he an escapee or something else? Lockertsen was mystified. If he did not report him, the entanglement with this man might have ill-fated consequences.

Around 6:30 a.m. Lockertsen moved quietly into the kitchen to start the morning fire in the wood stove. He liked to heat the kitchen before he did his barn chores and enjoyed the welcoming warmth of his home when coming in from the coldness outside. He had scarcely poked his head in the kitchen door when Jan flung himself about to a half kneeling position while at the same time grabbing his pistol and pointed it point blank at Alfred. In that moment Alfred was convinced Jan was no provocateur. This was the action of a desperate man.

Jan had been without sound sleep for 48 hours. Worn to a frazzle, he reacted like a wounded, frightened animal. The ruthless ordeals of the last four days were forcing their way to the surface. He had been half asleep drifting between consciousness and slumber when Alfred stuck his head in the door. Any slight unexpected movement put Jan on guard.

Alvin, the foster son, was sleeping in the room directly above the kitchen, known as the north-room. He woke up at 8 a.m., when Anatona started the milk separator that stood in the hall at the bottom of the steps.

Merging with the reverberation of the separator were two male voices coming from the kitchen. Effortlessly he distinguished his foster father's deep resonant voice with its enthusiastic Nordland's dialect, but to whom did the other voice belong? It was a gentler voice, and more careful. Alvin knew straight away, since he was from the South, that the other man did not have a Nordland's dialect at all, but that the stranger spoke with a distinct Southern tongue. He was amused listening to the two men; they spoke with entirely diverse dialects, yet they understood each other perfectly it seemed. Yes, the other man definitely had to be from Southern Norway.

Snarby was a rather deserted, almost forsaken, place north of Tromsø. There was neither road nor telephone communication out here, and Alvin could not remember that a stranger had ever dropped in like this. "So who was this man from Southern Norway? Why did he come in the early morning hours? How had he found them? Who had sent him?" He had so many questions.

Alvin started down the attic stairs but was met half way by his foster mother. Her face was sober.

"Who is that man in the kitchen?" asked Alvin.

"Oh that is just Astrid's boyfriend. He came to surprise her."

"At this hour of the morning? You are just kidding me?"

Anatona could see Alvin's doubts. "All right young man, I'll tell you the truth. But you breathe a word to anyone, and we are all dead! He is a Norwegian commando soldier, the only escapee from the battle in Toftefjord."

"Wow! Why did he come here? How long will he stay?" Alvin found this exciting.

"I am afraid I can't answer any of your questions. You must understand that we can't talk about this, not even to your best friend. It might mean the soldier's and our lives if word gets out. Do you promise not to tell anyone?"

Alvin thought for a long time. Though he was young, he grasped the severity of the situation. Should the Germans come, there were no possibilities of escape and the adults would be shot. The women would probably also be shot or sent to a concentration camp.

Alvin looked into Anatona's unyielding eyes and knew this was serious business. He feebly reassured himself that the Germans probably would extend mercy to him because of his young age and because he really did not belong to the family.

"What is your answer, Alvin? You must not reveal this secret to any other human being. Do you promise?"

"Yes. You have my word," vowed Alvin.

On Sunday afternoons, Alvin's friends from neighboring farms came over to play with him. Today was different.

"You must keep your friends away from the farm today. You go to one of their homes."

Alvin understood and did as he was told.

Intent on continuing his escape, Jan hoped to leave Løvli farm within a short period of time. The fear that innocent people would be harmed or sent off to a concentration camp because of him was ever in his mind, and it made him uneasy.

"It means a lot to me to be on the mainland at last," Jan said happily. "I'm impatient to put my new skis on and begin to climb these forested mountains. I want to head eastward en route to Sweden."

"Jan, you don't have any conception of what the terrain is like out there. It is not a good idea," said a skeptical Alfred. "I'll find you a better alternative." The older man produced a map and spread it out on the table. "Look Jan, this is Løvli farm." He pointed on the map. "Right here, at the outermost part of a huge peninsula, there are miles of steep, precarious Alpine mountain terrain, beginning just to the back of the farm with cavernous clefts. There are no natural paths for a skier to follow. And the weather is unpredictable. Masses of loose, deep snow, and nowhere you can seek help or shelter from the storms."

Jan listened intently, following Alfred's finger on the map.

"The southern part of the peninsula tapers to a narrow neck of land where the German watch posts are strategically stationed," Alfred continued. "On either side of the peninsula, the fjords cut deeply through to the innermost part of the region. If you attempt that route, Jan, it'll all end tragically for you."

Jan relaxed somewhat with this new information. The Lockertsens wanted him to have some rest before he continued onward and showed him up to an attic room, with a window toward Grøtsundet Sound, where he could get some sleep. This room belonged to the Lockertsen's married daughter and son-in-law, but both she and her husband were away. The husband was fishing in Lofoten, and the daughter was in the hospital. From the Cape Cod window in the attic Jan had a splendid view of Grøtsundet Sound, which unfolded before him like a rich blue carpet. He sank down on the bed, and watched as a German patrol boat, probably the same boat that the Sørensens and he had outsmarted the night before, moved unmenacingly past.

The wintry weather had been cold and nasty for some time, but today it had dawned with a bright Northland sun and azure skies. The view from the attic window blessed Jan with peaceful moments while reclining on the bed, though the burden when recollecting the fate of his friends was a hurtful memory he was unable to erase.

Sunday dinner at the Lockertsen's home was always at 12:30 p.m. sharp, and this day was no exception. Jan had been invited to join them. He savored every bite. Jan couldn't remember the last time he enjoyed food to this degree and such a large, warm meal.

The Lockertsens had locked the outer entrance door, just to be sure of no surprises today. Jan looked handsome dressed in his Navy uniform with the Norwegian flag on his shoulder, the pistol by his side. The German patrol boat was returning and everyone thought it came conspicuously near, but it glided past on its way northward.

Save for the patrol boat and Jan, the afternoon was like any other Sunday at Løvli farm. Every now and then it was difficult to remember the war was raging all around, yet in this home, this afternoon was peaceful and consoling, almost serene.

The Lockertson Family

Astrid, the Lockertsen's younger daughter, had done her best to care for Jan's wounded foot. She washed it with tender care, and applied salve and a new bandage. Her experience in such things was minimal, and she worried that with its appalling coloring, the foot was infected. The nearest doctor was in Tromsø, three hours away by motorboat. The Lockertsens had a boat, but there was no way they could bring a doctor to Løvli farm without someone prying and wanting to know why, not to mention the risk of being stopped by the Germans.

Jan returned upstairs and fell into bed following dinner. Although the Lockertsens had made him extremely comfortable, his mind was ever rehashing the harrowing experiences of the last few days. When sleep finally came, he slept well for a few hours.

At this time of the year, Alfred was busy setting fish nets out in Ullsfjorden. They were set at the innermost part of Jøvika Cove in the Kjosenfjord. To get there, he had to row northeast toward Grøtsundet Sound around the promontory into where the Ullsfjord cuts inland toward the south. Further in, it divides into Kjosenfjord toward the east and Sørfjord toward the south. The distance of travel round trip was almost twenty miles.

Alfred owned a remodeled dory without a deck. A small wheelhouse was built toward the front of the boat, close to the motor. Below the wheelhouse a modest little cabin was embodied. They called the boat Bloffsen, but its official mark was "AKT-T28 TD." Her crew, in addition to Alfred, was his son Jon, who lived in a neighboring house on the south side of Løvli farm, and Peder Nilsen from Svarvaren a little further south.

Monday mornings, it was Alfred's habit to sail into Jøvika Sound. On this Sunday he changed his schedule. He and Jan had come to a possible solution. They would put to sea late Sunday evening after dark, and plot a course for Nordkjosen, in Ullsfjord. From there Jan could ski by way of Lyngen, with Sweden as his final objective. Alfred would bring his usual crew. Earlier in the day he had sent his daughter Astrid with a message to Peder Nilsen. She walked south on the beach along the fjord, then cut across a field below Peder's home, and knocked on the door.

"Mr. Nilsen is it possible for you to come a little earlier today? The weather forecast is not promising and Papa said they could not postpone the fishing trip to Jøvika until Monday morning as planned earlier."

"No problem. I'll be there."

Peder, a husband and father, worked a small farm in Svarvaren in addition to being part of Bloffsen's crew. Just at this time Peder and his wife were deeply sorrowing. Their two-year-old son Norman had accidentally burned his foot on the wood stove. The burn got infected and fever set in. They took him to the hospital in Tromsø, but little Norman never returned home.

This crushing sorrow enveloped the Nilsens when Astrid came visiting them. Nonetheless Peder was a kind, remarkable human being, sober minded and selfless. He would never turn his back on anyone who needed him, no matter what the situation. He liked working unnoticed. He was a good friend, honorable and courteous.

Peder had an early afternoon dinner with his wife before he went northward. When he reached Løvli farm, Alfred was out in the farmyard pacing back and forth, chewing tobacco and spitting. He did not say a word to Peder though he had seen him coming. Peder guessed something was wrong.

Alfred was aware Peder knew the Toftefjord story. Suddenly he turned to him and shared his burden. During the night a stranger had come, the only survivor from the Brattholm tragedy in Toftefjord. He was on a desperate flight from the Germans and was trying to reach Sweden. Lockertsen wondered if Peder would help with the further transport of this man. Peder expressed instant willingness to help. They agreed they would transport him to Tyttebærvika (Lingonberry Cove) in Kjosen.

Later that afternoon the weather changed and strong wind gusts brought snow showers and awful visibility. In reality, the weather was in their favor since they had to travel across Grøtsundet Sound in the channel where the German patrol boat traveled. Between four and five p.m. they made ready. Jan wore his uniform and he was wearing a thick, Russian style leather cap. A few days earlier Alvin had found it on the beach. It had been washed and dried, and he gave it to Jan.

The dock at Løvli from which Bloffsen *set out.*

Jan was eager to leave, knowing he would soon be able to try out the skis and ski boots he had received at Bjørnskar. Peder noticed the boots were just a smidgen too small, and he was concerned the cold would harm Jan's already disfigured foot. He cut soles to fit inside the boots made from cellulose. Cellulose was a material easily obtainable during the war and used for many purposes; it is the chief substance composing the cell walls of fibers of all plant tissue. He stuffed the soles into Jan's boots. Though they crowded Jan's feet, Peder hoped they would prevent the cold from penetrating the bottom of his boots.

Anatona readied several small food packs and Jan put them in every pocket of his uniform. He accepted a small knapsack this time. It was filled with a change of clothing and extra food.

The wind nipped at the four men as they made their way down to the dock. Alvin followed all the way to the wharf but was not allowed to go aboard. He thought this had been a most action-packed Sunday.

Bloffsen's rope was unfastened and Alfred went into the wheelhouse and navigated the boat into the open waters. Jan spent most of his time below with Alfred's son. Amid their small talk, Jan readied and polished his pistol.

The heavy snowdrifts and wind and Bloffsen with no lanterns were ominous signs. Intermittently the snowfall ceased, the sky cleared, and at that moment the brilliant stars and moon shone forth. The celestial bodies are brighter up close to the North Pole, and there was no place for Bloffsen to hide during those moments. Peder kept watch in those brief intervals of cessation. He could dimly make out the patrol boat pressing toward Grøtnesodden. The Germans aboard the patrol boat knew most of the fishing vessels that went back and forth in these waters; seldom were any of them stopped. If they were called toward the patrol boat, it was usually on the way in from the sea, and most likely because the Germans wanted to buy some of their newly caught fish.

The men had loaded a sizeable quantity of fishing nets and other fishing gear aboard Bloffsen. They intended to hide Jan under it should the German patrol stop them. Jan insisted this was too risky for them, and felt the Germans would assuredly look underneath the fishnets if they were hunting an escapee. Instead he had Alfred navigate close to land, so that he could slither right into the water and swim to shore without the Germans discovering him. They did as Jan wished, but no one believed he would survive on the mainland very long after such a swim. Coming ashore soaking wet, in deep snow and freezing wind where the houses were scarce, and no one to give him help, he surely would freeze to death in such a situation.

Even Alfred could not help. It would be impossible for him to turn towards the shore after a German inspection, they would at once become suspicious of them. At the first opportunity after sailing around the northern end of Ullstind Peak, they set the course into the Ullsfjord, relieved that the most dangerous area was behind them. They had made good time and were a little earlier than expected. As a result Alfred slowed Bloffsen, not wanting to arrive in Kjosen before midnight. They wanted to take advantage of the darkness.

The men worked their way to the innermost section of the fjord before they ventured over toward the eastside. A short distance past Storsteinnes, on the north side of Kjosenfjord was Tyttebærvika. A deserted place, Lockertsen owned a small boathouse in the cove with fishing yarns draped over wooden racks in front. He headed Bloffsen straight in that direction.

Near midnight they reached the boathouse. The tide was out, and Bloffsen's motor was shut down some distance from the shore, the water being too shallow to continue all the way in. All the men were willing to bring Jan ashore, but Jan asked Peder to help him these last remaining yards.

Aboard Bloffsen they had a small dinghy. It was hard for Jan to say goodbye again, to people he had gained such respect for and to whom he owed so much. He climbed over the railing into the ready dinghy, seated himself in the stern, and was handed the skis and the poles. On his back he had his little knapsack.

Rocks were everywhere. Peder rowed carefully, but they kept colliding with them. At last he pushed with one oar on the bottom to help move them along. Even that only worked for a few yards before the boat stranded. He jumped into the icy water and dragged Jan and the boat as far as possible. Then he went back and got Jan's skis, poles and the knapsack and brought them over by the boathouse. He re-entered the water, and carried Jan on his back, an arm around each of his legs, and with Jan's arms around his neck. When they reached the boathouse Peder turned his back to the boathouse and the ladder enabling Jan to climb up dry-shod. Jan was of a much larger stature than Peder but Peder kept a good balance amidst the slippery rocks while bringing him ashore in the dark. Peder now returned to the dingy, waded into the water and dragged it to safety on the shore.

The two men visited under the cover of the fishnet for about one hour. Peder mentioned some relatives he had in Lyngseidet, and suggested Jan look them up should he have difficulties. He gave Jan good pointers and directions. He also updated him about the surrounding terrain, where he should go, and where there might be danger.

When the subtle light from the midnight sun became visible in stark contrast to the serrated mountain peaks in the distance, Jan reached out and clasped Peder's hand firmly, "I know no names," he assured him. Peder understood it to mean that if Jan was taken a prisoner he could not reveal any names, because he did not know them, and they did not have to be concerned.

"No German will ever catch me," he continued. In his gun he had one cartridge left, saved for himself should it be necessary. Jan heartily thanked Peder, and slipped away into the darkness on his skis.

A NARROW ESCAPE

APRIL 5, 1943: The loneliness of Tyttebærvika (Lingonberry) seeped into Peder as he stood and watched Jan vanish into the shadows. Jan had come into his life only a few hours earlier but he had left a deep impression. The two men had communicated spirit to spirit, and with his whole being Peder wanted Jan to reach Sweden unharmed. Having just lost his son Norman, Peder did not want to lose his newfound friend as well. A narrow motor-road snaked along the

Peder Nilsen, 1999

Peder Nilsen being interviewed by Tore Haug.

Kjosenfjord a few feet up from the shore. Traffic was sparse on this road. Sometimes the whole night could pass without a car being seen. A few miles ahead Lyngseidet Village was crawling with Germans and who could know when they would show?

Jan was jubilant. For the first time since Toftefjord he did not have to fight the elements and wade through deep snow or cross mountain plateaus. Ahead lay the open snow-covered road with great skiing conditions. It was the middle of the night and running into people was not a concern. Should he notice approaching car lights it would be an easy thing to fade into the woods bordering the road. In truth this was the first time he felt a road beneath him since he broke away from the Germans. He had food and other necessities in his knapsack. The weather was fairly good, and he was an excellent skier. Re-energized by the circumstances and the hope of soon reaching Sweden, Jan glided across the smooth roads. Sheltered by the darkness he moved rapidly toward Kjosen at the end of the fjord, not quite four miles from Tyttebærvika.

Jan was able to move so quickly that it surprised him. A feeling bordering on euphoria filled his being. His every need was met; he had dry clothes and plenty of food. While people slept he would work his way through the populated areas. During the days he would seek cover in barns and boathouses along the way and ski mostly at night. With this extraordinary speed he would be at the Swedish border in no time.

His first goal was to get through the villages of Kjosen and Lyngseidet, then ski along the magnificent Lyngenfjord south toward Elvebakken, a small snugly populated area five miles from Lyngseidet.

Jan remembered Peder's words: "You must stay off the road going east toward Lyngseidet, Jan. You will be safer back up in the hillsides."

"I'm sure you are right about that," Jan had agreed.

"German soldiers as well as the Norwegians will find it peculiar to meet a skier on the road during the night hours. And be aware that in Kjosen there is a road barrier. To pass it, people have to call the guard, a German soldier. He is up at a nearby house. He comes down to check the person's identification card to see if all is in order before they are allowed to enter the village. You know what you have to do, Jan," Peder had warned.

Jan passed through the barrier unnoticed.

During the nearly two miles between Kjosen and Lyngseidet Village, Jan climbed the incline hidden away from the built-up areas on several occasions.

As Jan neared Lyngseidet, one of his ski bindings snapped. Although it took him a while to fix it, his watch showed the time to be 4:30 a.m.

Jan felt confident he could get through Lyngseidet before people began to stir. But his confidence was misplaced. The watch had been along on three swims in salt water and through many wet storms. Jan neared Lyngseidet center with a marvelous elongated downhill road enabling him to click along at a good speed. Suddenly, two-dozen rowdy German soldiers poured out of a school and swarmed into the road blocking it. The soldiers carried plates and utensils instead of grenades and guns – they were heading for breakfast.

Jan couldn't stop abruptly without having the whole troop pounce on him. Having no where else to go, he did what all Norwegians do when skiing and they meet up against people. He kept up his speed and shouted, "Tracks! Tracks!" The soldiers did not move fast enough and Jan was right on top of them. He pushed his way through them shouting "Tracks! Tracks." trying his best not to act flustered.

The soldiers must have been half asleep. They neither resisted nor tried to stop him. Jan was amazed they didn't notice he was wearing a Norwegian Navy uniform with "NAVY" and "NORWAY" insignias emblazoned on his shoulder. It all happened so fast that they, like Jan, probably had no time to react.

Immediately after skiing through the troop, Jan neared an even steeper downhill road a few hundred yards ahead. The road approached a crossroad down by the fjord. Jan saw another barrier in the middle of the crossroads with only a narrow passageway open on the left. Three German soldiers were inspecting identification cards of Norwegian civilians.

Jan butted his skis to slow down and veered slightly off the road, coming almost to a standstill. A few yards ahead, he saw a narrow road turning to the right in the direction of a small cottage not far from the barrier. Jan seized the narrow road with his skis, moving as naturally as possible so as not to show the fear of a hunted man. He forced himself to appear relaxed, as if he was going about insignificant business.

This little side road and his quick decision to take it saved Jan. He continued to move away from the main road and the German guards, and worked his way up the mountain slope. After a while, Jan felt safe enough to stop and think the situation through. He could see the mountain slopes were too close to the German guards and the fjord, and he had to be careful not to reveal himself. Jan remembered the map he had studied which showed an old Sami summer trail used in times past when their reindeer flocks were on the move. This trail went from Lyngseidet over into Lyngsdalen Valley and Furuflaten. Jan was confident he could follow this same road on skis.

His original plan was to follow the road along the fjord – first to Elvebakken, then later along the road past Pollfjellet Mountain in the direction of the village of Furuflaten. Jan planned to travel only when his surroundings looked safe and mostly at night.

After his narrow escapes with the Germans that morning, he reconsidered. The area was crawling with Germans, and the first plan no longer seemed prudent.

ALONE IN THE MOUNTAINS

APRIL 5, 1943: Jan began his ascent into the high mountain plateau in the early morning hours. He climbed diagonally up the hillside in a southerly direction and stayed well away from the built-up areas of Lyngseidet and other small settlements. He had decided to take the Sami summer road toward Lyngsdalen Valley and Furuflaten.

Some distance up, Jan reached the Fyenelv River. He stayed close to the riverbed. The hilly terrain rose continually, and in the end, the river became but a small creek hidden under the deep snow and impossible to follow. In his steady climb he had risen some 1500 feet above the fjord. To the west he saw the mighty peaks of Kavringen and Kvalvik.

The sun shone brightly and below him, to the east, shimmered Lyngenfjord. Staying oriented in this landscape would be easy with such good visibility. Jan hoped to travel far while the weather was so clear. When he reached the top of the plateau, the terrain stayed fairly level for the next two miles.

Jan maintained a southerly direction, working his way around the tall peaks. He then turned west in toward Kvalvik Mountain's south wall. From here the Kvalvik Valley spread out. Jan scanned the landscape and saw no other possibility but to cross the valley. He worked his way down the abrupt slope toward the Kvalvik River, crossed it, and began climbing the south wall of the valley. Viewed from the plateau on the north side, it had looked fairly simple but he found the valley to be much steeper than he'd thought.

The south wall was too precipitous to use his skis in a herringbone fashion; instead, Jan had to side step his way up from the river. This slowed him down considerably. The Kvalvik Valley forged its way toward the Lyngenfjord in the east. Jan admired and was invigorated by the lofty view.

His own situation stood in stark contrast to the power and the magnificence of the nature spread before him. Jan had always enjoyed spending time in the mountains. The mountain ranges here in the Troms District, interspersed with sharp jagged peaks and glaciers, were quite different from the ones he'd roamed before the war in southern Norway. The many mountain hikes he had enjoyed with his parents and siblings during his childhood taught him to love and respect nature.

When he reached Kvalvik Valley, a second valley, possibly Fugledalen, stretched southward. He felt that was the direction he needed to follow. Jan could not remember all the details from the map, but he believed it would take him in the direction of Lyngsdalen Valley.

Steep mountains bordered Fugledalen Valley on both sides. Jan passed to the east by Bredalsfjellet Mountain and the Vestbreen Glacier. The rugged, varied terrain amazed him and he guessed that the mountain wall he saw to the east was part of Rundfjellet Mountain. The Fugledalen Valley eventually blended with another wide valley that Jan neared as he continued his southerly trek.

The majestic terrain thrilled him, but it also slowed him up. In the midst of this beauty he was taken off guard when the wind suddenly bore down on him. Until now, not even the smallest breeze had whispered by him. Within minutes, the snow whipped around him at an alarming speed. The mountain peaks he'd admired moments earlier were now cloaked in ominous clouds. Steel-gray clouds moved in fast and tumbled down the mountainside. Before Jan had time to think or plan, he was in the midst of the storm's fury. The downwind was unbearable. He struggled to keep his balance. The heavy mist and the whirling snow became so thick Jan could not see the tips of his skis. Sharp snow particles scraped his face.

Jan turned his back to the wind and crouched to a half-sitting position but it gave him no relief. The wind blew straight through his clothes and chilled his flesh. He had to keep moving. His only escape was to descend the mountain and find his way back to the sea.

Even as Jan inched his way forward, the ground beneath him began to slant steeply downward. He worried that the skis would just take off, perhaps over a cliff? The snow gales made seeing ahead impossible. But Jan remembered that at the end of the Bredals Lake, the vertical mountain wall sheared down to a small flat plateau. Jan feared he might be right on the edge, but he had no way of knowing. He was caught in the fury of the penetrating wind and whirling snow. Like a helpless toddler, Jan fumbled around lost in a world of giant mountains and glaciers.

How to avoid the edge? "Snowballs!" exclaimed Jan. Now and then the raging wind ceased for a moment to gather strength for its next onslaught. In those fleeting moments, Jan would throw a snowball a few meters ahead. It was impossible to follow its trail in the thick snow, but he strained, listening for its muffled landing. If Jan didn't hear it hit the ground, he reasoned he was too close to the edge of steep and dangerous terrain.

It was a tedious process. Jan threw many snowballs during the storm. Many times he retreated and edged his way forward far away from what he believed to be a precipice, all the while descending steeply. Jan methodically worked his way down the treacherous mountain. He had no idea how steep the mountain was, but he had to side step most of the way down. Jan couldn't see where he had come from or where he was going. After many hours he felt the terrain flatten beneath him. He crossed the even plateau where, without knowing, he was nearing the edge of another precipice, which ended in Lyngsdalen Valley 450 feet further down. The terrain before him was even more difficult than that above. The loose snow rushed madly away from beneath his skis. He leaned heavily on his poles and sidestepped gingerly as he kept moving downward. When he threw a snowball he seldom heard it fall anymore. Perhaps they had outlived their usefulness? The ground unexpectedly evened out once more.

Jan wondered how far he had come. Could he possibly be in Lyngsdalen Valley? It was pure guesswork; he did not know. If he stopped concentrating for even a moment, he became aware of his suffering body. His wounded foot pained him and his hands were stiff and frozen. Even after all his struggles, the possibility remained that he could still freeze to death in the wilderness unless he could find a way out soon.

The chill he had felt after going ashore to Vårøya had eased somewhat, but now it returned in full force. At the time he thought it impossible to ever be that cold again, but the dreadful freezing had returned. Jan trembled uncontrollably.

Overcome by bitter cold and exhaustion, Jan yearned to stop and rest. But there was no place to hide – and besides, if he did, he would surely freeze to death.

"Ski on Jan," he said to himself. "Somewhere you will get down to the sea." His strong will and naturally confident attitude enabled him to forge ahead yard by yard.

The terrain became extremely smooth and he wondered if he had reached a lake. It felt good to ski across this smooth surface. His skiing quickened and a gentle hope began to rise. It wasn't long before the ground rose again. The snow became powdery and he sank deep. He used considerable strength pushing hard on his poles to keep moving.

STORM IN LYNGSDALEN VALLEY

APRIL 5, 1943: Without realizing it, Jan had reached the base of Lyngsdalen Valley. He fumbled around totally bewildered; his sense of direction was gone. In his disorientation Jan began the upward climb. The incline escalated with each step, forcing him to turn his skis and tramp sideways up the gradient.

Jan's foot throbbed with pain. He yearned for relief. The raging wind stirred up the snow around him and icy particles abraded Jan's face and eyes. The sharp Arctic air chilled his lungs - each breath he took smarted.

Jan had no idea he was climbing the lower part of a precipitous mountain stretching upward 500 feet. The mountain was encircled by other snowy giants, except where it butted up to the Lyngsdalen Valley from where Jan had come. Some were over 5000 feet high. No matter where he turned, the snow and fog engulfed him and he could not get oriented in this murky gray and white world. Jan's body was numb. His blood felt as if it had turned to ice.

The buoyant optimism he had felt leaving Kjosen a few hours earlier evaporated. It would be so easy to give up here. No one would blame him. His strength was waning and maybe it was best to end it all. But negative thoughts never lingered long in Jan's mind. "Where am I? There will be a way out! I must find a way!"

The precipitous mountain he faced was weighted down with deep, loose spring snow. Jan could not see it. Suddenly snow, ice and dirt broke loose and moved down the mountain, slowly at first, then rushing madly toward Jan. There was no escape.

The avalanche roared downhill, deafening and awe-inspiring. Helpless, Jan did not know in which direction to move nor did he grasp what was happening. He was offered up, a sacrifice to the crushing snow masses.

The mountain of snow swept him off his feet, catapulting him down, backwards, sideways, then head first. Tossed like a rag doll, Jan flipped, jerked, and was propelled ever downward until he landed on the valley floor he had crossed a short while earlier.

All went black.

View of Lyngsdalen

Jan opened frost-covered eyelids. His breathing was shallow and came in short spurts. As if through a foggy glass, all he could see was white snow wherever he looked. His mind was vacant. The snow masses enveloped him. Only his head and one arm were free. It wasn't clear to him what had happened, but he'd received a concussion. No matter how hard he tried to focus, he could not remember. The last thing he recalled was how he carefully worked his way down the mountainside. He didn't recollect crossing the valley floor or that he was on his way up the opposite mountain.

Jan struggled to remember. Slowly his consciousness returned. He knew he must have received a terrible blow to his head, but he did not know how long he'd been unconscious. Nausea swept over him and he was clammy and disoriented. Struggling to free himself from the snow masses, Jan discovered both of his ski poles were gone, and one of his skis. The other ski was broken in half, with part of it still fastened to his boot. His mitten and cap were gone. Red spots dotted the snow. Jan touched his face. He looked at his fingers, covered with his own blood. He realized he'd survived an avalanche.

Jan looked around and tried to focus. He saw nothing but high mountain peaks and snow. Where was his knapsack? Gone, and all the food with it. Jan was isolated in a world of snow and ice.

The last few hours before the avalanche Jan had managed to keep moving ahead though his ability to see was impaired. Working his way down precipitous cliffs, being able to see only a yard ahead, he had arrived in Lyngsdalen Valley without knowing it. Unwittingly, he had turned right across the valley floor. He'd gone further into the wilderness and up into the mountains on the opposite side instead of turning left toward the sea. Jan was lost. The raging snowstorm had blinded him, making it impossible to know in which direction he was moving. All he knew was that he had to keep moving.

The unseen power that had preserved him so many times before, again kept him alive against the odds. Yet, life seemed to be at cross-purposes. He was alive, but barely. Nonetheless, in his wretched, deplorable condition Jan was driven to continue onward.

The part of his face that had rested against the snow was scraped and bloody. It burned and stung. The avalanche had also robbed him of his mittens. His hands were turning blue. The boots that Einar Sørensen had given him at Bjørnskar cramped his feet, and the thin socks were not on a par with the Arctic weather. He blessed Peder Nilsen for making him the cellulose soles. Without them…it was too much to think about.

Jan turned from the mountains and headed east across the flat valley floor. Each step depleted his strength. Sometimes he sank so deep into the snow that he had to dig around his leg to free himself or use his hands to lift his leg out. His fighting spirit stirred him on.

"Onward Jan. You must keep walking," he told himself.

Jan battled against the frigid elements for hours. When he tried to orient himself to his surroundings, the white terrain and white vertical mountains blinded him. He was able to make out that the valley had narrowed. Towering mountains stood guard like sentinels on each side. The sound of a rushing river was near and he followed close. The terrain was hilly and rough, up for a few feet, then down, then up.

Jan tried to concentrate but felt like a spectator watching his own drama.

And the cold – the bitter cold penetrated every nerve, every cell of his body. He knew he had to get warm. He came to a large rock and, in his despair, he began digging with his bare hands, down, down. He crawled in, but the bitter cold intensified. It was hopeless. Lying there, Jan knew he would freeze to death. He struggled out of the dent.

Despondency overshadowed him again. It would be so easy to give in. Nature would do the rest, and it probably would not take long.

"Jan, keep walking. You must keep walking!" he demanded of himself.

He trudged through the snow, sinking down to his hips, pulling himself back out again. He fought for his life minute by minute. Eternity could not last this long.

"Jan, you must keep walking."

"Walk!"

What happened during the night when darkness fell was not clear to him. His thoughts blurred. He only knew that if he stopped he would die. Wet, and frozen clear through, beset with pain, Jan forced his body to obey.

"Don't stop! You will die if you do!"

"Just one more step!"

"And another. And another. And another…"

His inner voice refused to give him peace until he obeyed.

"Where am I? Where am I going?"

He lost all sense of direction in the avalanche. Jan waded through the snow hour after hour. He became aware a new day was dawning.

His mind raced, and then it abruptly stood still. He battled to stay alert.

He had won against the hostile night, but the weather conditions did not improve. Several times he tried to dig himself down in the snow, but was unable. The next day came and Jan still fought the elements and his demise.

He continued wandering, but he did not know where he was going. He only felt snow, ice, cold and wind. He had no goal anymore.

"Walk!"

As the day joined with the evening, he heard voices. He didn't see anyone. But the voices were real, and he thought he knew them.

"Yes, it is I. Over here! Yes! It is I, Jan!"

He exerted his last ounce of strength to move toward them.

The voices kept calling for him. But they did not answer when he called back to them. Nonetheless, they instilled in him courage and fortitude to continue. As the night shadows crept in over Jan and eclipsed the confined valley, Jan grappled with reality.

"Am I losing my mind? Maybe I am sleepwalking and dreaming? Am I really wandering about in a storm, alone somewhere in the Arctic? How will it all end?"

Reality had slowly merged with imagination. The nightmare he was living got jumbled up with the voices. At that moment the Brattholm men walked toward him. One by one they came close.

"Jan!"

"Ja, Per, it is I!"

"Jan!"

"I have missed you terribly!"

"Jan!"

"Ja, You can see me, can't you, Sigurd?"

"Over this way. It is I!"

Jan plunged forward trying to grab his pant leg.

"Over here. Oh please!"

Jan cried into the howling storm.

April 8, 1943: During the afternoon the weather eased. The heavy clouds loosened their grip on the mountains and a pale glow of blue sky came into view. Jan barely saw the mighty bordering mountain walls.

He was in a valley that continued downward, ever downward. "Was it moving toward the fjord? People? And hope?"

Jan continued to follow the valley, staying close to the ravine. The voices he'd heard so clearly earlier came and went. In the end he tried not to pay attention to them. They never answered his call anyway. The snow was deep. In places he sank to his waist and felt imprisoned when he did. He dug and twisted and turned to free himself, just to take the next step only to have the same thing happen all over again. But something deep inside urged him on.

"Walk!"

"What am I doing here? Where am I?"

"Jan, you must keep walking."

"Per! Is it really you this time?"

"Keep walking!"

"Why are my eyes burning? Why do they hurt so when I try to open them? Why are the mountains so dim?"

The answers never came.

About four miles from the avalanche in Lyngsdalen Valley, Jan emerged at the upper end of Furuflaten. The river rushed headlong down to the village and Jan eagerly followed along as fast he was able. He reached a clump of birch trees and wandered helplessly. A steep gradient rose before him. He gathered there was a plateau not too far up because he could make out the black marks of many birch trunks. He climbed upward, slid backwards, but continued on.

His whole body was wracked with pain. Hunger pangs continually gnawed at him. His hands were frozen stiff and blue. He hardly felt his feet anymore, but his eyes caused him the greatest agony. "How much longer can I hold out? Is there an end to the misery?"

He reached the plateau and could distinguish a dark block a few feet ahead of him. He pushed forward. It was almost within reach. A wall! A wall!

LOVING HANDS

APRIL 8, 1943: The Lyngsdalen Valley cuts a deep and narrow channel into the mighty massifs guarding it on either side. The valley's head, near the immense glaciers, is spread wide. Winter cloaks the valley with a covering of pure white at the feet of the impressive mountain peaks Jiehkkevarri and Balggesvarri, tapering off as it weaves its way four miles eastward in a relaxed "S." At its final point, the valley gives way to the Lyngenfjord. Close to the fjord, the valley opens up wide again and creates space for scattered homes near the water's edge up to the highest plateau in the lower valley. This is the country settlement of Furuflaten.

On the north side, the steep rock wall of Pollfjellet Mountain rises up more than 3600 feet. The vertical mountain wall on the east plummets headlong into the Lyngenfjord. Far down along the water's edge, the narrow road curves with the coastline and connects Furuflaten to the hamlet of Lyngseidet nine miles further north.

The area at the foot of Pollfjellet is extremely dangerous in the winter, because of sudden violent snow slides. The snow masses crash down, one after another, and block the roads. Since open travel year round between Furuflaten and Lyngseidet was of strategic importance, the Germans felt it imperative to keep this thoroughfare open throughout the year. Subsequent to a snow slide, the Germans marshaled manpower to quickly remove the snow and keep the traffic moving.

Because of this, many German and conscripted Austrian soldiers were stationed in Furuflaten. They were quartered at the country school. Near the local road, there was a large depository filled with snow removal equipment and other machinery needed to keep it open. On the road outside of the depository, armed soldiers stood guard.

Uppermost in Furuflaten, on a nearly flat plateau, was the site of the Grønvoll farm. Marius, thirty-three, lived here with his widowed mother and two of his sisters. Gudrun was a few years younger than Marius and Ingeborg was a teenager.

Straight across the farmyard from Marius lived another sister, Hanna. She was married and had two sons of her own, Johan, 16, and Ottar, a couple of years younger. They lived in an old, grayish-worn log cabin with a small enclosure that stored overcoats, boots, and food. The ceiling was low and the one-room cabin had only one door, which opened up toward Marius' house.

The Pedersen family had just enjoyed a weekday meal together in their unpretentious little home. Hanna's husband Alfred was away at Lofoten, fishing. The kitchen table still held a plate of potato peels and fish scraps, leftovers from their just-finished dinner.

They heard something scratching along the wall outside their cabin. Unable to make out what it was, they listened more intently. The door bolt began to move, it creaked and grated, but did not open. The scratching along the wall repeated itself as it moved further away, before it moved back towards the bolt again. There were no windows by the door, so they couldn't look out. Hanna's frightened eyes stared at the door.

"Johan, open the door quickly!" The boy did as he was told.

Hanna gasped! She stepped back and let out a stifled scream, half covering her face with her hands. A frightening being tumbled in, took a couple of faltering steps and ended up standing, barely, in the middle of the room. His body swayed from side to side. His filthy clothes were soaked. He had no cap. Particles of ice, dried blood and sedimentary grains of rock clung to scruffy coal-black hair and stubs of beard, white with frost. His face was all scratched up, dirty and bloody. His eyes were nearly swollen closed, bloodshot and watering. Frost clung to his eyelashes. Dried blood and scabs covered his cracked blue lips and his breathing was heavy and came in short spurts. He groaned and trembled violently.

His boots were entombed in ice that extended well up his legs. It was obviously difficult for the creature to open his swollen eyelids, fire-red around the edges, but he exerted himself, and two horizontal slits appeared.

He spied the plate with the potato peel and fish scraps on the kitchen table. The frozen man toddled over to the table and sank down on a nearby chair. The chair slid toward the wall and he lay half diagonally against the table, grabbing the leftovers and cramming them into his mouth with both of his bluish swollen hands - a starving man out of control. Frightened, Hanna and the children stood speechless, staring at the creature half-lying at their kitchen table. They were watching Jan Baalsrud.

"Johan, run to fetch Uncle Marius." Johan took a couple of seconds to react, then dashed through the door and toward Uncle Marius' house a few feet below the farmyard.

Johan took the four steps up to the door in one big jump.

"What's the matter Johan? It's not like you not to come in. Come on in!" encouraged his Aunt Gudrun.

"Uncle Marius you must come at once, there is a fugitive in our house!"

Marius did not believe him at first. He was sure Johan was teasing him. They had fun outsmarting each other at times. Having delivered his message, Johan darted back to his home.

As he watched Johan sprint across the farmyard, Marius was not quite sure whether or not the boy was teasing. It all sounded a little unbelievable that a fugitive would come to their house, the uppermost house in the valley.

Still unsure, Marius decided to make an errand to the barn. On his way there, he would have to pass Hanna's house. As he drew close to the little cabin, Hanna appeared on her front steps and frantically motioned for him to come in, "You have to hurry Marius!"

He realized Johan had been telling the truth and rushed to his sister's side.

Jan was lying on the floor with a mouth full of leftovers. His remaining strength had deserted him and he had fallen from the chair to the floor.

Marius stood motionless inside the entrance door, gaping at the heap of human being on the floor. Terror stricken, Hanna and her sons looked to Marius then to Jan and back to Marius. They felt totally helpless and bewildered.

"What shall we do, Marius?" Hanna got her voice back. "Who is this man?"

Marius sized up the situation and what to do. Ingeborg and Gudrun joined them from across the way. Marius stopped them in the entryway amid the winter boots, work clothes and coats hanging on pegs.

"We have a very ill man in the kitchen. Please wait here a minute," Marius said.

He pondered what to do with the ill stranger. The young man looked like a prisoner of war, tortured to the brink of death. He could not have known that this time it was the forces of nature that had been at work, not the Gestapo.

The ghostlike chafed face starkly contrasted with the disheveled coal-black hair and beard, covered with frost and ice just now beginning to melt. Jan covered his eyes with his hands shielding them from the light. He had difficulty keeping them open. It looked like someone or some thing had dragged him across the ground, as scraped up as his face and hands were. But the worst was his ice-covered boots and legs. Marius was simply stunned.

When Jan fell, Hanna thought he was dead. The fish scraps still filled his mouth; he had not the strength to swallow before sinking to the floor. She leaned over him to see if he was still breathing.

Marius took control of the situation. Flashes of the rumors he'd heard about Toftefjord ran through his mind. He called for his sisters in the anteroom. They were anxious to help.

"What if the Germans should come?" Hanna went in and out of shock.

"They are so close, aren't they Uncle Marius? What shall we do?" Ottar asked.

"Yes, they are near. But we will find a way to help this man. We must do this," Marius whispered.

Jan struggled to say a few words. It was difficult to understand him as he struggled to move his lips. "I am on my way to Balsfjord. Are there any Germans around here?" He tried to keep his eyes open while he was speaking.

"You are among friends, and have nothing to worry about," Marius tried to ease his fears.

"What is your name? My name is Marius Grønvoll."

Jan ignored the question about his name. "Did you say there are no Germans around here?" Jan was anxious.

"You only have to worry about getting well. We'll take care of you."

The family went to work to try and save him. Marius started by chipping the ice off Jan's legs and boots. Hanna heated water on the wood-burning stove. He had to be cleaned up. The boots had frozen to his feet and were whittled off in small pieces. The socks were cut off in strips. The sight of his feet and legs was shocking! The girls became queasy. They had never seen flesh with such terrifying colors, mostly an off-color blue, but in places covered with darker bluish-black-purplish spots. Other parts were a white-rosy marble-like color. Despite his agony, Jan didn't complain as the family worked feverishly to try and bring circulation back into his body.

Hanna and Marius got him cleaned up and changed his clothing. Gudrun and Ingeborg gathered pails of snow; they knew the best treatment for frostbite was to rub and massage the affected area with snow. It made no difference if they touched the ice or his legs, the temperature was the same.

Marius stayed in command. He placed Hanna's son Johan outside to keep watch. No one could be allowed to surprise them. The cabin had no place where they could hide Jan. Clear to them all was that they were laboring under the threat of a death sentence. The Germans had brought fear to the settlement in Furuflaten with their many posters attached to telephone poles and anywhere there was room, warnings to anyone who worked against them that should they be discovered the result would be death by an execution squad.

The girls began their work. Taking a leg each, they rubbed and massaged as gently as they could. Jan moaned, but it had to be done; it was the only chance to get his blood circulating again. Their backs hurt, their hands were chilled and yet they kept at it, hour after hour.

Hanna and Marius took their turns. Jan was massaged continuously into the early morning hours. When one tired, another took over. They were encouraged when Jan first began to respond; how they wanted to save this man.

Gradually he was able to say a few words. Marius quickly gained his trust. Jan said his hometown was Oslo where his family lived and that he was the only survivor from Brattholm.

Marius was now able to put all the pieces together; this was a fugitive from the Gestapo! "Incomprehensible that this man is still alive," he told himself. Even at that, Marius was completely in the dark about how many times Jan had escaped death, nor did he have any knowledge of the mental agony Jan had already lived through. All Marius knew was that this man needed help, and as long as it was humanly possible, he vowed he would be there for him.

Two courageous men, Jan and Marius instantly bonded. The head of the Furuflaten underground, Marius wondered, "Was it just chance that led Jan to me?" Marius did not think so. Once Marius gave his heart to a person, or a cause, he was fiercely loyal. He cared about people. A warm, loving human being who knew when to help, Marius never pushed himself on people and only stepped in when needed. If someone was in need, no risk, no German, no threat of death, could stand in his way.

When he graduated from elementary school at the age of thirteen, his education was over; so like most of the other young men at that time he had to help supplement the family income. The early 1900's were an extremely difficult time economically for the people of northern Norway. Marius helped his parents provide the necessities of life by fishing, but he also had a deep interest in photography and writing, and after awhile became a reporter for the newspaper Tromsø.

Marius' lack of education, however, was not a hindrance to his curious mind. He was well read, and was familiar with the works of the Norwegian literary giants. He often quoted from memory the works of Ibsen, Welhaven and Bjørnson, as well as Kipling and others.

Marius deeply loved Norway. Extremely patriotic, he was a leader, respected and trusted by the two hundred people in Furuflaten. To him, it was his civic duty to help another Norwegian in need.

That evening, Marius took a break and returned to his home across the farmyard to eat dinner with his mother. Filled with love and concern for her children and grandchildren, she was skeptical about helping this stranger. There were no blind spots in her eyes - she knew the danger and what it might do to her family.

Marius sat down next to her and in his warm understanding way explained the situation. When she resisted, he asked her, "If I, your own son, should end up wounded and helpless in Oslo – and no one would come to my assistance – what would you do?" His mother turned silent, looked admiringly at her son who had displayed such wisdom, and said not a word. After a brief interval she expressed her change of mind. Her son was doing that which he ought to be doing, that which was good and decent. She agreed with her Marius. The stranger had to be taken care of, no matter what the cost. She looked at him with moist eyes and patted his hand.

"Son, you are a good man. We must do that which is right. You have my blessing."

The situation was extremely tense at the Grønvoll farm. Many Germans were quartered at Solhov School in Lyngseidet, the German headquarters for the whole Eastern Front, and only nine miles away. And down in Furuflaten, close to the fjord, the Germans had confiscated the local school, which was now being used for a German billet. The soldiers, when not busy, milled around Furuflaten, and it was not unusual for them to come unannounced to the farm to purchase eggs and milk. The Grønvolls tried to avoid selling to their enemy, but most often the choice was not theirs.

Marius, Hanna and the two girls counseled together and made the decision to give their all to help Jan to freedom. The safest place to hide him was in the barn, up in the hayloft where there was presently an abundance of hay. No one but the family was to know about this; not even their nearest neighbor could know they were hiding and aiding a fugitive.

The girls had done their best for Jan, tending his hands, feet and legs. Old clothing, sheets and such were scarce during these days when any old piece of clothing was altered for many different uses, but having gathered what could be found, the girls and Hanna tore them into strips. A salve with a cod-liver oil base, a healing compound much used by Norwegians, was applied to Jan's body where needed, after which the strips of sterilized cloth were wound around his affected limbs until they were completely protected.

His general condition was so poor and his pain so insufferable that he was totally helpless, unable to stand on his own legs. The situation looked bleak. Even after all the Grønvolls' efforts, Jan's atrocious suffering in the mountains had taken its toll.

IN THE HAYLOFT

IN ONE of the outbuildings was an old sled. Around two in the morning, Marius and the two girls lifted Jan onto the sled. Johan kept watch outside, and when all was pronounced clear, they pulled Jan across the farmyard in the dark. They towed and pushed him up the steep barn bridge. The barn was furthest away from the other buildings in the farmyard, and the barn bridge, the only way they could get him up into to the hayloft, was in the opposite direction from their neighbors, facing Lyngsdalen Valley from where Jan had come.

Marius had brought an old mattress up earlier and placed it in the far corner of the hayloft. He and his sisters transferred Jan to the mattress and tucked wool blankets around him. They left him there, hidden behind the haystacks. All went home, but none of them slept. Throughout the night Marius pondered and the girls were frightened. What would happen to them if the Germans came and found Jan? Of a truth, they knew, but they were too frightened to share their thoughts with one another. Morning emerged without the girls having been able to squelch their fears. The experience was all too traumatic for them.

The assignment given to the saboteurs in Shetland was code-named "Martin." The Grønvolls decided to call Jan by that name. He had been in the hayloft for a couple of days, and in spite of the Grønvolls' nurturing, Jan's feet didn't show any signs of improvement. He remained unable to stand on them. Marius puzzled over what to do next.

During the many days Jan was detained in the mountains, snow blindness had set in. His cornea and eye membranes were damaged and inflamed, infected by the reflection of the sun's ultraviolet rays on the snow. His eyes pained him terribly. Sunlight caused a burning sensation. Tears flowed continually. His red, swollen eyelids were roughly attached to one another. When he tried to open them, only a narrow slit appeared, but it enabled him to hazily see the people around him and some of the surroundings. Relief came only when he closed his eyes.

Gudrun and Ingeborg's main assignment was to bring food to Jan in the barn. To be sure, they never took the barn-bridge up to the hayloft. No unnecessary tracks were to be made in the snow. Instead they went in through the barn door, past the cow barn, up the ladder and through the hatch in the ceiling up to the hayloft. They were aware that Jan always kept the loaded pistol close by his side; when they neared the top of the stepladder, they called out, "Martin, I am bringing your food." Three times a day they brought him food. Gudrun often prepared and cooked the food, such as potatoes and other root vegetables, meat, fish and tea if available. Whatever the family ate they shared with Jan.

Being young, it was a highlight of Gudrun and Ingeborg's day to go and visit with this commando soldier. He was good at camouflaging his own pain and the sorrows he carried. At the same time, they were shy and reserved, and hardly dared exchange any words with him. They knew, above all, he needed to rest. The girls did not know how much their visits meant to him. Jan always had a smile and a friendly comment for them. He felt their selflessness and their eagerness to help him. Jan was overwhelmed with indescribable gratitude when he saw these beautiful genuine girls who risked so much on his behalf. The world and its cruel ways had not, to a great extent, intruded upon Furuflaten.

Helpless, ill, and at the point of death, he had been brought into the safety of this barn and had been shown the greatest of care and concern. It was unavoidable that Jan had become very fond of the Grønvolls and all who had helped him.

Likewise, the girls felt pride each time they visited the hayloft with food for Jan. Knowing they played a small part in saving the life of a Norwegian saboteur, taking him away from the Gestapo so to speak, made their hearts joyful. In spite of that, they were careful not to spend too much time with him. They wanted to be sure he got the rest he needed.

Marius felt unsafe. During periods of good weather, without snowfall, the German and Austrian soldiers living at the school in the valley did not have much to do with their time. The road between the Pollfjell Mountain and Lyngseidet did not have to be cleared and plowed on those days, and the soldiers' days seemed tiresomely long. To lessen their boredom, they would ski up into the countryside, and they often made their treks close behind Marius' barn where there was good skiing in the sloped fields.

Jan's tracks still remained in the snow; they led straight to the farmyard only a few hundred feet away. Marius thought with great alarm of the consequences should the soldiers discover them.

The day after Jan came to the Grønvoll farm, Marius decided to do something about the tracks. He put his own boots on and followed in Jan's footsteps from the barnyard down the steep hillside towards the riverbed. Marius made a frightening discovery; the trail revealed a fight for life beyond anything he could have comprehended.

A short distance from the farm, Marius noticed Jan's tracks disappeared into a circle in among a grove of stunted, windblown birch trees. Jan had walked round and round in circles! He must have been partially unconscious, Marius thought, unable to see much, but determined not to lie down and die. He had to keep himself erect; he had to keep walking. If he stopped, the exhaustion would overtake him; he would sink into the snow and perish.

Marius saw before him, like a moving picture, the unsteady stride of two feet transformed into two hunks of ice. He felt Jan's pain, fright, exhaustion and despair, and his struggle for consciousness. In many places he noted how the footprints had taken off from the circle. Jan's trail showed confused side trips from the pressed-down circle; a couple of them turned close to the Grønvolls' barn before they took off down into the valley. Totally bewildered, Jan had fought for his life in a circle. He had spent hours around and in between the birch trees.

Jan had been near the farm without ever knowing how close he had been to relief. Marius realized the man in his barn was no run-of-the-mill soldier. Eager to help Jan anyway he could, Marius retraced his footsteps back to the farmyard. Let the Germans come. Let them ask about the mysterious tracks in the snow! He would have no problem explaining that as a farmer he, from time to time, had to go up into the valley for wood. Marius hurried to the hayloft.

"Hello Martin, it's me, Marius!" he called out, as he neared the top of the ladder leading to the loft. Excited by his discovery, the farmer laid out for Jan his visit to Lyngsdalen in great detail. Jan was overcome by the news. It all seemed so distant and hazy. All he remembered was the one thing that had remained crystal clear during his fight against fatigue: if he had not been able to place one foot in front of the other, or if he had sat down to rest, he would never have been able to get up – and would have lain there and frozen to death.

Jan did not want to die.

This helped Marius understand why Jan had continued for hours in the circle among the birch trees. Jan expressed his appreciation for all Marius' family was doing for him, and his concern for them. The resistance leader's answer was simple and direct. "It might cost me my life, but what of it? You have to say 'Yes' or 'No' to life."

Marius gave a resounding "Yes" to helping Jan.

Everyone on the Grønvoll farm, especially the young girls, fought a constant battle with fear. Ingeborg, the youngest, was almost in shock. Jan's appearance and need for help had torn the safety net of the farm away from her in a dramatic way; it was a difficult experience for her. The war had now entangled her family. Any talk about death and danger and risk terrified her. The adults' concerned and troubled looks only added to her fears. Ingeborg knew they were afraid the Germans would raid the farm. She also knew they were afraid for what might happen to Jan, and also the family, should the Germans find Jan in the hayloft. They didn't talk about it, but the fear hovered over all of them. It was in the air around them. Ingeborg could even see it in their actions: the many times they looked out the kitchen window and scanned the country lane leading to their house, and how they tensed when the telephone rang. Yet she knew that no matter how afraid her family was, they would never think of turning their backs on Jan, or on any human being in need just to save themselves. Ingeborg was near tears continually, and food held no temptation for her. She tried to act brave like the rest of her family.

Jan was thankful for the help showered upon him and was thrilled with the comfortable mattress behind the haystack. He felt safe. He slept mostly for the four days and nights he had been at Grønvoll farm. He had had no strength when he arrived here; sleep had been a welcome gift.

Marius, as often as he could and when he felt it was safe, entered through the hatch and visited with him. Jointly they made their plans. They had so much to share and tell one another. Marius was able to reiterate the Tromsø rumors and what he had heard about the fate of Jan's friends. Jan lay still and listened, saddened, as again the terrible tragedy was verified. Jan surmised that the two men taken prisoner were Moursund and Knudsen.

The merchant at Bromnes, a few days after the battle in Toftefjord, had received a package in the mail. The package held a rope with a noose in one end. On a torn off paper slip it said:

This rope is meant for you. Should it
be too difficult for you to use, I will be
happy to come and assist you.

The sender was anonymous and nothing else happened.

After the Toftefjord tragedy, the Germans had been around the district arresting people, looking for radios. They imprisoned family members of young men who had been able to escape to Sweden.

German Schnell boats patrolled the fjord often around the inlets of Furuflaten. It was risky for Jan to remain in the barn for long. Sooner or later the rumor mill would begin to buzz. Even if the Germans didn't figure out that the elusive Jan was in their midst, Marius' neighbors would soon begin to wonder about all the trips to the barn.

One could not expect everyone to be tight-lipped – that would be a fatal mistake.

BUSY DAYS ON
GRØNVOLL FARM

THE GHASTLY man that had fallen through Hanna Pedersen's door a few days earlier was not horrifying anymore. He was not a stranger, but a friend. Tending Jan and taking food to the barn three times a day was not a chore, but a highlight for Gudrun and Ingeborg as intense and bright as the summer midnight sun.

The young women were filled with pride each time they returned from the barn. They admired Jan's courage and fortitude and were impressed with his knowledge and his work as a saboteur. The Gestapo was hunting him. Yet they were the ones who had him.

As strong and skillful as Jan was, now when he was in danger and vulnerable, he depended on them. This brought them happiness. Each morning they looked forward to their visits with him, though they were usually brief. Jan had brought with him glimpses of a world they knew little about, a world they had only read about. He made that world real to them. And sometimes Jan wanted to talk. They were all young, they all had dreams and hopes for the future, and they enjoyed sharing them. Their lives had been divergent, but now they met at a crossroad. Jan needed caring and tenderness; he had experienced the evil and terror war brought. Gudrun and Ingeborg needed a chance to serve and to show compassion, which is so much a part of a woman's heart. Jan's and the young women's needs met as moments of gentleness in a cruel world. It was good for all of them to make new friends.

As the days passed, a routine of sorts developed; having Jan hidden in the barn was not as frightful as it had in the beginning. They were, of course, still aware of the danger, but a quiet peace settled back over the Grønvoll farm as everyone went about their daily chores.

One day, the peaceful atmosphere was shattered. Within seconds, horror replaced the tranquility and paralyzed all in the little log cabin. Two German soldiers with shotguns over their shoulders were headed straight for the cabin where Marius was visiting with Hanna. As the soldiers crossed the farmyard, Marius went out to greet them.

They told him they had come to re-examine the farm for illegal radios. In 1941 the Germans attempted to confiscate all the radios across Norway. Many Norwegians hid their radios rather than give them up. Aware of this, the Germans carried out raids unexpectedly, often revisiting places they had been just a short time earlier. The laws were strict; no one was allowed to listen to a radio. Heaven forbid that a Norwegian should hear the enemy's messages from London! If caught, the punishment was swift and cruel - torture or the concentration camp, or both.

Though they had recently ransacked the Grønvoll farm, the soldiers announced they'd returned to re-examine the barn. The girls froze. Someone must have reported them - they had been betrayed! Jan would be found and shot! And so would they. Ingeborg could not help herself; tears streamed down her ashen cheeks. She went to the bedroom and sat down in a corner to hide. All was over.

Marius and Gudrun were told to come to the barn with the soldiers. The soldiers walked two steps behind them. It was difficult to keep a nonchalant appearance. Gudrun also fought tears. A few years older than her sister in the cabin, Gudrun was still just a young woman. As they neared the barn she wanted to shout, to tell Jan to run away. She knew it would be impossible; poor Jan could not even stand on his feet, much less run.

The cow barn and the piles of hay were meticulously inspected. The Germans poked their guns into places they could not get to and lifted and pushed farm tools aside. The stress became unbearable.

Marius stood and watched them dispassionately with his hands in his pocket. His face did not reveal the fright within. They neared the stepladder and one soldier began his ascent. He pressed his helmeted head against the hatch, lifted it up and peeked around the hayloft. The hatch was heavy and he grunted trying to hold both his gun ready for action and the hatch up with his head. With great effort he took one more step – and another; his upper body came through the hatchway. He turned in every direction, breathed heavy and groaned, irritated by the heavy hatch leaning on him. Below, retreating a few steps, Marius and Gudrun stood helpless next to the other soldier glancing upward. The German soldier turned and studied their faces, holding the gun ready. The siblings thought for sure it all was over.

The future flashed before their eyes: they would be executed, as would Grandmother, Hanna, Ingeborg, Johan and Ottar. Even their innocent neighbors would be imprisoned or shipped off to concentration camp somewhere in Germany. Their beloved Furuflaten village might be burned to the ground. No one would have a home to return to. Jan would be the first one they would grab. They would haul him in for interrogation and torture.

The German atop the ladder fumed and hollered, coughed and spit. He took a step back down on the ladder, stooped and the hatch slammed shut. Down on the floor he brushed the dust and chaff off his uniform.

"No need to ransack up there," he commented to his buddy. "There is only some dried-up hay." He turned to Marius and Gudrun.

"Danke," thank you. "We hope we have not interrupted your day," he said in broken Norwegian. The soldiers clicked their heels, and nodded stiffly.

"No problem."

The inspection was over and the soldiers left.

Had the soldier not been slothful, he would have found the catch of his military career, an enemy commando.

The plans for Jan's continued flight could not be put off. The unseen power that protected Jan from the beginning had sheltered him yet again. As Marius looked ahead, his duty seemed impossible – nonetheless, he would find a way. If Jan had been well and could walk without help, things would be different. But it was too much to expect that Jan could recover quickly. His cheerful manner covered much of his anguish but it all would take time.

Hanna and the girls continued their nurturing care of Jan. He lay in the barn bandaged up, unable to stand and unable to see much. And in this condition, it was Marius' duty to find a way to get him to Sweden past the German guardposts. Obviously there was no time to waste; the just-completed inspection was proof of that. This challenge was Marius' greatest test.

Marius thought and schemed the whole day through and into the evening. He had many ideas but one by one he rejected them.

Then one idea burst forth. "Could it be possible?" He headed to the barn to share it with his friend. This was too important and risky not to discuss with him. Jan listened intently. He agreed that the plan Marius presented was daring. They would need help from several courageous men and a generous portion of good luck to succeed. But what other choice did they have? Jan was grateful that Marius would even have such thoughts. After all, he could not just take off on skis anymore.

Marius went to work. Their plan was to remove Jan from the barn during the darkest of night, pull him on a sled down the valley to the fjord, then row him diagonally across the Lyngenfjord toward the northeast, a little over six miles.

On the opposite shore in Revdal, a short distance from the water's edge stood a little log hut. It was the only remains of a burned-down farm except for the scarred fireplace clinging to a broken-off chimney jutting heavenward where the farmhouse had stood. The untrimmed grass poked through the snow in small tufts here and there. A deserted spot five miles from the nearest neighbor, it was an ideal hiding place.

No road passed through the little place called Revdal, quiet except for the whispering waves and the rushing wind. The little windowless hut could be Jan's hiding place – a place no one would suspect, stranger than anyone could expect, and surely no one would inspect. Jan would be safe in the hut until they worked out the next phase of his journey to Sweden.

From Furuflaten, Marius could see the log hut with his bare eyes. It was a little black speck just back of the water's edge. It stood a few hundred feet north of two rivers which plunged down the steep mountainside and emptied into the fjord. The mountain towered nearly 3000 feet behind the hut. Close to the plateau, a narrow valley snuggled into the granite masses. The gorge was called Revdal (Fox Valley), like the little place by the fjord, named after the many foxes which made their homes there.

On the other side of the Revdal mountain plateau, the massive mountains drop steeply, fringed by the elongated Manndalen Valley, stretching into the interior from the Kåfjord. Marius planned to enlist some men from the Manndalen Valley to help get Jan to Sweden. Deep within, he hoped that Jan would improve enough to be able to ski along with them, but that was a wish, not reality. By human standards the flight seemed almost impossible, but desperate men seek desperate solutions.

Even with this hopelessness, Marius never considered quitting; he was not that kind of a man. In a brief time, strong ties had formed between him and Jan. He had tremendous compassion for his new friend, mixed with genuine admiration. Saving Jan was not an option anymore. Marius had determined many days ago to give his all to save Jan, even his life. He had promised Jan that if he had to die, he would not die alone.

THE THREE siblings at Grønvoll farm had another sister, Petra Solberg. She lived a short distance away with her husband. She knew nothing about Jan, and was not told. She was trustworthy, like the rest of her family, but everyone involved felt that the fewer people who knew about Jan, the better the chances of keeping the secret. They felt no need to involve people unnecessarily and risk their lives.

Like most Norwegian women, Petra was an expert knitter. Most Norwegians knit for pleasure, but during the war they did so out of necessity. Gudrun knew that Petra prided herself on knitting her husband's long underwear, doing all she could to keep him warm and comfortable during the Arctic winters. One day, Gudrun got the sneaky idea to pay her sister Petra a visit; this would be a different kind of a visit. She realized her plan was not kind, but the need was desperate. As

Gudrun set out on the 15-minute walk to her sister's home, she hoped that when she told Petra the whole story in the future, she would be forgiven.

Happy to see Gudrun, Petra welcomed her warmly, ushering her in to the living room where she set the coffee table with home baked goodies and a warm drink. They talked of everyday things and shared thoughts and happenings as sisters are apt to do. This time, however, Gudrun's heart was not in the visit. She could not get her mind off her brother-in-law's long underwear. Petra's husband was a powerfully built man just about Jan's size, and his underwear would fit Jan perfectly.

Gudrun consoled herself that Jan had to have that well-knitted underwear, knitted with gray yarn, if he was to stay warm on the terrifying journey ahead. As Petra chatted, Gudrun knew she couldn't ask for a pair outright. Petra had two pairs for her husband. While he wore one, the other was washed and hung to dry on the clothesline stretched between the inside walls of the little outbuilding not far from the main farmhouse.

It would be difficult to get her hands on them, but Gudrun had a quick mind and was determined. She parted from her sister and set out in the direction of her home. Nightfall covered her as she rushed back to the outbuilding, snatched the long underwear off the line, crammed it under her winter coat, and dashed all the way home.

Jan had his long warm underwear.

As for Petra, her hatred for the Germans grew. The following morning when she went to retrieve the underwear and discovered it was gone, she immediately "knew" it was in German hands. In telling her sister Gudrun about the incident later, Petra vowed she would never forgive them!

A TENDER FAREWELL

THE RESISTANCE group in Furuflaten received an important assignment. Many men were needed and all had to be tight-lipped. Marius realized how essential it was to find the right people.

Marius had several reliable friends, some from his boyhood days. One young man, Olaf Lanes, was only 17 years old. Olaf lived at the northern end of the village. A powerfully strong young man with broad shoulders, Olaf was energetic and trustworthy. His father Hans owned a fishing boat, and Olaf had gone fishing with him in Lofoten many seasons already.

Amandus Lillevoll, an unmarried farmer and skipper of his own fishing vessel, was a few years older than was Marius. Amandus was reserved, but had a strong will and always finished what he set out to do. Following his father's death, he took over the responsibility of supporting his mother and sister. He had a great wit and enjoyed telling stories. Marius wanted him to join the group because he was tough, energetic and trustworthy. But Amandus was still fishing in Lofoten.

Alfon Hansen, 30 years old and Amandus' cousin, had attended Solhov folk high school in Lyngseidet. His interest was carpentry and he was a skilled craftsman. He also was strong and dependable.

The fourth man Marius wanted for his team was Alvin Larsen, a wise and physically powerful twenty-five-year old who never shunned hard work. When he turned thirteen, Alvin began accompanying his father on frequent fishing trips to the Lofoten Islands. He got his coastal captain's license when he was only eighteen years old. The rough Arctic seas and climate coupled with heavy work had molded him into a mentally and physically strong man. Alvin preferred to live on the sea.

Olav Bakkevold, the oldest of the men Marius sought, lived on a small farm north of the river. He too was unmarried. Like the other men at Furuflaten, he often fished to help with living expenses. And like the others, he was patriotic and dependable.

Artur Olsen was a post official in Furuflaten. Marius hoped for his help during Jan's transport down to the fjord. In addition to these men, the resistance leader involved teacher Longva. To a man, all stood ready to help.

Monday, 12 April 1943: The plan was to remove Jan from the barn during the night. The next phase of his flight to freedom was risky but necessary. He had felt safe at the Grønvoll farm, hidden behind the hay up in the barn, and strong ties had formed between Jan and the Grønvolls.

The leave-taking disheartened Jan. The success of the transfer rested on Marius' shoulders. He came to the barn to wash Jan up. Gudrun and Ingeborg heated water on the wood-burning stove and carried it up to him. Jan would leave with new undergarments, hand knit of pure wool. Jan tried hard to act upbeat and uncomplaining, but Marius sensed his low spirits.

"I am also despairing, Jan. I would have liked for you to stay on," said Marius.

"Don't worry, I'll do fine. And I am impatient to get closer to Sweden."

"I wish I could stay with you all the way, my friend."

"It's just that I…I hate goodbyes. All of you have become dear to me. I am so indebted, Marius."

"Nonsense Jan, we are just happy you found us. We've got to get ready now."

In the late evening, Olav Bakkevold and Alfon Hansen arrived. Still snow-blind and too ill to stand on his feet, Jan was bundled up in wool blankets and placed on the sled. His jovial spirit evaporated. The resistance workers opened the barn door just enough to get the short sled through. Jan's head and bandaged feet hung over the ends. The wounded commando was too weak to hold his head up, so Gudrun and Ingeborg bent over and cradled it in their hands. They rushed sideways down the steep barn bridge while the three men controlled the sled's descent.

Jan cried.

The five shadows hurried across the farmyard, pulling the sled bearing a bundled up and strapped down Jan. The men guided the sled from the front while Gudrun and Ingeborg steadied the back. The girls strained to support Jan's head, stooped over as they were.

At the end of the farmyard, they veered the sled to the left, ending up in a long, narrow hollow bordered by scattered trees and bushes. Further down they crossed a belt of crusty snow leading to the moraine-covered riverbed. A few darkened homes revealed no activity.

Creeping among large rocks, bushes and scraggly trees, they hurried downward to the sea. The chill wind swept over them unnoticed. Though the darkness shielded them, their senses stayed alert to any hazard.

Two places along the route were particularly dangerous: the school where the German soldiers were quartered, and the warehouse near the local road, guarded by the Germans. Key pieces of apparatus, machinery and snow removal equipment were kept safe in the storehouse. The narrow two-lane country road that snaked its way along the water through Furuflaten was the Germans' main supply route to Finland and the Eastern Front. It had to be kept open; therefore, they guarded the snow removal equipment very protectively.

Marius had surveyed the escape route several times in advance. He knew every foot of it, and what he and his friends faced. They had met and worked out detailed plans.

Artur Olsen had been sent out in advance to stand guard on the moraine hill north of the river. The river ran underneath the road bridge and spilled out into the sea. The bridge was near where the German guard was stationed. Artur's exact position had been carefully chosen. An armed soldier kept watch down on the road, walking between the bridge and the store at Hamvik. From his lookout point, Artur could see the bridge. When the German soldier turned by the bridge to go south, Artur was to strike a match as a signal.

Johan, Hanna's son, had been eager to help Jan in some way. He was proud that his Uncle Marius had asked him to be part of this effort. Uncle

Marius had loaned his flashlight to him. And to have a flashlight - with batteries - was something unusual in war-torn Norway of 1943. Johan was excited to be on a par with the adults.

Quietly, the young man trudged through the snow. Johan crawled up the moraine hill to his appointed place on the south side of the river. His heart pounded as he peered into the darkness, alert to danger. Johan felt the tension more than did the others, perhaps because of his youth. He kept looking behind him. Unusual noises seemed to come from everywhere.

All was quiet.

The small country store a little further down was a sociable place. Friends and neighbors met and chatted about happenings in their village. These days, the havoc the war caused always crept into their conversation. Before the war, the men-folk centered their conversation on fishing vessels or their latest catch important to their livelihood. They focused on the success or failure of their crops and livestock, weather being all-important here in the Arctic. The latest news of world or around Norway was also important to them.

The women looked forward to gathering at the store. They discussed new ideas on homemaking and rearing children. These were women of substance for the most part. By and large their men were fishermen, often spending weeks or months away fishing, while the women cared for children and attended to farm duties.

Most walked to the country store, though some bicycled. In the wintertime they used kick sleds or skis. The country store was their meeting place, a place for sharing the latest goings-on in their lives, stories they were bursting to pass on, joyful tales.

Closed tonight, the townsfolk safely home, the country store lay quiet.

A shadowy figure stood near the store. Wearing a leather cap with earflaps tied underneath his chin, a homemade knitted sweater and scarf, teacher Longva kept his hands warm inside knitted mittens. Standing guard with matchbox in hand, he would strike a match to signal danger to the five pulling Jan.

Marius had placed teacher Longva by the country store because it gave a good overview of the paths on which they were transporting Jan.

Marius, Olav, Alfon and the girls neared the end of the hollow. The land spread flat at the bottom of the moraine riverbed. The closely guarded school where the Germans slept sat on top of a ten-foot embankment. A soldier kept watch close by. All they could see of him was the upper part of his rifle and his helmet moving along the snow mound.

The five crept gingerly along the riverbank below the soldier, all hoping that the sound of the rushing river drowned out the scraping of the sled. Marius had described the escape to Jan in detail. Jan knew their location, and he wanted to assure the girls. It was clear they were nervous by the way they looked around, glanced up at the snow bank and at each other.

Gudrun Grønvoll

"We are almost there, girls. They cannot hear us because of the river," said Jan, though he was not totally convinced of that himself.

The off duty soldiers in the school were lethargic and heedless. None of them had any idea of the daring activity playing out below them. Raucous laughter erupted from the school and over the snow bank. It jolted

Ingeborg Grønvoll

Marius and the others. The German soldiers were enjoying their time off.

Carefully, Marius' group distanced themselves from the school, and when they neared the county road, they stopped in a thicket. A German soldier a short distance away was guarding the warehouse.

Gudrun and Ingeborg parted company with the others. They walked boldly out into the road and conversed loudly as if sharing an exciting experience. They headed straight for the soldier with the machine gun.

"Guten Abend," good evening, they smiled.

The soldier was somewhat surprised that the two Norwegian girls would talk to him. He was pleased with this interruption, breaking the monotony of his watch.

"Guten Abend," the soldier smiled broadly. "What are you young girls doing out so late at night?" he continued in German.

The girls shrugged their shoulders and laughed.

"Ich nicht verstehen," We don't understand. Ingeborg tried out the few German words she knew.

"Aah!" the soldier nodded and eagerly labored to make himself understood in his broken Norwegian.

The girls kept him busy pretending they had a difficult time understanding him. Slowly they turned southward. The soldier accompanied them. They chatted as they distanced themselves and the guard from the sled. Reaching a narrow path, they stopped and talked a few more minutes.

The soldier by the bridge had turned. Artur lit the match. Marius hardly saw the weak flame north of the river. Gudrun and Ingeborg turned off on the side road.

"Auf wiedersehen." They waved.

"Auf wiedersehen." The soldier saluted the girls.

Marius checked the road. Clear of Germans, it was time to pull Jan across. The men crouched around him.

"Let's go!"

They darted across the road and rushed down the embankment on the other side into the safety of another thicket, stopping only momentarily to catch their breaths. The boat lay ready by the shore, oars, sail and mast tucked away in the bottom. Jan was freed from the sled and lifted into the boat. Like Viking king Olav Tryggvason's warship, Ormen Lange, The Long Serpent, the boat carrying Jan headed into the wind, swallowed by the darkness.

Ingeborg and Gudrun turned to go home. The wind played with their hair. Gudrun brushed a few strands away from her face with a mitten-covered hand. Ingeborg pulled her knitted cap further down her face. She could not bear to look at her sister.

"Did you see how careworn and sad Jan looked?" ventured Ingeborg.

"Ja."

"I hope he will make it." Ingeborg sniffled.

"He will."

In their sadness it was difficult to find words. They walked on in silence, the snow crackling underfoot. In the short time Jan had been at the farm, he and the girls had grown very close. The girls' deep love for Jan had grown out of the care they had given him. They admired his strength and courage and they had suffered with him in his pain.

Jan, on the other hand, loved the girls because of their wholesome youthfulness. When he needed tenderness and a listening heart, one or the other was there. When he needed care it was offered to him. During the brief moments they shared, the sisters helped Jan forget his ordeal and he loved them for that. The girls reminded Jan of his family and happier times.

"Do you remember how emotional Jan was when he said, 'I have ruined everything for all of you?'"

"Ja."

"I don't think he did; do you, Gudrun?"

"No. We are Norwegians and we must help each other."

The tears that had been brimming spilled over and flowed in a steady stream.

"Why does it hurt so much, Gudrun?"

"Because we love him."

They went home to an empty barn.

The tragedy of war is that
it uses man's best to
do man's worst

— Harry Emerson Fosdick

HOTEL SAVOY

APRIL 12, 1943: Thoughts of the farewell scene at Furuflaten filled Jan's mind as they crossed the Lyngenfjord. The tender moments stayed with him and made him melancholy.

When the boat was pulled up over the small rocks on the east side of the Lyngenfjord, new hope filled him. Freedom was one step closer.

His eyes were slowly healing. They did not water as much anymore, the swelling was nearly gone, and the redness was beginning to disappear. But the shooting pains in his feet made it impossible for him to walk or stand, even with help. The men lifted him out of the boat. Jan wanted to help.

"Relax Jan, we'll handle this."

"This is no problem. You're not that heavy!" They chuckled.

Olav pushed the boat back in the water and rowed away from the hut. He would wait further south by the Innerelva River until the men returned. They did not want someone discovering a boat lying at the very door of Jan's hiding place.

Marius and Alfon were careful not to cause Jan additional pain. They carried him the short distance up toward the old log hut and paused by the door. Jan was placed in a sitting position on a knapsack.

From the snow pile where they stood to the threshold of the entrance, it was another couple of feet. There were no steps. Marius stretched to remove the bolt and the door squeaked open. The darkness made it impossible to distinguish any contours. Marius climbed up and crouched to get through the door. The small door opening only reached to the top of his chest.

With outstretched arms he felt his way around the room. On the south wall his knees bumped into something resembling a small cot. As his eyes adjusted to the dark he made out the outline of long narrow boards with a slight edge. It could be used as a makeshift bed. Several articles, some of them farm implements, lay strewn around the floor. The wood cot was much shorter than was Jan, but Marius was sure it could be used. Jan's helpers added a couple of the wooden planks which lay on the floor and gathered some loose hay stacked in one corner of the hut. They lifted Jan into the cottage and up into the makeshift bed.

His friends at Grønvoll farm had packed a knapsack with food, some alcohol and a small kerosene burner so he could heat his food. The men laid it all out neatly within easy reach of his bunk.

Marius and Alfon were troubled over leaving him. Jan reassured them he was comfortable and would be fine until they returned.

"Take care, Jan. We'll be back in a couple of days and bring you a little extra food."

"Ja, takk for alt," thanks for everything. Give my best greetings to everyone."

"So long, Jan."

By the water's edge they signaled Olav to come pick them up.

Jan felt good. He was happy with his new living quarters and expressed his gratitude to Marius. He was dry and he had a roof overhead, food, and clothes, even a kerosene burner. Most important though, he knew he had good friends that would stand by him no matter what. And he was nearer to the Swedish border than he had been yesterday.

Jan moved the planks beneath him a little and felt rather contented. Far away from the Germans, he could relax a little and again reminisce over the happy time he had spent in Furuflaten.

Jan expected his feet to improve quickly. Before long Marius would return, as he had promised, and with his help he would climb the mountain behind the hut toward the east. When he reached Sweden, Jan knew his suffering and fear would be a thing of the past.

Hour after hour he philosophized in the dark. The sharp light that forced its way through the cracks between the logs and around the ceiling told him that a new day had dawned. The details in his surroundings became more visible. On the floor and in the corners there were thick layers of dust, hay and cobwebs. The wall planks were carved into square beams by ax. The workmanship varied, allowing the daylight to break through the large cracks. Moss had been stuffed into the larger cracks, but even at that, the hut was far from being well insulated. About four feet above his head there was a heavy crossbar between the walls. Jan could not figure out its usefulness. The ceiling was made from flat, wide boards.

The hut was about nine feet long and six feet wide. As Jan lay there, hour after hour, he discovered new details of workmanship. It gave his mind something to mull over. Every board and beam had different size knots and patterns as he compared them with each other. Soon he knew them all. As he familiarized himself with the hut he felt more at home and he began to feel safe and comfortable.

Jan kept his mind busy learning all about his surroundings. His thoughts also wandered back to his earlier life and the happy times he'd experienced as a youth in Oslo with his friends and family. Reliving these scenes of happiness calmed him, and at the same time, infused him with a longing for home and family. Often he reviewed the reasons for ending up in this hut and he rehashed every detail of how the war had come to Norway.

Past midnight, April 15, 1943: As promised, the men from Furuflaten returned to the hut two days later.

"Hallo Jan, how are you doing?" Their cheery voices greeted him before the door was fully open.

"I am doing great. It's like living at Hotel Savoy!" They all shared a hearty laugh.

Jan felt good, and he was happy and expressed gratitude for his new living quarters. His foot still bothered him, but it was nothing he could not live with. He expected it to keep improving.

Marius had attempted to reach the doctor in Lyngseidet to learn more about frostbite, but the doctor had been away. Instead, the bus driver, Lars Utgård, drove to Tromsø in an unsuccessful effort to get professional advice.

"Let's wait a few more days, Jan."

Hoping that his feet would continue to heal, they agreed to return in another few days with more food and provisions. The plan still was that Jan, with Marius' help, would make it over the mountains on his own two feet.

Once more they said goodbye, but seeing how well Jan was doing, it was easier for them this time. They had to cross the fjord and return home before the people in Furuflaten began their day.

ANOTHER DAY forced its light through the cracks in the hut. Jan's legs suddenly hurt terribly. The burning sensation and throbbing increased at a startling pace, and did not let up. Never before in his whole life had he ever felt such terrifying pain. An unexplainable inner alarm took hold of Jan. Within an hour pain and fear wholly overpowered him. He groaned. Jan pulled up to a sitting position, then laid back down, turned over, rolled from side to side and back again. He cried out for relief, but the pain only intensified.

Grabbing his legs just below the knees he squeezed hard. It gave him slight relief. He pulled the bandages off his feet. Horrified, he saw his toes were a dark grayish-black. When he stroked them he could not feel his

Hotel Savoy stands close to Lyngenfjord.

190

own touch. The large toe on his right foot was pitch black and the skin was cracking. Fluid trickled out, some clear, some yellowish and thick.

"Oh my - my feet! Gangrene! No! Yes - it is gangrene!"

He knew the consequences of gangrene, but at that moment he did not want to believe it. He knew how quickly it could spread, and that it could end in death. Alone in this dim place with not a friend to turn to for help or comfort, he panicked. Even his trusted friend Marius would not be back for another couple of days.

For three days Jan suffered through agonizing pain. Sleep was impossible. As the minutes turned to hours and the hours into days he could only lie there and struggle with his pain.

Surely Marius would come soon; did he not promise he would be back in three days?

No one came.

A new day dawned and dragged on, then night came; Jan's suffering continued. Another new day and another night came and moved onward. Five days had passed since Marius and Alfon's last visit. Jan gave in to his fate. For him all hope was gone. He assumed the Germans had arrested his friends, and no one else had any idea of his whereabouts. He would die here in this little hut, a slow painful death.

AMANDUS LILLEVOLL returned home to Furuflaten from a fishing excursion in the Lofoten Islands two days after Jan had been taken to Revdal. He ran into Marius and two other men on his way home.

"Amandus I need to talk to you. It is a rather serious matter." Marius looked earnest.

"Go ahead, I have time." Amandus studied Marius as he explained about Jan.

"Frankly, dear friend, I am in desperate need of help. Would you be able to help us get him to Sweden?"

But Amandus had heard of the happenings in Toftefjord and felt that it was too risky.

"I have to think about this Marius. This is not child's play."

"Take your time, it might mean our very lives," said Marius.

Amandus pondered the pros and cons, and what to do.

"I'll take the risk. I'll help you," was his final answer.

Furuflaten, April 20, 1943: A dreadful spring storm made it impossible to cross the Lyngenfjord. Finally on April 20 the weather eased. Alfon and Amandus packed their knapsacks. They would have to cross the fjord in daylight; they needed to get food to Jan. At Røykeneset, straight across from Furuflaten, was a German guard post. From there they could observe the whole fjord. Even Revdal to the north behind Foraneset was in their field of vision. The men were uneasy; there was no place to hide.

Alfon and Amandus took fishing gear along and stopped often, pretending to fish. They were concerned that the Germans might have found Jan by now. They had not seen him for several days.

They came ashore on the sandbank south of the Revdal hut and hid among the tall turf.

"I'll run over the grassland," Alfon suggested since he knew Jan from before. He worked his way over to the hut. Jan was armed, and kept the gun close by his side. They had agreed that they would knock three times on the wall when they came. He knocked and heard creaks from within. He waved for Amandus to enter.

Jan crawled from his cot, pulled himself across the floor and opened the door.

He greeted Alfon warmly and shook hands with Amandus.

"We've brought you some food."

"All I have left over is bread crust. It will taste good. Thanks."

They noticed how pale and worn Jan looked. He showed them his feet – all his toes and both heels were black.

"If this is gangrene, I am finished. I am too young, I don't wish to die."

The men looked at his feet in horror.

"Is it possible to reach a doctor when you get home and bring him to me?"

Jan was in despair. It hurt them to leave him, but time was of an essence. They "fished" their way back home across the fjord and contacted a doctor.

The doctor did not have the courage to cross the fjord with them to Revdal.

Wednesday, April 21, 1943: Jan shuddered with pain. Big drops of sweat trickled down his face. In an instant his body chilled, then it turned hot again, and back to cold. Fever ravaged. All he could do was watch his murky gray toes turn black and new cracks appear on the skin. But it was the stench, the putrid stench that rolled over him in waves and nauseated him, that scared him the most. His feet were rotting away! "If I could only lose consciousness and allow death to come unnoticed," he thought.

With all his might he pulled his knees close up to him, grabbed his ankles and pressed them against the back of his thighs. This helped to relieve the pain somewhat. At intervals he had to let go and rest, then he repeated his efforts for fleeting moments of respite from the excruciating pain.

As he struggled emotionally with his situation, his inner will again came to the forefront. He had been close to death many times and somehow he had survived. Lying there in his lonely state, a thought formed in his mind. He pondered his circumstances and what, if anything, he could do to change them. His legs would soon be covered with black spots as the gangrene worked its way upward.

"I have to stop it! I refuse to die here in this hut!" Jan began to fight back. He was still not willing to give up on life and he told himself he would not give in to inaction, pain or panic. He would will himself to function, even to take drastic steps.

He looked around. His eyes fell on the sheath knife close by. He stared at it. Grabbing the wooden edge of his bunk with one hand, he pushed the boards beneath him until he came to a half-sitting position, with the other. The sheath knife was on the makeshift stand next to the bunk. He pulled it out of its sheath and laid it on the bunk with the handle toward him. He calmly folded the bed covering aside toward the wall. Jan bent forward and examined his feet, focusing on his large toe. It was all black, including the rough edges on the bottom where the gunshot wound had begun to grow together. He squeezed the toe in several spots but he felt nothing.

Jan's mind was made up.

"What other chance do I have?" he asked himself. No better answer came to him so he reached for the alcohol bottle. Pouring some into his hands, he rubbed it between his fingers and over his hands and wrists. He put the bottle to his lips and took a couple of large gulps.

Jan repeated the procedure twice. The second time he poured a little alcohol over the knife blade and rubbed it clean. He took a few more gulps for final courage and to hopefully soothe the pain.

Two, three times he rubbed his large toe with alcohol. He took a firm hold of it with his left hand. Jan picked up the knife and resolutely held it. He placed the blade of the knife where he felt it to be the best angle. Sweat resurfaced on his forehead.

Jan began to cut. He inched his way ahead as the blood began to trickle out, grateful the bleeding was much less than he had imagined. The knife butted up against the joint. Jan continued the sawing motion and then quickly cut the last piece of skin, severing the toe from his body. He was shivering and dripping wet.

Jan placed the toe by a crack in the wall timber, and then fell backwards in his crude bed. His chest heaved with each breath and moan. The knife fell from his hand onto the floor. With his elbow he wiped his soaked brow. With trembling hands he covered his face and wept.

Minutes later his clarity of mind returned. He again pulled himself up on his elbows. With alcohol he washed his hands, the knife, and then carefully dabbed his toe. The first joint of the next toe was black; with his left thumb and index finger he grabbed hold on each side of the nail. It was easy to place the knife blade now that the large toe had been removed.

Though the edge of the knife was in place, Jan was unable to slit the skin and had to start sawing before the blood was released.

His head shook - his whole body shuddered. Sweat poured from his twisted face – but Jan's hand held steady. Half of the joint was cut when he had to stop. The pain was intense – alcohol was not the best pain reliever.

"You must finish the job, Jan!"

He began to saw again. Jan broke the last piece of the joint and pushed it to the side. The cut gaped. The knife moved easier. The tip of the toe fell into the folds of the covering together with the knife. Jan fell backwards.

Outside the wind howled and beat Lyngenfjord into a fury. Huge white-capped waves angrily flogged the shore near the little hut.

Snowdrifts engulfed Jan's shelter, leaving just the upper walls and the roof visible. The whirling snow crashed into boulders and the bare trees leeward thrashed all about as the forceful wind gusts pounced on them.

Jan was oblivious to the storm.

On the opposite side of the fjord, a restless Marius and his friends had to return home. The raging sea was too dangerous. Their little boat was no match for the colossal waves and the wind; they would never reach Jan. Marius could dimly make out the black mountain wall close to the hut, only five miles away. It was so close, yet in this weather so very far.

SEVERAL MORE black spots had to be removed. Jan cut, fell, and cut again several times. No one could have stopped him. His only chance for life was to mutilate his own body. The nightmare lasted several hours.

Motionless, Jan lay on his back. His right arm hung over the edge of the cot. Close by him on the floor was a bloody knife.

Thursday, April 22, 1943: Soon after 2 a.m., Marius and two men hurried from the boat up to the hut. Since Alfon's and Amandus' last visit with Jan, Marius had been frantic. He ran in front the last few steps, knocked three times on the door and rushed in.

"Hello Jan! Have you been waiting for us?"

The moonless April night blinded Jan when Marius opened the door and disrupted his aloneness. He groaned and shaded his half-shut eyes with a hand blotched with dried blood. Even the early morning light pained him. It took minutes before his eyes adjusted to the change after the days of darkness.

A foul odor greeted Jan's visitors. The stench rolled through the door, so fetid it nauseated them. They turned toward the door for a breath of fresh air.

"Jan!" Marius moved toward the cot. No response. The farmer looked down on his haggard friend, moved the blanket aside and gasped. Then he saw the bloody knife on the floor. His eyes traveled to the crack on the wall. A black toe!

Jan did not move. He was dirty and bloody, and his skin resembled a corpse. The sores from his incisions had not healed, and secretions mixed with blood seeped out. The offensive smell filled the tiny hut. Below Jan's knees, his legs and ankles had turned brownish-red.

With the arrival of his enthusiastic friends, a glimmer of hope returned to Jan's wasted body and desolate spirit.

"We're here to take care of you Jan."

Jan moved and slowly opened his eyes. The men cleaned him up and fed him some of the food they had brought. In time the conversation turned to small talk. Jan quickened. Even seriously ill, he was able to find hope in the smallest things. The Furuflaten men were amazed at what their visits did for him. Their visit had restored a flicker of hope to him before they left him alone again.

View from Hotel Savoy across Lyngenfjord toward Furuflaten

HAPPENINGS IN
LOFOTEN ISLANDS

ON APRIL 24, 1940, Reichskommissar Terboven became Hitler's highest civil authority in occupied Norway. A man explicitly trusted by the Fuehrer, and into whose hands were poured unlimited, concentrated power.

Lofoten Islands, March 4, 1943: The British and Norwegian forces launched a successful raid in northern Norway, in the Lofoten Islands.

Immediately following the raid in Svolvær, Reichskommissar Terboven flew from Oslo to Lofoten for briefing. Terboven's punishment of the people of Svolvær was swift; several innocent hostages were taken and many homes were burned to the ground.

Two young men from the village of Furuflaten, one of them Alvin Larsen, were in the Lofoten Islands at the time of the raid, having just purchased a fishing boat.

Subsequent to Terboven's terrorism of the people of Svolvær, he did something unusual for him. Terboven expressed a wish to see some of the Norwegian fishermen in action. The Germans used huge amounts of fish to feed their soldiers. In spite of his power, Terboven felt it essential and beneficial to have a good relationship with the fishermen. Alvin was among those chosen to be present for Terboven.

A few men were gathered in a fisherman's shelter repairing fishnets when Terboven appeared. He explained he was curious to learn a little of their everyday life.

Terboven was feared. His power was absolute. He was of medium build and slender of stature with a rather handsome face; his dark piercing eyes looked through unframed glasses. While in the fisherman's shelter he displayed a congenial demeanor, and he was almost likeable had his reputation not preceded him.

As he was leaving he stopped abruptly in the doorway, turned toward the fishermen and placed one hand on his hip, the other above his head on the doorframe.

"Do you have any special wishes? Or perhaps, I could serve you in some way?"

A hush fell over the men, they all had wishes but only one dared voice them. Alvin had a blazing desire that could not be extinguished: "I would like for my fishing boat never to be requisitioned into German service," he said, looking straight at Terboven.

The Germans' common practice was to take possession of whatever they desired and they had confiscated many fishing vessels. Terboven lingered momentarily without saying a word, saluted and left.

Reichskommissar Terboven in Lofoten.

There was a stir of excitement in Alvin's home when, several days later, an envelope with the Reichskommissar's logo came. Alvin, a little uneasy perhaps, pulled out a document bearing the German eagle, Terboven's signature and stamp. It stated that Alvin and his companion's fishing vessel were not ever to be requisitioned into the German service. Alvin let out a howl. With such a document he could take his fishing boat anywhere.

Later when German patrol boats stopped him for inspection, from out of nowhere as they often did, Alvin gleefully produced his valuable document. As soon as Terboven's signature and stamp were noted, the military boots clicked together and a rigid military greeting was afforded. Alvin and his crew sailed on triumphant.

GEARING UP FOR REVDAL

WHILE JAN languished in the log hut at Revdal, Marius constantly devised ideas on how to best transport him to Sweden. It was an overwhelming challenge. Jan was extremely ill, and Marius knew that the most comfortable way for Jan to be transported would be by car or truck, along the main road. Even before completing the thought, Marius knew they would not be able to pass the German border guards leaving Norway, nor cross the northwest corner of occupied Finland without being discovered. It was useless to think he would ever reach Sweden by that route.

As the days elapsed, Marius realized that only one way was left open to them, the mountains. The task would be Herculean for the resistance workers to pull off, and for Jan, almost merciless. But it was Jan's only chance for survival. And, without daring, how would they know that it could not be done? They had to try. There was no alternative.

It became obvious to Marius that transporting Jan to Sweden was too risky and too big of a job for the men of Furuflaten alone. They needed to contact the other men working within the resistance movement in the neighboring localities.

Telephones in these outlying areas were few; only party lines were available. Telephones were extremely dangerous to use for illegal work because people listened in. Any veiled stories could be embellished and passed on to other itchy ears.

State roads were non-existent in Birtavärre, Olderdalen and Manndalen Valley. Many of the people central to the resistance movement lived in these places, and a tight-knit communication system was essential to their success. Sometimes because of the distances between localities, it took days before a message reached its intended recipient.

Soon after Alvin returned from Lofoten, he was pulled into the midst of the master plan to rescue Jan. With Reichskommissar Terboven's blessing, unknown to him of course, the document he had granted Alvin suited him superbly. The task of delivering messages among the fjords and inland waters of the Troms District became Alvin's job.

Alvin readily agreed to have his boat at Marius' disposal and suggested they bring along Alfon Hansen. Being a commercial fisherman had its advantages. Once the season was over, or when they came home for a break, the time was theirs to do with as they pleased. Alvin felt good about using his boat in Norway's service.

Furuflaten, April 19, 1943: Alvin Larsen, Marius Grønvoll and Alfon Hansen readied to leave Furuflaten for their inland trip. Alvin called his girlfriend and apologized that he had to break their date, but promised to make it up to her. Alfon told one of his funny stories to his mother before leaving the house. He enjoyed seeing her laugh. Marius was the last to come aboard, having had to finish up some barn chores before leaving.

It was good weather with a brisk wind, and the men were in good spirits as Alvin took to the tiller and set the boat out to sea.

"Jaja." The words came quickly. "When several Norwegians band together, the green devils don't stand a chance," Alfon laughed contagiously.

"You're right. We are going to snatch Jan from the Gestapo yet," Marius agreed.

They crossed the Lyngenfjord and sailed northwest around the tip of Odden. The wind was picking up a bit and it felt good; the air smelled of seaweed and fish, always invigorating to the men. Crossing Kåfjord they soon reached Olderdalen, where they met with resistance member Peder Bergmo and discussed the possibilities of securing help to transport Jan to Sweden.

"No problem. Count me in."

Peder was the contact person for Manndalen, Birtavärre and Olderdalen.

They sailed south to Birtavärre, innermost in the fjord where the Bjørn brothers lived. Stalwarts in the resistance movement, and always willing to offer all they could, the brothers offered advice and provided help whenever it was needed.

Continuing on, they cruised northwest to Manndalen and met with teacher Nordnes, a tall handsome man with deep set clear blue eyes in his early forties. The positive answer came as expected. Many alternatives for transporting Jan were discussed with all of these men. Ultimately, however, they all reached the same conclusion. Satisfied with their work, Alvin's crew returned home from their outing.

Marius now had a well-defined plan. The men from Furuflaten would bring Jan, tied to a sled, up the Revdal Mountains in back of the little log hut. At a designated spot up on the mountain plateau, they would deliver him to the more rested and vigorous Manndalen men, who would come up on skis from the opposite side of the mountains. The Manndalen men would be responsible for Jan's safe passage to Sweden. The plan would be put into action as soon as it was practical and the weather was accommodating. They had to move swiftly. Marius set the day for April 24 and they were to meet at midnight. A message was sent via teacher Leigland at Lyngseidet on to Peder Bergmo in Olderdalen. Jan's life hung in the balance. He was in desperate need of proper medical treatment.

The Solhov School was located a short way up from the Lyngenfjord in the southern part of the village of Lyngseidet, some nine miles from Furuflaten. The school was famed in the Troms District because of its excellent curriculum and also because its majestic building was the largest wooden structure in northern Norway at the time. The Germans had confiscated the building and installed their headquarters unit for the entire Eastern Front. As the building was strictly guarded, no one approached it without a just cause. The school caretaker, however, lived in one of the wings of the building.

As the preparations for Jan's further transport continued under the strictest secrecy, caretaker Jensen was called on to help. An excellent carpenter, Jensen was assigned to make a strong wood sled sturdy and of adequate size to transport Jan on.

In a basement corner of Solhov School was Jensen's modest carpenter shop. A small carpenter's bench squeezed up against the corner window and made it possible for him to partially see the school grounds outside. One of his shop walls adjoined one of the soldiers' quarters. They came and went at all times of the day and sometimes they dropped in on Jensen for a chat while he worked. Despite these circumstances, on his little workbench he managed to build an excellent ski sled, 6 feet long, 4 inches high and 22 inches wide. It was suitable for a grown man to lie down on.

A couple of days after Alvin and his friends' boat trip to secure aid for Jan's transport, Jensen had the sled ready. Alvin had been given the task of transporting the sled to Furuflaten. One of Alvin's uncles, Johan Johansen, also owned a fishing boat and just that day he was with his son in Lyngseidet to repair the boat's motor. Alvin knew this, jumped on his bicycle and pedaled quickly toward Lyngseidet.

He went straight to the "lion's den" – the German headquarters at Solhov School. Like Daniel of old, Alvin went undaunted and filled with faith. It was a threatening situation but he believed the outcome would be favorable. He hastened over to one of the guards. Knowing a little German he said, "Guten tag," Good day.

"Guten tag," replied the guard.

"Ich suche Jensen," I have a meeting with Caretaker Jensen.

The soldier quickly understood; nevertheless, he was a little annoyed at being disturbed but brushed it off.

"Danke sehr," thank you, said Alvin.

All the soldiers knew of Jensen, but regarded the carpenter as harmless. As a result he didn't question Alvin further. He gave the go-ahead with a nod of his head and waved him over in the direction of the stairs leading to the large windowed entrance door. Alvin thanked him, closed the heavy doors behind him, and continued down the few steps to the basement. As he walked along the corridor, he noticed the guardroom door ajar where some soldiers were relaxing; they paid no attention to him.

Jensen waved Alvin on and closed the door behind him to the workshop. The sled was ready to be moved. But knowing an assembled sled would lead to many questions, Jensen had constructed it like a building set. He carefully explained to Alvin how to piece it together.

"Easy to transport, easy to assemble," he whispered.

They tied the twelve-foot long un-planed boards together into a pile. These planks were quite a bit longer then the rest of the pieces so that both ends could be stuffed with the un-planed sawed-off pieces for the wooden braces, making it all look like 12 foot long planks when tied together and wrapped. The package was extremely heavy, but also fragile, so had to be handled with care.

The workbench at Solhov School where Caretaker Jensen made the sled on which Jan lay when he was taken up into Revdal Mountains.

The two men decided it was best for Alvin to bicycle ahead down to the docks in Lyngseidet to wait by his uncle's boat.

"Auf weidersehen," one of the soldiers waved through the cracked door as he walked back down the hall.

"Auf weidersehen."

Within half an hour Jensen arrived with the horse and sleigh and a long well-wrapped package of wooden planks destined for Furuflaten, and eventually to be Jan's transportation to Sweden.

Soldiers patrolled the Lyngseidet dock. The air coming off the fjord was biting cold, but their compensation was the magnificent view of the Lyngen Alps in the distance. The tide was out and Alvin struggled to get the cumbersome package down into the boat, which lay several meters lower than the edge of the dock. The German guard saw his predicament, removed his machine gun which, up to now, had been loosely flung over his shoulder, and carefully placed it on the dock.

"Ich helfe," I will help, he said, hurrying over to Alvin. With care, the two placed the valuable package up in the bow of the boat.

Quivering nerves never disturbed Alvin; he was a feisty young man. On the contrary, he was stable, wise and daring. With his cheerful disposition, both friends and strangers took an instant liking to him.

"And where is the crew to the boat?" the soldier queried.

"They'll be along shortly. I'm just hitching a ride with them."

Alvin crawled back up on the dock and chatted with the soldier in his broken German. With a thick German burr, the soldier made an effort to speak Norwegian. A pleasant conversation ensued.

"I long for my family and home in Germany. May the war soon end so I can return to my homeland." The soldier was melancholy.

Alvin agreed. He fumbled through his pockets as if trying to find a cigarette, though he didn't have any. The soldier unbuttoned the breast pocket of his uniform, took out a package of cigarettes and seemed pleased to offer one to him, though he was forbidden to smoke on duty.

Soon Alvin's uncle and his son arrived, ready to return to Furuflaten.

"I guess I can come along?" Alvin queried.

"Ka har du der?" What have you got there? His uncle stared, and pointed at the long package up in front of the boat.

"Just some material from Solhov School."

"You are a lucky man to have contact with Jensen." His uncle removed his cap, smiled and scratched his head. "There is such a shortage of material these days."

Alvin lifted his bicycle and put it down on the deck. They loosened the ropes, and as the boat distanced itself from the dock, Alvin raised his hand and thanked the soldier for his kindness.

"Bitte sehr," My pleasure! The soldier saluted.

Arriving at Furuflaten, the package was left aboard the boat.

Furuflaten, April 22, 1943: Alvin's friend, Hans Olsen, picked up the package with the twelve-foot-long boards and loaded it into his rowboat. He rowed along the coast a little further south in the village. Upon his arrival Alvin was waiting. They wrapped the set in burlap and hid it in a

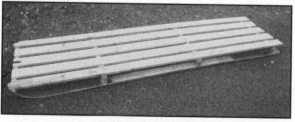

secure place close by the water's edge. It would be picked up again when they set out toward Revdal to transport Jan.

Replica of the sled

204

ON THE OTHER SIDE OF
THE FJORD

KÅFJORD, LYNGENFJORD'S 15-mile arm, stretches southeast toward the mountainous village of Birtavärre at the head of the fjord. Birtavärre lies on the southeast side of Manndalen Valley; to the north lies Olderdalen Valley. West across the Lyngenfjord lies Lyngseidet and nine miles south of Lyngseidet lies Furuflaten. These communities form sort of a quadrangle on the map.

Daring patriots from each village were active in the resistance movement. Each village had established its own sensitive and secret communication nets. Communicating by telephone was risky

Kåfjorddalen Valley

because one never knew who would be listening in. The only roads were between Furuflaten and Lyngseidet. There were none between Manndalen, Birtavärre and Olderdalen. A ferry ran between Olderdalen and Lyngseidet and sometimes it was utilized to send secret messages. Other times the resistance members rowed half way out into the Kåfjord between Olderdalen and Manndalen to meet and exchange messages. From Samuelsberg, on the outskirts of Manndalen, over to Olderdalen, the distance was around four miles to row midways into the fjord.

Peder Bergmo, a thirty-one-year old father of five, lived in Olderdalen. His oldest son Asmund was only six. Peder was known as a loving and attentive dad, firm, but fair. He appreciated nature's beauty and loved to be outdoors in any season.

In 1943 Peder managed the communal office for medical insurance. A compassionate man, he cared deeply for the poor, and anyone who faced difficult times. He was of great service to many in the rural community when hard times or disaster struck in its varied forms.

In his youth Peder become acquainted with the Bjørn brothers in Birtavärre. Through this friendship he was later drawn into the resistance movement when the war came. As time passed, he became the leader of the group in Olderdalen. He was the key person in the village's connection with the schoolmaster Leigland in Lyngseidet.

After Jan Baalsrud arrived in Furuflaten, resistance leaders in the area discussed plans for his evacuation to Sweden. In Olderdalen, there were rumors that fundraising to obtain money for Jan's transport to Sweden had begun. The Gestapo got a whiff of this, and Peder Bergmo was arrested and imprisoned in Tromsø. Suddenly his wife was left alone to care for their young children, fearing all the while for her husband's life.

Sheriff Marvold heard about Peder's arrest. He and Peder had been in the same class all through folk school and had spent much time together in their youth. Marvold took pity on his old school chum and his family. Being friendly with the Germans, he traveled to Tromsø and sought out the Gestapo. Since Marvold had an in with the Gestapo and they trusted him, he tried them out.

"You have Peder Bergmo from Olderdalen imprisoned here. I believe you have the wrong man."

The Gestapo agent straightened up and stared at Marvold. "Are you questioning our judgment?" The sheriff ignored the question. "Peder is a school buddy of mine, a father of five. He keeps busy seeing to the need of the villagers through his work and he is law abiding!"

They discussed the issue back and forth without coming to an agreement. When Marvold readied to leave he turned and resolutely stated, "I vouch for this man."

After a short imprisonment, Peder was set free. He returned to Olderdalen, and unafraid despite his misadventure, he continued his work with the underground.

In Manndalen, it was a 43-year-old bachelor, Aslak Fossvoll, and teacher Nordnes who were the contact persons. Aslak was totally trustworthy and an extremely polite man. He owned a small farm that he nurtured with care. He loved nothing more than fishing in the clear streams of the nearby majestic mountains, with his faithful dog by his side. People in the valley said that if you saw Aslak you would also see his dog. The two were inseparable and often went out into the wilds together. Aslak was happiest if no one knew where they were going.

Peder Nordnes was Manndalen's revered folk-school teacher. The rural community considered him a man of sterling character. He was a tall, well-built man and very strong, with Nordic blond hair and intelligent blue eyes. Like Aslak, he was unmarried. All the youth in the valley had had him as a teacher, and he was greatly respected. He had impeccable manners and was known for his ability and willingness to cooperate with others.

When Marius, Alfon and Alvin visited Olderdalen, Birtavärre and Manndalen on April 19, they had worked with these men and made plans for Jan's transport to Sweden. The final date for putting the plan into action was the only thing that was not set.

Furuflaten 23 April 1943: Marius decided it was the right time to carry out the well-laid plans to begin Jan's transfer to Sweden. The weather, something that always had to be considered in the North, was good. The wind was calm and it was not too cold - and all the men were ready. On that day, Marius sent a message via Lyngseidet to Peder Bergmo in

Ankerlia and Moskogaisa Mountains

Olderdalen. It read, "He will be delivered to the Manndalen men early Saturday, April 25, between two and four in the morning."

Peder Bergmo was working at his office when Marius' message arrived. There was no way he could just close his office and leave, since people depended on him to be there. At the end of the workday, it was too late to reach the Manndalen men and organize the climb up to the Revdal Mountains. The men hadn't been sought out and told in advance in order to keep the plan secret. If someone should make a slip it could be catastrophic for all. No one was to know anything before the time was ripe.

Olderdalen, April 24, 1943: It was early morning when Peder set course for Manndalen. He rowed across Kåfjord and tied his little boat at Samuelsberg, at the edge of Manndalen. Time was of the essence – he had only one day to find four men who were able and willing to take on this dangerous assignment.

A chill wind blasted Peder as he walked briskly toward the post office to inquire of a trusted friend as to whom he should approach. He received names of people who could possibly help. Another friend loaned Peder his horse to make his trip around the hilly village faster and easier.

From the post office, Peder went straight to the school to see teacher Nordnes, who also was helpful with names. Teacher Nordnes himself desired to be part of the team, but felt he was not in good enough condition for the fatiguing climb. Teacher Nordnes was plagued with a stiff body and was often wracked with pain. He felt that his participation would be a hindrance and possibly cause failure for all.

After Peder left Teacher Nordnes he went to Aslak Fossvoll. As the leader of the resistance movement in the village, he would surely be the right man to ask for help.

The two men discussed able-bodied men who could make the hike. After a short discussion, they both knew they had the right man. Peder left Aslak.

The horse trotted along the wintry road to Hans Oppevold's little house further up in the valley. There Peder found that Hans had cut his foot the day before while working in the woods. It was impossible for him to take on the assignment.

By the time Peder left Oppervoll's home, it was late afternoon and he had yet to find the men he needed for the job. The next man that Aslak had suggested Peder see lived nearby. Peder gave the horse a little rap with the reins and in a small gallop headed toward Nils Nilsen's house. The horse slowed down after awhile, and Peder had to continually smack the horse with the reins to hurry him on. The horse leaped ahead and kept up the speed once more. Time was short.

Nilsen was a tireless and hard working man. Married with a house full of children, his friends called him "Nigo." He ran a small farm and fished on the side for extra income. Everyone admired his ability to handle strenuous work and his diligence long after all others quit. He was a man who could work hard for 48 hours without a bite to eat. On the other hand, Nigo could easily eat a whole loaf of homemade bread once he got started. His unbeatable optimism, no matter the situation, was also well known.

Nigo was working outside when Peder arrived. Peder explained the urgency and the secrecy of his message and Nigo brought him over to a quiet place away from the children. As quickly as possible, Peder laid out what needed to be done and the danger of it all.

"Ja, I'll go," Nigo responded, without a moment's hesitation. He knew the mountains, the terrain and the danger at this time of the year; he asked for a companion, one who was both strong and persevering.

Peder was elated knowing Nigo would see this assignment through, but he needed one more man. He had started out from Olderdalen early in the morning and worked all day. Now the day was gone. And Peder Bergmo had been unable to find two men who could climb up to Jan in the Revdal Mountains. He had to leave the responsibility to find the second man with the Manndalen men. Knowing they would not be able to meet the Furuflaten men up in the Revdal Mountains at the appointed time, Peder's heart was heavy. He returned the horse back to its owner and walked down to the dock. He climbed into the rowboat and began the journey home. The rowing home seemed extra long and strenuous.

On the west side of the Revdal Mountains, the Furuflaten men had already begun their climb up from Hotel Savoy with Jan tied to a sled.

PUSHED TO THE BRINK

THE TRANQUIL spring evening with its warm breeze was welcome respite from the harsh winter storms. Quiet waves gently lapped the shore and vanished over nearby rocks. A few puffy clouds hung suspended midway up the nearby mountains.

Despite the peace that surrounded them, Marius Grønvoll, Alvin Larsen, Olaf Lanes and Amandus Lillevoll were apprehensive. They motioned to one another and spoke in whispers when they had to communicate. German soldiers were quartered at Furuflaten School a short distance into the village. The young men hoped the soldiers were unwinding for the day. On the village road a short way from the docks, a lone German soldier patrolled; he might hear any accidental noise. The village was quieting down with families relaxing at home. This was the evening the three men had prepared for. This was the evening Jan had been waiting for.

The men, to the minute of the prearranged time, brought the long wrapped package with the sled material aboard Amandus Lillevoll's boat. Inaudibly they rowed out into the fjord, knowing the first few hundred meters were the most perilous. The open water magnified every small sound and could easily be heard in the village.

Cautiously they slipped the oars into the water. Drops formed on the oars and fell back into the water like tinkling silver bells. Too big a splash could give them all away. With the stealth of their Viking ancestors, the Furuflaten men glided smoothly into the nocturnal shadows of the unknown future.

Tension eased as they distanced themselves from the land. Once they were well out in the fjord they felt safe in raising the mast and sail, a noisy proposition. Knowing they would be easier to spot from land, they had waited to hoist the sail for as long as possible.

The wind was almost still and the sail provided little momentum to the boat's forward thrust. But Jan's friends were prepared for any contingency and their sail had a totally different purpose. Should a German patrol boat surprise them, they would have difficulty explaining the long package in the bottom of the boat. Under such circumstances, they planned to sink the package, to which they had attached a heavy rock. Next, they would get their fishing lines out.

As an added camouflage they had brought nakkeskudd, which literally means a shot in the head from the back. Nakkeskudd was Furuflaten's own homemade brew, a hard liquor with caraway seeds added. The drink derived its name from the violent effect it had on the bodies of those who dared. They had brought several bottles. The plan was to pretend as if they were on a genuine rabble-rousing party out in the fjord.

If necessary, they would pour a little nakkeskudd on their clothes; they would take a gulp or two as well. All this, designed to fool the Germans, would happen quickly and behind the sail. Surely the Germans would find nothing suspicious aboard their boat: only provisions, fish gear and liquor. As it turned out, the Norwegians pulled the boat up on the shore opposite Furuflaten, in Revdal, after an hour of hard rowing and without incident.

A stone's throw away from the beach, up a small incline, stood the forsaken wood hut almost buried in snowdrift. Within, an ill friend wasted away, yet the hut sat there gawking over the fjord, utterly void of human feelings, dark and threatening.

Behind the rough wood door, Jan battled in solitude against pain and fear. Even after his self-operation, the pain in his feet troubled him. Loneliness pricked his heart and never let go. Unfulfilled longing for human contact made the wound deeper and the solitude harder to bear. For Jan, panic was never far removed. Sometimes it prevailed.

During the day a few rays of light crept through the narrow cracks around the doorframe and along the wall, but they were narrow and sparse. From his cot, Jan pulled out some of the moss which had been stuffed into tiny fissures of the walls to prevent drafts. These gaps were miniscule, the size of small coins. He mused over which spot of moss he should remove next. These small openings had been his only source of light. In some places where he had pulled the moss out, no light came through. The soldier realized the snowdrifts reached far up the wall.

Jan yearned for news from his friends. His recurring worry was that something had happened to them. He was genuinely concerned that the Germans had arrested them, and that they would be tortured. All he wanted was a hint of them, a small piece of encouragement to make his own burden easier to carry. Jan drifted in and out of consciousness from the pain.

Icy fingers of fear left him little hope. Why this prolonged suffering? What was its purpose? Why had he not perished in Toftefjord with his friends? Why could he not just die now?

Agonizing in his bed, Jan felt forsaken. He did not know that only a few feet away four men trudged through the snow toward the hut. They carried clothing, a couple of wool blankets, an old military sleeping bag, food, drink and some cigarettes. Olaf carried coils of rope over his shoulders.

Alvin brought the long package with the unplaned boards. He fought his way a little past the cottage, up towards the incline, and put the package down. The muscles in his arms ached and his neck felt stiff. Alvin stretched and bent from side to side to loosen up after toting the heavy load. Above, he discerned the outline of clouds hanging low up against the mountainside. He thought back to the kind German soldier who had helped him earlier in Lyngseidet. He had been unaware, of course, of the package contents. The soldier, a young man about his own age, who longed for his own home and loved ones, had been so trusting. Alvin opened the package and set the pieces out in order. Jensen's directions on how to assemble the sled were excellent. Screws, bolts, boards and runners fit together perfectly and swiftly completed the ski sled. Alvin laid down on it to try its strength. He stretched out; it was both long and wide enough and sturdy.

Earlier in the day Alvin rummaged through his house to find the Navy jacket he had worn with pride. It had hung in the back of the closet since his leave in 1940. He had never been recalled. Tonight he dressed in his uniform jacket once again. Alvin tried it on in front of the small mirror at home and was pleased with how well it fit. He looked good. He knew Jan was wearing a Navy uniform. Alvin hoped dressing in a Navy outfit would contribute to Jan's well being, and make him more relaxed and comfortable.

MARIUS OPENED the door to the hut; Amandus and Olaf were right behind. Jan was very ill. The putrid smell of rotting flesh still lingered in the air. The men tried to cheer him. After all, he would soon be on his way to Sweden.

"We will get you out of here as soon as you have eaten, Jan."

"Before too long, we will have you in Sweden. The Manndalen men are meeting us up on the plateau."

"By the way, my family sends warm greetings and wishes you their heartfelt best," Marius added.

Jan barely managed a smile.

The men went to work. They cleaned him up and tended to his feet. They changed his clothes and disposed of the waste. With something warm to drink and a slice or two of bread, a little of Jan's strength returned. Mingling with his friends cheered him. They reassured him that his worst trials were behind him. Jan's inherent optimism began to return.

His admiration for these men, these courageous giants, knew no limits. His gratitude for their sacrifices and the risks they were taking overwhelmed him. He was keenly aware that these men had put their own safety and comfort aside to save his life, and by so doing they might give up their own. They wanted neither payment nor praise for their effort. Their reward, as they had expressed it, was in seeing him brought to safety. Most of them did not even know him. Life, even in the midst of the relentless trials and evils of the war, was good. His mood and confidence rose.

A short time earlier, Jan felt like he'd reached the end of his road; with a little food to comfort him, tenderness, warm friendship and joviality, his outlook changed to near euphoria. His friends had brought with them a plan of action, a new hope. Jan had learned that one cannot live without hope. With the faith and hope the men brought, Jan returned to the man he really was, a courageous man who could withstand most anything, a gentle man who possessed the strength of the granite mountains he had traversed.

The men bumped into each other as they readied Jan. They removed the door from its hinges and put it out of the way. Six strong arms gently lifted Jan out from the contracted bunk bed. There were no stair steps but Alvin stood in the snow outside, ready to help, and they lifted him down toward him. Soon they placed Jan on the waiting sled. The fresh sea breeze was like a tonic. Jan began to feel alive!

This was the first time Jan and Alvin met. Alvin bent down toward him with outstretched hand.

"I have been looking forward to this meeting. My name is Alvin Larsen, I live in Furuflaten."

Jan slowly reached Alvin's hand and held it in both of his.

"Many thanks for joining us." Jan smiled warmly.

"I'm just happy to be of help."

"I see you are also a Navy man." Hotel Savoy launched a lifelong friendship between the two soldiers.

The resistance men wrapped Jan in two blankets and placed him in the sleeping bag. They then tied him securely to the sled, intertwining the ropes in and around the braces of the sled up to his armpits and down to his ankles. From time to time, especially when they tied his legs and feet down, Jan grimaced – but not a word of complaint escaped his lips. He resembled a mummy tied to the sled as he was, but this was his happy choice. Soon, with the help of his friends, he would be over the mountains and into Sweden where freedom and medical support would end his ordeal. He longed to be there.

The two pairs of skis the men had brought were tied to the side of the sled. Everything had to be absolutely secure for the vertical climb they faced. Jan looked up at the men and again expressed his gratitude for their service to him.

He looked toward the nearly vertical mountain ahead of them.

"If I survive this, I will be able to live through anything," he said.

Shortly before midnight they began their climb up the Revdal Mountains. The path they had chosen was the ravine that tended upward from the hut. Marius, Alvin, Amandus and Olaf had examined the mountain from the fjord and later from the shore and found it to be the only logical way.

Closest to the fjord, scattered brush dotted the gently sloped terrain. The men reached the thicket where the incline rose sharply all at once. The snow was heavy and deep. In some places they disappeared into the mountain-snow up to their waist. Two of the men were at the front of the sled. Fifteen-foot long ropes were secured to each side of the front of the sled, which two of the Furuflaten men held. A six-foot length of rope was attached to each side of the rear of the sled and held by the other two men. In this way, two men on each side ensured the sled's stability.

The four young men were all in excellent physical condition. In spite of that, they soon realized that the climb would require more energy than they had imagined. They pulled and pushed, slid and fell, and climbed again. All along, they did their best to keep the sled steady to minimize Jan's suffering.

In the midst of the thickets they had difficulty getting the sled through and around the dwarfed timber. Olaf pulled out a small ax and chopped at the stunted trees, clearing the way while the others steadied the sled. These moments gave them brief respite. These were also the times when Amandus kept them all in good humor with his stored-up anecdotes.

"Have you heard…?" or "Did you know…?" he'd begin.

They forged ahead, scrambling over stony outcrops, pulling on boughs, stumps, and exposed roots. Jan helped when he could, grasping at nearby branches and rocks. Sometimes, when the men needed it the most, they'd find a small, strong tree strategically located for them to throw their arms around and pull themselves up with. The complexity of the mountain increased as they scaled upwards, but the men refused to give in.

Just above the tree line they rested on an outcrop. Below the mighty Lyngenfjord came into view. They were amazed at how precipitous the mountain was, compared to their view from below. Each man watched his steps carefully on the ice-encrusted granite. A slip here and the next stopwould be the fjord. Looking backward a few yards on the tracks they'd made, the men saw only air, an abyss, and the fjord below them. The loose snow they had waded through further down now had a crusty surface. When they sank through it up here, it sounded like the crushing of gravel.

The mountain accentuated everything, including itself. It was appallingly rugged and steep. The situation worsened with every few steps. They no longer could just pull and push, though that had been strenuous enough. At present they had to force an entrance to the more difficult passageways, then through absolute determination, the two men in front grabbed a rock or whatever was accessible and pulled themselves up. In a kneeling position, they hoisted the sled up behind them while the two in the rear struggled to lift it up above their heads.

Other times, one man led the way and kicked holes in the crusty snow, providing those who followed a foothold. Cinched down tight, Jan focused on the group's objective, rather than his own pain. When the going was unusually tough or bumpy he let out a stifled groan, but he never complained.

When the men thought they should be nearing the plateau, they discovered that another crest rose higher. The struggle, far from over, tested their faith and determination to the limit. It was too discouraging to look up,better to concentrate on one step or foothold at a time.

The terrain dropped so steeply that the sled hung almost vertically, and the stumps on Jan's foot began to bleed again. Jan thought his feet would burst from the unbearable pain. He frequently lost consciousness; each episode was a moment of relief, then he came to and the horror began yet again. He was torn in his own suffering. How could he complain? His selfless friends were exerting themselves beyond human endurance, but they went on. So must he. But when the pain became utterly insufferable he gave in.

"Is it possible to turn the sleigh? "

They gladly did anything for Jan to give him even a moment's relief.

It eased his pain momentarily as he hung there upside down, suspended in space as it were. Soon the pressure to his brain became overwhelming. Marius and the others returned him to the original position.

The men panted and puffed, spit and pulled, went through the crusty snow, pulled themselves out and pressed upward.

And Jan just hung, tied to the sled.

The time came when the men were spent. They had no more to give. Their arms trembled from exertion; their knees refused to hold them up. The muscles in their legs and thighs cramped and wouldn't respond. Soaked through from perspiration, tumbling in the snow and grappling with the mountain, they were burning hot and thirsty. They prostrated themselves in the snow and closed their eyes. All the while they kept a sure hold on the ropes that kept Jan's sled close by. They lay there, desperately needing rest and renewed strength.

As soon as they laid down, they noticed the freezing wind gusts, more penetrating up here, closer to the plateau. And when physical exertion forced them to stop, their bodies quickly chilled. Only a few moments' relief was all they dared give themselves.

They climbed upwards.

When they reached the edge where the ravine unfolded itself onto the plateau they knew it all would become easier.

The terrain leveled off and they trudged through the snow instead of crawling and clawing. Before they got far, they realized they would have to cross a cleft in the mountain, sideways, beneath a huge overhang of ice. It was vertical and the snow was so hard and cumbersome that the men had to work out minute details each step of the way. They had to force their way through. Because of the gradient they could only place one sled-runner on the snow close into the cleft. Two men sat down and guided it along foot by foot. The other two kicked repeatedly to get a foothold in the iced-over snow while suspending the outside runner in the air.

This way the sled lay perpendicularly. Jan's friends carried the carefully balanced sled over to the other side, one measured step at a time. These were committed men; no obstruction seemed too dangerous, and relinquishing the fight was not part of the plan.

Jan now hung in open air, the determined efforts of the men the only thing between him and a terrible abyss. Even if only one of the men, for one split second, lost his foothold, all five would plummet violently downwards. In long free falls they would be thrown about in a wild breakaway toward the fjord some 2500 feet below. They were somber men struggling to concentrate on their own and their friends' movements. The only words were of the details of their next step.

Jan was, for the most part, quiet except for his occasional moaning. He tackled his own problems as best he could. The excruciating pain continued, almost beyond his ability to endure. Yet through it all, he was aware that his survival depended fully on his friends' endurance.

They had almost reached the plateau when they heard the drone of an airplane. The noise increased rapidly. Almost straight overhead, it reverberated amid the mountaintops. A plane came into view at a low altitude. Alvin recognized the big black swastika painted on its side at once.

"A German Junker!"

Jan reacted like lightning, knowing exactly what to do.

"Throw yourselves face down!"

Hopefully they would look like rocks from the air, and be camouflaged by the mountain terrain. The Junker disappeared as quickly as it had come. They had succeeded.

In those moments Jan felt a heavy responsibility for his friends. The four men knew anything could happen when they took on the commitment to help Jan to freedom. This was just part of their commitment. They were proud to be part of this rescue effort to help a countryman to freedom. It gave a deep purpose to their lives. And to outsmart the Gestapo would bring them many a story to tell after the war. Such thoughts added determination to their endeavors.

The mountain plateau spread before them. Some three hours after they had tied Jan to the sled outside the hut in Revdal they reached their destination.

Like a white carpet, the next 2000 feet lay before them with hardly a rise. In actuality it began with a lengthened gentle downgrade, which flattened out, then gradually eased up to an extended slope where at the end another dark-walled bluff rose straight up.

The sled moved slowly on its own power, the men needed only to guide it along. Across the level plain they were able to pull the sled with two men walking on each side. Here and there they fell through the snow but not as often as earlier. The last steep stretch was difficult, but compared with the cliffs they considered it easy.

The men of Furuflaten were nearing complete exhaustion. But they had accomplished what most would call humanly impossible; their minds and bodies had been pushed to the brink, and they were beginning to pay the price.

In addition to their own exhaustion they were greatly concerned for Jan. He too was totally spent. But he was their inspiration, their reason for completing the deed. He had suffered right along with them in silence. He kept all his fears and pain to himself. Jan was deeply moved and most grateful for their self-sacrifice.

On the south side of the plateau a steep mountain wall rose some 2700 feet. At the foot of this black wall was a large stony wasteland.

"This is the place! We have reached our goal. This is where the men from Manndalen will come!" Marius was jubilant.

They found a level place to rest the sled. For the first time in four hours the resistance men let go of the ropes. They felt free knowing the sled would not rush away from them. Beneath them the babbling river hurried by, but they were safe on thick ice and a layer of snow.

The four men settled down in the snow close by Jan to rest. Even now they did not say much, too exhausted to carry on a conversation. With a quick movement of his arm Olaf pushed his cap back, the brim pointing straight skyward. The others also adjusted their caps and wiped their sweaty faces. They peered across the plateau looking for the men from Manndalen.

Turning away from the plateau they glimpsed the frigid six-mile-wide, Lyngenfjord. Just north of Furuflaten, on the opposite side of the fjord, they observed the outline of the headland jutting out into the fjord. When they moved a few more feet in a northerly direction they could make out the rooftops of their homes in Furuflaten.

The agreement had been to meet between 2 a.m. and 4 a.m. and they became concerned for the men from Manndalen.

Marius questioned if he had the time right. Were they too early, or had the men already been here and left? Were they delayed, or a little lost perhaps? He wondered if something serious had happened to them. Innumerable thoughts ran through his mind, but none of them gave answers to his questions.

Luckily they had thought to bring two pairs of skis along in case of an emergency. Amandus and Olaf strapped them on and searched for tracks in an ever-widening circle. There was no trace of either man or animal. No one could have been near the place for days. Where were they? Marius asked if they had strength to go toward Manndalen to try and meet up with the other fellows.

"We'll do it."

Rocks and boulders lay sprinkled throughout the plateau as if a giant hand had snatched handfuls and scattered them around. Some rocks were several feet high.

Amandus and Olaf trudged among these rocks into the plateau. They disappeared from sight far up in the inner terrain. Mountain distances seem small until one watches a person moving away. The person gradually shrinks, but is never totally out of sight, until at long last he vanishes. Then one begins to understand the immensity and the power of the mountains.

The men moved in a northeast direction toward Kjerringdal Valley, a precipitous side valley on the west side of Manndalen where they assumed that the men from that side had, or would be coming up.

They skied to the very ridge of the mountain. From here they had an overview of the whole landscape as it stretched before them. They looked up and down the surrounding mountains, back down in the valley and across the valley floor, scraped flat by ancient glaciers. They saw no sign of life. Moreover they saw no tracks. They stood there forlorn, unable to speak. Taken aback, they just looked at each other. The disappointment was acute. All they could do was turn back.

Marius and Alvin tried to hide their restlessness from Jan, but he understood. After about an hour, two forms heading in their direction took shape. Uneasy, Marius knew something was seriously wrong.

As Olaf and Amandus returned and told their story, the other men were filled with misgivings. The mood turned gloomy. All of the men were exhausted. The struggle up the mountain had been difficult, but not without hope. Total bewilderment and disappointment swept over them as they considered this snag in the plan.

The men had an enormous emergency on their hands and they were miles away from shelter and help. A decision had to be made. But what solution could they find? Most choices were eliminated before they were even thought through.

To continue on to Sweden without enough supplies was suicide. Fully expecting to meet the Manndalen men, they had only brought two pairs of skis along for an emergency. Two men could not pull an ill man over the difficult terrain. None had an abundance of strength left after the strenuous climb, and spring snowstorms still raged up here in the mountains.

Jan was too ill to be moved down the mountain. The thought of imprisoning him in the hut again with the appalling memories he had of the place was unbearable. That also would be suicide. Jan was unable to take the stress of the descent in any case. Also, the men themselves were near spent. They shared their thoughts and tried to figure out how best to handle the situation. There was no solution, at least not an easy one.

After much discussion, the four came to the agreement that they had to leave Jan behind in the mountains. Heavy-hearted, they presented the plan to him.

"We have no choice."

"Of course we don't." answered Jan, without a moment's hesitation. "I already came to that conclusion when Olaf and Alfon scouted after the Manndalen men."

"Jan we are so very, very sorry." Marius spoke for all.

"Don't be. You have done everything humanly possible for me. There is no other way. It'll all work out. You'll see." Jan sounded brave.

When they had stopped to rest they were a short distance north of the black mountain wall. They noticed a nine-foot high boulder, which stood out from all the rest midways between them and the wall. It was flat on the south side, and measured roughly 15 feet by 18 feet. It was the only rock of this size and shape in the immediate area. It stood as a sentinel over the landscape. They agreed that this would be a good

The Gentleman Stone

The Gentleman Stone seen toward the east with the river delta on the left.

hiding place for Jan and pulled the sled up the slope towards the rock.

Snowdrifts surrounded the boulder. Toward the east the wind had forged a large gaping hole in the snow, a natural cauldron that almost reached the moss below. A thick snowdrift had formed an overhang from the top of the boulder pointing east, a lid for the cauldron.

The men examined the hole and, using the back ends of their skis, cut large square blocks out of the snow. They cut out a shelf in the snowdrift and into the snowfield southward so that Jan and the sleigh could be pushed sideways onto the shelf, placing his feet toward the rock with his head away from it. They used the snow blocks they had removed to wall up the opening to the shelf, making Jan invisible inside his cave. A small round hole was drilled through the layers of snow so that Jan would have air to breathe.

The remaining food that had not been eaten was gathered. There was a little leftover drink and it was all placed close by him. The snow cave muffled his voice and they could hardly understand him without straining, but they were able to make out Jan's upbeat courage.

"All is well in here," the enthusiastic voice said. "Be careful on that mountain. Get down it safely."

Helpless, the four of them stood there, wanting to encourage him. But they had lost their own courage. Were they signing Jan's death warrant leaving him up here in his condition? They faked optimism for him.

"The Manndalen men are bound to come shortly. If not right away, at least by tomorrow, Jan."

"Good-bye and take care."

"We wish you the best." Empty words meant to be pleasant.

They said their goodbyes through the little opening in the snow, then crawled out of the cauldron. The four young men turned around and looked down on the place where they had left their friend. No one was able to say a word. No one could give an explanation for this turn of events.

The men were bitterly disappointed. They did not cry – they were men of steel, but tonight their eyes were moist, their hearts torn apart. They had concentrated on cheering Jan up as much as possible. Considering the circumstances, they felt this amazing man was in surprisingly good spirits. In the midst of this unthinkable situation, he did his best not to show them he was concerned. This was Jan; he made the impossible seem achievable. They took courage from his resilience.

The Furuflaten men struggled to keep their emotions in check. They stood there on the edge and looked down at the miniscule opening where they were leaving a helplessly ill man; none of them really believed he could survive. They hated themselves.

Near the riverbed, about thirty feet away, they placed a ski pole in the snow. Surely if the Manndalen men showed up they would have an easy time finding Jan with the pole sticking out of the snow. One by one they headed for the abrupt cliffs.

In one big sweep, reality had changed and existence became emptiness and a heavy loss. Marius agonized. He could not be blamed for this mishap; still, a helpless man had been left behind, and he felt responsible. Marius had but one desire, to turn back. He did not want to climb down the mountain. He wanted to go back to be with Jan to let him know how much he cared. How could he leave? It all seemed so meaningless, so futile. What kind of a friend had he become?

Revdal, April 25, 1943: It was past 6 a.m. when the exhausted and dispirited men rowed back home to Furuflaten. They had given all that was in them, but it had not been enough. They had failed the courageous man who had put his trust in them. The loss hurt them deeply. Would another door open for them? They would give up all to be able to rescue Jan. They had to find a way.

They rowed on until Hotel Savoy faded on the horizon, until all that was left was a small speck in the snowdrifts across the fjord. Daylight bathed the surroundings. It was the Sabbath and their intent had been to sneak home and get to bed before their families arose, but they knew that plan had also failed. Their strength had dissipated during the ordeal and the rowing was harder and took longer than usual. At this hour all their families would be up. As they neared the shore, they noticed a crowd of people gathered by the dock. A "welcoming committee." The fearless resistance workers cringed at the thought of confronting their friends and families.

The four of them had left the village many times before, and had returned unnoticed. None of their family members knew that they were entangled in illegal and dangerous work. The families were close friends, yet neither parents nor sweethearts had ever been told. During the past evening however, they had begun to wonder.

When they had been unable to find the men the night before, they had become quite concerned. They had spent the early morning hours together and had decided to walk down by the water and there spotted a boat far out in the fjord.

How they had all prayed that it would be their missing men. After a long time, when the boat came close enough, they recognized both the boat and the men. They did not realize how quickly their humble, sincere prayers had been answered. Instead their concern turned to anger.

The men in the boat realized their homecoming would be less than pleasant.

"We have to outsmart the welcoming committee waiting on the shore," Amandus whispered.

The three older men knew they would be held accountable for allowing 17-year-old Olaf to participate in such a rousing party. Once again they were left without a choice. They had to take the responsibility.

The top secret assignment could not be shared. Not an iota of the drama surrounding Jan and his transport up the mountainside could ever be whispered. Their whole trip had been disastrous.

This was just another set of problems to overcome, though far different than anything they could have anticipated.

They rowed to the headway that stuck out into the Lyngenfjord, north of Furuflaten. As courageous as these men were, they were totally unnerved at the thought of telling Olaf's parents that they were responsible for him staying out all night. They did not have the courage to bring him with them toward the welcoming committee. As a result, they put him ashore at the tip of the headland and out of sight of the committee. Olaf walked the long way home. He crept into the village from the north, away from the main road, and stayed a good distance away from the neighboring houses and the people he knew.

The three others sprinkled their clothes with nakkeskudd; some ran down their chest. They also gulped down a couple of swallows for courage and let some run down their chins.

Their families had to be convinced that they had partied all night and had enjoyed lots of goodies. Would they believe they could have had fun fishing all night?

When they reached shore, though sober, they enjoyed acting as if drunk with the smell of liquor burning in their noses. Alvin's mother was enraged. She walked down to her son and in a shrill voice, gave him the verbal lesson of his life.

"Son, how could you have left without letting anyone know where you were? I have taught you better than that!"

"Have I not endowed you with any sense? Are you able to understand the grief you have caused everyone? And furthermore, what kind of a man are you? Leaving your sweetheart on a Saturday night to go fishing and partying with other men?" His mother had worked up a full head of steam and quivered with indignation. Not too far off, Alvin's sweetheart stood feeling both humbled and sorrowful.

Alvin straightened up. He went close up to his mother's face and stared right into her eyes. He stood erect, and was deliberately calm - his look unyielding, but friendly. Not for a second did he take his eyes off her and he did not say a word.

His mother quieted down. And in that moment she realized her son was not drunk. But rather, extremely sober! She realized he had tried to act as if he had been carousing, but she knew him too well. His eyes told her. She knew he had been involved in something dangerous, something important and highly secretive. She also knew the war had now invaded their family life. She was silenced without a word being spoken. She did not ask questions. Slowly she turned away and started walking home. Her eyes brimmed with tears. Like Alvin, she knew that secret operations against the Germans were extremely perilous. If something was revealed, the threads could unravel and the whole village could be wiped out. Alvin's mother became part of the small army of people who helped Jan, without being directly involved.

At once she was involved in a secret she knew nothing about, but she had to carry it in silence, a heavy burden for a mother. Women have for centuries been called upon to carry such burdens in wartime. Alvin's mother died before the war ended, and she never knew the story of her son's involvement nor how very courageous he was.

All four men reached their homes without further incident. Each walked off to cope with his anguish. Sadness and weariness were in themselves a heavy load. The men's thoughts dashed back to the plateau and the soldier in the snow cave high up in the Revdal Mountains.

The exact spot where he was could not be picked out from across the fjord, but they could approximate. They worried about every little detail. Was he distraught? Frozen? Scared? Depressed? Or had he succumbed?

Marius in particular had a difficult time. He took full blame for what had happened. Had his instructions not been complete and clear enough? He had never known teacher Nordnes and Aslak Fossvoll not to follow through.

He rushed to the telephone on his return. Resolutely he lifted the receiver and placed each call. Within seconds the lady at the telephone central answered.

"Aslak Fossvoll in Manndalen, please." Marius was in a hurry.

Aslak picked up the phone, and got a clear and firm message. "The fish yarn you ordered is ready to be picked up immediately. It is waiting at the appointed place, dug down in the snow behind a rock."

"We will get it as soon as possible. Thank you." The phone clicked.

Marius looked out from his house in upper Furuflaten. From there he was sure he could see exactly where Jan was. He felt powerless again; his own worthlessness flooded over him. It would make it so much easier if he could only talk with Jan.

Sundays were always peaceful on the Grønvoll farm, a special day. This was not such a Sunday. Thoughts of Jan rolled over Marius and weighed him down with anxiety.

It was amazing how the surroundings had not changed. The mountains and Lyngenfjord lay there untouchable and silent, an overpowering presence.

From left to right: Amandus Lillevold, Olaf Lanes, Alvin Larsen, and Marius Grønvoll, the team that carried Jan up the Revdal Mountain on a sled, 1960.

THE MANNDALEN MEN

MANNDALEN, A level and narrow valley one and a quarter miles wide and 18 miles long, cuts deeply through the massive surrounding granite mountains. Some of the mountains reach heights of 3500 feet above sea level. The spirited Manndalen River rushes down its hilly center and spills over into Kåfjord Sound. On the northern tip, the valley meets up with the hamlet Samuelsberg, bordering Kåfjord Sound; the innermost valley to the south gradually joins the mountain slopes stretching upwards into mountain walls and ends up on the undulating plateaus.

In 1943, there were no roads connecting the communities with each other in this area, only narrow country roads within the valley itself. Traveling by sea, hiking or skiing over the mountains from a neighboring village was the only way to reach this remote area of the Troms District. The people who lived here were hard working farmers, fishermen and hunters. Tradition passed on through their families taught them to care for one another and any strangers who might enter their village.

Unspoiled by worldly sophistication, the people of Manndalen were fiercely patriotic and fully understood those things that enriched life: family, friendship and the importance of education. For the most part, the war had not intruded much on life in Manndalen, except that necessities and food were more scarce – and ten German soldiers, rather passive men or lazy perhaps, had confiscated the valley's youth center and moved in. The soldiers did not bother with the villagers much, and they frightened no one. However, from time to time, the German soldiers from Lyngseidet came over by boat and performed a house-to-house search. The Manndalen people were much more respectful of them and concerned when they were in the valley.

Manndalen Valley

The Arctic growing season being short, mainly potatoes and root vegetables were cultivated in Manndalen. Many families also had a few domestic animals, enough for their own needs. Often, many children were born to families in those days, and it was not unusual for siblings to be divided up and taken in by other family members. Peder Isaksen was one of those children, the third of a flock of ten siblings, taken in by his grandparents. Though there were no luxuries, they lived a good life on the little farm they owned. During the summer their cows grazed in the isolated fields around their modest home, or in the wilderness; at close of day the tiny herd was gathered in the barn.

Aslak Fossvoll

In the late winter of 1941, at the age of twenty, Peder was fishing in the Lofoten fishing grounds some one hundred and twenty miles from Manndalen. He was there when the Svolvær raid took place on March 4.

Following such raids the Germans heaped reprisals on the Norwegians and many chose to escape to England to avoid them. Peder considered escaping, not so much from fear of the Germans, as from wanderlust, and also to possibly help Norway on other fronts. In the end he decided to stay.

Manndalen, Sunday, April 25, 1943: Life in Manndalen continued its traditional rounds. Many of the men were anxious to play a larger part in the war effort. On Sunday afternoon Peder Isaksen left his grandparents' home for a leisurely walk. He passed his good friend Nigo's home and continued down into the valley. A couple of miles from his home he ran into Aslak Fosvoll, who also was the uncle of Peder's betrothed, the pretty, soft-spoken Eliva Hansen. Except for his experience in Lofoten in March of 1941, Peder Isaksen had little feeling for the war raging around them, and no involvement. In the span of a few minutes he became an active player in the game of war. The peaceful days he'd enjoyed became a life of intrigue and fear.

Aslak worked furiously to finish the work he and Peder Bergmo hadn't completed the previous evening. Marius Grønvoll had telephoned early in the morning from Furuflaten, saying urgently, "The fish net is ready to be picked up immediately."

Aslak understood the implications. The soldier the Manndalen men were supposed to have rescued was left out by himself on the frozen, snow covered tundra, waiting. Aslak worked desperately to find someone to go with Nigo, who had readied himself the night before. He had just dropped off his skis for Nigo, who did not own any. They had packed a knapsack full of provisions necessary for the trip into the treacherous mountains and food and drink for the soldier in the snow cave. Aslak had also given Nigo an exact description of the rock where Jan lay. He warned Nigo that the soldier was armed, and that he had to use the agreed upon password, "Hello Gentleman," which they were to shout loud and clear.

Aslak and Peder Isaksen greeted one another and stopped for a chat. Aslak's mind revolved around the soldier in the mountain, and knowing Peder Isaksen to be a trustworthy fellow, he suddenly became thoughtful. He looked straight ahead into the valley while rubbing his chin.

"Peder, would you be willing to take on an assignment for me? It might be a way to earn a few extra kroner, but it will be with your own life as a pawn."

"I can't promise you anything before you tell me what this assignment is, Aslak."

Aslak was desperate. There was no more time to lose; the wounded soldier needed to get to Sweden for medical help. The responsibility rested heavy on his shoulders. Assuming Peder would say yes, Aslak took the chance, and brought Peder up to date on the secret mission.

Peder listened intently as he learned of the happenings in Toftefjord and how one of the commando soldiers from Brattholm had managed to escape. Now seriously ill, he was hidden in a snow cave up in the Revdal Mountains. It was imperative that he be found before long and transported to Sweden. Once Peder had been filled in, no hesitation clouded his mind.

"If that's the situation, it's okay," he volunteered his readiness right then.

"You can't go into the mountains alone this time of the year, Peder. Nigo is ready to join you. He is ready, packed and waiting," Aslak said. "You have to go tonight."

"No problem. I'll get ready."

Hope and energy returned to Aslak after he spoke with Peder. The heavy burden he had been carrying vanished, and he was filled with triumph.

Peder's leisurely walk ended abruptly. He hurried home with a long quick stride. Memories of childhood lessons to give food and a place to any guest came to his mind. The soldier in the mountain surely was such a guest, even though he had arrived in an unusual and dramatic manner. Peder saw it as his Christian duty to help.

Halfway home Peder dropped in on his friend Nigo who sat ready waiting for word. They agreed to go their separate ways through the village and to meet above the tree line at 10:30 p.m. The two friends gave each other strength of mind and vitality. Both were elated about the mission they had accepted. Finally they would be of service to Norway.

Peder hurried home and changed his clothes. He readied his skis and started for the woods and up into the mountains. The two men went unnoticed as they skied through the Arctic darkness, and met as planned high up on a slope just above the tree line.

It was a difficult climb up the steep mountain, dark and quiet. They advanced steadily, hardly speaking, concentrating on their every move. Young and strong, they made good time. Within two hours they reached the plateau. Ski conditions were good, and it wasn't particularly cold. Only a mild wind caressed the tundra.

Mount Balggesvarri towered in the darkness. They made a path around it and turned slightly southwest to Revdalen. There was still quite a distance to their goal. Not attempting to conserve their energy, they sped along the plateau up over hillocks, and down again from the top of the plateau towards Revdal, dashing along in search of the boulder where the soldier was hidden.

The area they arrived at by following Aslak's instructions was strewn with large boulders and rocks. They hurried from boulder to boulder, searching. Their calls rang out into the dark quiet of the vast mountain plateau, "Hello Gentleman! Hello Gentleman!"

Their voices did not carry far in this immense domain.

The plateau remained silent.

The men of Furuflaten had left no tracks. A rock-to-rock search was of no avail. After two hours of fruitless searching, Peder and Nigo called it quits. It was four in the morning, and they needed to reach Manndalen before six when their neighbors started their barn chores. Would the soldier be able to survive another night? Or was he dead? Their unanswered questions troubled them deeply.

With subdued spirits they climbed back up to the tundra. Once on top, they raced downward to Manndalen and reached home in the early morning hours of April 26.

Manndalen, Monday, April 26, 1943: As soon as prudent, Peder Isaksen and Nigo cautiously contacted Aslak and teacher Nordnes. Both were deeply distressed over hearing the soldier was still in the mountains.

"There are hundreds of boulders and rocks up there," Nigo explained.

"The boulder where Jan is has to be marked clearly if we are to find him," added Peder Isaksen.

Peder Bergmo in Olderdalen had to be contacted at once. Peder Isaksen and teacher Nordnes hurried down through the village and rowed across Kåfjord to find Peder Bergmo. His surprise and shock when he saw them revealed he understood the reason for their visit.

"Will you get a message to Marius?"

"Yes, of course. I'll ferry across to Lyngseidet and take the bus from there to Furuflaten. But I have to find an excuse for leaving this office."

Unable to leave the following day, he troubled over how to get away, concerned the whole while for the soldier in the mountain.

Furuflaten, Wednesday, April 28, 1943: Finally arriving at Furuflaten, Peder Bergmo walked the last few miles to the Grønvoll farm.

"Marius, they didn't find him! The place has to be marked. There are too many boulders and the men are unable to find the place."

Marius grew tense. "Poor Jan! Buried three days in a snow cave. It'll be a miracle if he hasn't frozen to death."

Though Marius believed his friend to be dead, he had to find a way back up into the mountains.

GRAVE CONCERNS FOR JAN

MARIUS WAS reassured that the Manndalen men were ready to climb back up into the mountains to rescue Jan and bring him to Sweden as soon as his hiding place was clearly marked. He committed to doing so immediately. He knew, however, that the hike up into the mountain plateau was too dangerous to undertake alone should the mountains and weather reveal their fury.

He thought of his trustworthy buddy Amandus and his sturdy boat. No doubt Amandus would, without any ado, say yes. The weather conditions looked promising. But Marius also had an eye for a beautiful young lady who lived by the fjord at the northern end of Furuflaten village. Olaf Lanes' sister, Agnete, had incredible physical endurance, but beyond that, she had an understanding heart with a deep centered inner strength. Never one to shy away from hard work, she met challenges head on and saw them through to successful endings.

Agnete was admired by many of the young men in the village but it was she and Marius who enjoyed a deep friendship and spent much time together.

Marius felt the pressure of getting Jan to safety and he yearned to share his feelings with Agnete because she would know exactly how he felt, and she was trustworthy. As soon as Peder Bergmo had left for home, he contacted her. Agnete listened quietly to the astonishing story.

"My goodness Marius, I'll go with you," Agnete responded without a moment's hesitation.

"Are you sure Agnete? You understand the risk involved?"

"I understand."

"Our efforts might be in vain. The wounded soldier might already be dead."

"I'll go."

Marius embraced her. "This might be the most important work we will have the opportunity to do in this war."

He had wanted very much for Agnete to come with him and was positive that she could manage the stressful climb and the emotional strain involved.

Hurriedly they changed into their ski clothes and filled their knapsacks with food and provisions. Marius allowed a small flicker of hope to burn. Over and over his mind repeated, "We are coming Jan. Stay alive!"

Always aware that Nazis might be watching, Marius asked Agnete to walk along the beach a short distance from her home and he and Amandus would row and pick her up. The three of them set out across Lyngenfjord.

Agnete (Lanes) Grønvoll's identification card

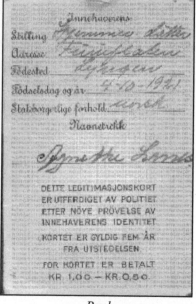

Front   *Back*

A good hour passed before they reached Revdal. Skis, poles and knapsacks were taken ashore. This time they chose a different route than the one they had used to transport Jan. Supposedly a few hundred meters south of Hotel Savoy, the climb would be a little easier. Amandus would wait for their return north of the Innerelva River.

Marius and Agnete ascended the first half of the climb rather quickly. As they mounted higher, huge boulders and vertical crags slowed them down. They pulled themselves up by birch trunks and branches and handed their skis and poles to each other enabling them to grip on to the outcrops with both hands. The rushing sound of the river hidden deep in the cleft to the south guided them.

Each mount above them gave the impression that they had reached their goal, only to find another higher one ahead. From their vantage point they could see a good stretch of Lyngenfjord below. Appearances were deceiving in the mountains. Mountaintop followed mountaintop; the plateau was so much higher than the impression they had acquired from the other side of the fjord.

Marius looked up and spotted the vertical mountain wall towards Larsbergfjellet Mountain. It loomed black and ominous against the night sky. The mountaintop they had reached gradually rounded off toward even terrain. From the plateau, the pass higher up became visible.

"Look Agnete!" Marius pointed. "Jan is hidden right inside the opening of that pass." The wind was biting and he tried to sound optimistic, though they still had a long climb ahead. Able to use their skis again, the distance quickly narrowed where the plateau was fairly flat. A few minor knolls here and there did not trouble them as they headed toward the last steep rising. Turning in a southerly direction to come nearer to Innerelva River, they followed the edge of the cleft on the northern side. Two hours of steady and difficult climbing had left them exhausted.

The huge boulder was in sight a few yards ahead on the rocky slope by the precipitous mountain wall. Their bodies tensed; was Jan still alive? Marius sped ahead the last few feet. Agnete followed in his tracks. He unfastened his skis and crawled around to the east side of the boulder. Marius saw that the ski pole they had placed in the snow on their earlier visit had blown down. Snatches of tracks from their last visit were still discernible.

He stood on his knees and began to dig with his hands. Close by, Agnete stood silently shielding her face with mitten-covered hands. The wind was sharp and cold and the snow was packed down hard. Below the whirling snow, and the top layer of new snow, Marius butted up to the snow blocks they had placed three days ago. He kept digging; suddenly the snow collapsed around his arms.

Agnete moved closer to look inside and caught sight of Jan's motionless bearded face.

"Don't sweetheart, move back a bit. I am afraid Jan is dead." Marius gently tugged at her arm.

From within the cave a weak, distraught voice responded, "Oh no! You can't fool an old fox!"

"Jan! Jan! Thank God you're alive! We were afraid we'd find you dead."

"I am okay. I've kept the hope that you would return." Jan whispered.

"We're here to take care of you, Jan. And we've brought you something hot to eat."

To see Jan alive gave new strength to both of them. They dug hard with their remaining energy and pretty soon the snow cave was open.

Agnete crawled into the opening and saw Jan's weary face close-up. Lifeless eyes peered from sunken cheeks and his pitch-black beard rendered his face colorless. Like a mummy, Jan laid on the wood sleigh, tucked into the sleeping bag. Slowly he began to move and freed his arms. Shakily, Jan reached toward Agnete.

He held her hands in his as he studied her face.

"You must be Agnete. Marius has mentioned you a time or two to me in the past." He gradually moved his head and winked at Marius then turned back toward Agnete and flashed a weak smile, "My name is Jan."

Agnete's eyes became moist. Unable to speak, she squeezed his hands.

With both hands Jan took the thermos bottle filled with hot soup. Marius lifted up his head to help him drink.

"I thought you already were safely in Sweden," Marius explained. "It was not until today that I learned that the Manndalen men had not found you. Two men have been up here hunting for you for hours but without luck." Jan just listened.

"Agnete and I are here tonight to mark your place more clearly. As soon as we've returned home, we will send a message on to Manndalen that you are ready. They will pick you up right away and bring you over the border."

With his friends close by, some hot food and the good news, Jan quickened. "This man is amazing," Marius thought as he looked admiringly at Jan. "His fortitude and will to live are astounding!" Marius emptied Jan's sleeping bag of waste and put him back in again.

Agnete placed the food from the knapsacks close by Jan's sled.

"What else can we do for you, Jan?" Marius found his own words rather empty.

"Oh thanks, but nothing really. Well, maybe there is something – a little hot water for a bath?"

Jan's humor had resurfaced – just like it had in the barn.

All laughed, but it was rather subdued. They knew the time for parting was at hand. Jan's friends kneeled near him, against his sled in the snow. Leaving him alone again was painful. Jan lay on his back and stared up at the snow covering above him. No one found the right words.

The whirling snow drifted around the boulder and down into the snow cave. The surrounding plateau was enormous, but the darkness camouflaged Jan's hiding place.

"Promise me, be careful on the way down and get home safely across the fjord." Jan whispered.

Agnete tied the hood tight around her face; she was wet from perspiration from the climb up, and now had chilled off.

A hush fell over all of them.

The whirling snow blew into the cave from all angles.

"Jan, keep up your courage. The men will soon return. We'll keep close track of you," Marius strained to smile at his friend.

"Thanks for all you have done for me." Jan turned his face toward the inner snow wall.

The two gently touched his covered up arm and quietly left and sealed up the cave behind them. Marius crossed two ski poles and stuck them deep into the snow a few meters away from the "Gentleman stone," and tied them crisscross at the top. They had to be clearly seen, especially from the direction in which the Manndalen men would approach. The wind tore at the two of them as they fastened the poles securely in the snow.

The force of the wind would have blown Agnete off her feet if Marius had not been close by to catch her. But even Marius had problems as they clung to each other. Once they left Jan's cave, they could find no shelter and they fought their way across the plateau and over to the mountain ridge. The wind eased a little as they started their descent, a strenuous, demanding climb.

Thursday morning, April 29, 1943: Agnete and Marius had been gone nearly five hours by the time they reached Amandus waiting for them in the boat. The trip home seemed drawn out, and the fjord seemed wider than ever for Marius and Agnete, both struggling to control their emotions. Agnete had been very quiet while they were in the mountains. The vastness of it all overpowered her in the dark. And now she was deeply concerned for Jan.

"Poor Jan is still up here, all alone behind that boulder." With her own hands she had helped Marius seal up his cave. "Will he have the strength to make it through?" Her conscience kept her doubting. "Did they do the right thing when they left him alone, or should one of them have remained with him?" Chilled and despondent, Agnete sat quietly in the back of the boat by herself.

No one in Furuflaten would ever know, at least not until after the war, of the selflessness shown by the three young people during the night – their friends and neighbors still slept as they returned.

Amandus parted from Marius and Agnete when they reached the shore. To avoid discovery at this undesirable hour of the night, they made new plans. Marius and Agnete flung their skis over their shoulders, picked up the other supplies and headed for Lyngspollen some two and a half miles north of Furuflaten. Marius' friend, Kristian Solberg owned a fishing boat with his son Alf. The 48 foot boat was moored at Lyngspollen. The Solbergs lived north of the river about 50 yards from Alvin Larsen's home.

A brisk, biting wind quickened their gait. Weary, Marius and Agnete trudged through the snow alongside the edge of the road in the darkness. Marius knew the Solbergs well and felt sure they would not mind he had found refuge aboard their boat.

Marius and Agnete crept aboard quickly. In the stern, they placed their skis, the two empty milk pails and the two blankets they had brought from their visit with Jan. Suspicious people in Furuflaten would not find a reason to talk should they be seen when they headed for home.

Marius looked at Agnete. Admiration shone in his eyes. She had endured an arduous ordeal without complaint. Marius noticed she was shivering mercilessly. He picked up one of the blankets and lovingly enfolded Agnete in it as he guided her toward the wheelhouse for shelter. She looked so fragile, yet she had a resolute will coupled with courage. They spoke in whispers.

"Marius do you think Jan has a chance?"

"A slim chance." He studied her face, fraught with concern. He wanted to spare her, yet he could not lie. "It all depends on if the weather holds and if the Manndalen men can find him in time."

They remained silent, each struggling with their own emotions.

When the early dawn pierced the darkness on the Eastern horizon, Marius pointed, "Look Agnete, the morning is breaking. The people of Furuflaten will begin their labors soon."

"Ja, that we can be sure of, " she smiled.

"Let's go home, Agnete. I believe it will be safe now." They left behind their skis and the supplies, planning to pick them up later. Marius saw Agnete home. They hugged. "Thank you, Agnete. Thank you."

They stood quietly a moment before she tore herself loose and went inside.

Marius ran up the steep hill toward Alvin Larsen's home. This could not wait until morning. "We have to get to Manndalen in a hurry. Can you possibly take me across the fjord in your fishing boat?"

"I only need a minute." Even without an explanation, Alvin realized the urgency. Marius, between deep breaths, told him the whole story. This early in the morning, it was impossible to disguise their telephone

Teacher Nordnes

messages, and time was of the essence. Jan was seriously ill.

While Alvin readied, Marius rushed home to change into dry clothes. The boat was tied to a stake a little distance from the shore. Alvin needed another man to help with the large boat. He ran to Alfon Hansen's house, the man who had been with them on the trip across the fjord on the 19th of April. It did not take them long to row out to Lyngspollen where the fishing boat was tied up. Marius was waiting on the dock when they came to pick him up; they set course for Manndalen. Crossing the Lyngenfjord, they sailed around the headland into Kåfjord and over to Samuelsberg at the tip of Manndalen. Marius went alone up into the village to talk to teacher Nordnes.

School was in session when Marius arrived. He went straight to the classroom. Nordnes instructed the students to study on their own while the two men went over the plans in muffled voices. Marius drew an outline of where Jan was kept and explained in detail where they could find the "Gentleman stone." He explained how he had crisscrossed two ski poles and placed them a few meters away. Teacher Nordnes nodded and promised they would find Jan this time.

Marius trudged back toward the dock. He could relax – his mission was accomplished. Yet he knew he would have no peace of mind until he was certain that Jan was safely in Sweden. A sudden exhaustion overtook him.

THE FOLLOWING day, a German soldier walked briskly up the steep hill leading to the Solberg's home and knocked on the door.

In broken Norwegian he explained that a snowslide was blocking the road between Furuflaten and Lyngseidet. "You me understand?"

"Ja, ja," Alf understood. "But what does that have to do with me?"

"Your boat needed now! Germany needs to bring mail and packages to Olderdalen. We go immediately. Come now, schnell!" He motioned for him to come. "We take mail to Olderdalen now."

Alf's good friend Eilif Sørsand was visiting, and offered to come along with them. The German soldier followed after them. The three leaped into the rowboat and rowed the two and a half miles north to Lyngspollen where Alf's fishing vessel lay moored.

Climbing aboard, Alf noticed the skis, milk bottles and blankets. His blood chilled. He knew someone from the underground had been there. How could he explain this? Somehow, the German soldier either didn't notice or found nothing strange about it. They returned southward to Furuflaten.

They docked the boat and the soldier explained he would be gone just a short while. "I pick up mail at blockhouse. You wait here."

Earlier that morning, Agnete, on her return home from the mountains, shared with her brother Olav the expedition she and Marius had made to Jan's cave during the night. She told him they had left their skis and supplies on the Solbergs' boat.

From his kitchen window Olav noticed Alf's boat approaching the dock with a German soldier aboard, and he feared trouble was brewing. He saw the soldier quickly leave the boat. Olav raced to the dock to help his friends. The three young men brought the skis and other provisions ashore and hid them. Alf and Eilif climbed back aboard the boat just before the soldier returned with the mail. They set off for Olderdalen and returned without a hitch.

PEOPLE IN the northland are accustomed to looking after each other and neighbors form warm friendships. Young children especially like to visit with neighboring families. Such a child was Roald. The tousle-headed nine-year old lived close to the Solberg family, and dropped in on Alf's mother, Sigrid, one day.

Roald and Sigrid struck up a nice conversation when Roald suddenly silenced. He twisted and turned while dragging his finger along the edge of the kitchen table, then blurted out, "Fru Solberg, did you know that a wounded Norwegian soldier came down from Lyngsdalen Valley? Marius hid him in his barn." Roald was pleased he could share this news with Fru Solberg.

"Hush child, what are you saying?"

"They took really good care of him. Marius and his sisters even brought him food every day. But it was too dangerous, so now they have found a new hiding place for him," Roald continued.

Sigrid was stunned. This was dangerous.

"You like Marius a lot don't you?" questioned Sigrid.

"Å ja! He is my best grown-up friend. He has taught me how to take care of the animals, and to clean the barn, and..."

"You would never hurt Marius, would you Roald?" interrupted Sigrid.

"Oh no! What do you mean? Why would I want to hurt Marius?"

"You must never – never – never again tell anyone about this." She was stern. "You have never seen or heard anything about this soldier. The Germans will kill Marius and his whole family if they find out about this. We all are in danger. The Germans could kill other families in Furuflaten and burn the village as well. Do you understand me?"

Wordless, Roald stared wide-eyed at Sigrid.

"You must promise that you will never talk to anyone about this until after the war." Sigrid looked intently at the overwhelmed youngster.

"Oh, I promise." Roald's eyes filled with tears.

"Come on boy, let's get your jacket back on and I'll walk you home. And remember this is our special secret." The woman patted the boy on the head as she spoke.

"Ja, this is our special secret."

CONCERNED FOR Marius and the people of Furuflaten, Sigrid rushed to the Grønvoll farm after she had walked Roald home. She breathlessly poured out Roald's story.

"You must stop him, Marius. We are all at a terrible risk."

"This is dreadful," Marius agreed. "There was nothing we could do.

He just dropped in on us unannounced one day when we were caring for Jan. I'll see what I can do."

Sigrid returned home and discussed the matter with Alf.

"Son, you must ski up into Lyngsdalen Valley and erase the soldier's footprints. They lead directly to the Grønvoll farm."

Alf bid farewell to his mother, strapped his skis on and headed for Lyngsdalen Valley.

Down by the riverbed, not far from the Grønvoll's, he found the footprints. Alf noticed that from the riverbed up toward the Grønvoll farm someone had either been frolicking in the snow or had already erased Jan's footsteps, but on the other side of the river and up where the valley curved into the lofty mountains, the tracks were fully visible.

Alf couldn't believe what he saw. Jan's footprints crisscrossed back and forth, traversed the frozen river, continued up the mountain side, turned back down again and crossed back over the river and up the other side. In places, his footprints disappeared and it looked like he had tumbled down the hillside, then re-crossed the river several times. The last mile, the prints revealed that the wounded soldier had dragged himself forward on all fours, lacking the strength to walk upright any longer.

Alf followed the footprints some three miles up into the valley where finally they had been erased by a heavy snowfall. He worked tediously to erase all the prints Jan had left, and returned home weary. An anxious Sigrid greeted him.

"What did you find son?" Alf told his mother the mind-boggling story.

"Are you sure you removed all the evidence? This is very dangerous for everyone in Furuflaten."

"I cannot be sure I got it all, but I did my best."

"Don't you think it would be wise to go back and make certain all the footprints are gone?"

Alf looked at his mother's troubled face and agreed to return. He returned to the valley and made sure every trace of Jan's prints was thoroughly rubbed out, leaving only his own ski tracks. The evening shadows had fallen by the time he finished. An expert skier, Alf reached home without any further incident.

There is a time for all things,
a time to preach and a time to pray....
There is a time to fight,
and that time is now come.

— Peter Muhlenberg

PEDER AND NIGO FIND
THE SNOW CAVE

LATER THAT day, Peder Isaksen and Nigo received a long-awaited call from teacher Nordnes. "The fish yarn is completed, and is ready to be picked up."

Both men were anxious and geared up for another trip to the plateau. They met above the tree line when darkness gave them cover, around 11 p.m. They had planned their trip straight up the mountainside toward the west and a bit north of Kjerringdalen Valley, a precipitous side valley to Manndalen. They headed straight for Revdal. Weather conditions were good with excellent skiing. Soon they reached the plateau and could see Revdalen stretch out before it extended downhill toward the west. To the south was the black vertical mountain wall rising upwards nearly 200 feet. North, the landscape was considerably lower and less steep with round hillocks punctuated by small round short valleys.

Below them, the valley floor flattened out and extended ahead with a wide outrun plateau. Under the snow, one might guess it to be a wide river delta or even a marsh. Marshes this high up in the mountains were not unusual and harbored diminutive cloudberry plants, the fruits of which are cherished by summer hikers. Beyond the outrun plateau, the valley shrank to a narrow gap in the surrounding bedrock, which joined the inhospitable mountain wall down toward Lyngenfjorden. At the bottom of the gap, the river plunged over the rocks by the looming mountain wall.

From where Peder and Nigo stood at the top of the Revdal plateau, they could look straight through the narrow chasm into the thin air above Lyngenfjord. Across the fjord on the other side sat stark and mighty Pollfjellet Mountain. Tucked at the base of the massive walls was Furuflaten.

Peder Isaksen

Peder and Nigo continued rapidly down Revdalen Valley, anxious to find Jan. Gradually, way down in the valley, where the terrain dropped steeply, two ski poles took shape in the snow to the left of a large boulder near the mountain wall.

"This time we've found him!"

"Let's go!"

The two men jubilantly pushed off down the rock-strewn plateau, faster than they were comfortable with in this difficult terrain, but tension and concern drove them on. The ski conditions were near ice and it was difficult to keep their speed in check. Every moment counted for the lonely soldier, and Peder and Nigo were eager to reach him and quell his anguish.

When they reached the ski poles, they realized they had not come far enough down into the valley on their prior search. The many hours they spent hunting for him four days ago had been too far up in Revdalen.

The ski poles were tied together at the top and there was no doubt in their mind that this was the place. A few feet to the side of the poles lay a huge boulder so thickly covered with snowdrifts from the mountain winds that it

Nigo Nilsen

could pass for one of the hillocks in the downward slope they had crossed.

Hesitantly they looked at the snow masses. It was difficult to believe that a human being could have survived underneath it all for four days - alone, surely frightened, ill and in pain. Wrapped in a sleeping bag, lying on a wooden sleigh and buried in snow, how had he managed? Was he still alive?

There was no movement. They heard no sound except for the wind as it swept over them, and all they could see was snow. The thought that close to their feet, underneath all that snow, lay a Norwegian soldier in flight from the Germans was rather incomprehensible to them.

Nigo, always the optimistic one, always believing in the possible, still believed the soldier alive even after all these days and the cruel circumstances. Peder, a more practical-minded man, was a little more skeptical. He found it hard to believe that anybody could survive under these conditions for five days, particularly a very ill man.

The snow was three feet deep, and even more so in places because of the drifts, which had been blown up against the boulder. They dug with their hands since they had not brought a shovel along. It seemed to them that they were digging a long time. Aware that Jan had a weapon, they continually called the password down into the deep hole, "Hello Gentleman! Hello Gentleman!"

The answer they hoped for did not come. They knelt and kept digging. They stopped for a brief moment and just stared at each other. Even for positive Nigo, hope began to fade.

"Maybe I have been a fool, but I really believed this man made it."

"Hello Gentleman! Hello Gentleman!" It was hopeless, but they could not just leave without seeing for themselves that he really was dead. So many had tried so hard to rescue him, so many wanted Jan to succeed in reaching Sweden.

They had dug down over four feet when a fragile, feeble voice answered their gentleman-call. Even when they stopped calling, the barely perceptible voice continued to answer in a low whisper, "Hello Gentleman, Hello Gentleman, Hello Gentleman!" The men froze.

They dug at top speed, and in record time they freed Jan from his entombment. To their astonishment, as best they could observe, Jan's mind was clear; nonetheless he was terribly weak. He was still dressed in his military clothes inside the military sleeping bag, which lay directly on the sled. He had no other clothing over him.

Inside his cave he had managed to fashion a small shelf about six inches long. On this shelf lay his most prized possession at the moment, a sugar cube! This sugar cube was the only food he had left. Before the Manndalen men arrived, Jan picked it up every so often, sucked on it a couple of times and carefully placed it back on the shelf.

"Were you able to bring a cigarette or two?" Jan wondered. He relaxed as he exhaled and the smoke swirled around him. Not until then was he ready for the food they had brought: some cured meat and bread, and some spirits to warm him up.

Jan eagerly ate the delicious food, recovering strength with each bite. Peder and Nigo tried to make Jan as comfortable as possible. They cared for him in every way, cleaned him up, and fed him until he was satisfied.

Morning neared and Peder and Nigo had to return to the valley before the people in the valley awoke.

It was time to return Jan to his snow shelf. How they hated themselves for having to do it. Peder and Nigo filled in the opening, leaving a small hole for air. They promised Jan that the next night, four men would come from Manndalen to transport him to Sweden and freedom. Jan was greatly comforted, cheered and encouraged by these thoughtful and generous strangers.

They said their goodbyes and Peder and Nigo started their ascent up the steep mountain to the top of the plateau and down again, to Manndalen.

The original plan had been to move Jan by reindeer transport to Sweden, but that seemed all but impossible at this point. They had to pass Skibotn, which was crowded with Germans, and in any case, the helpers were not near the Sami's regular travel route.

Manndalen, 30 April, 1943: It was daybreak when Peder and Nigo came down from the mountain plateau. Soon after, they contacted Aslak Fossvoll and teacher Nordnes. Four men had to retrieve Jan the following night and help transport him to Sweden. Peder Isaksen and Nigo Nilsen would return, and with them would be Nils Brustrøm and Olaf Olsen.

Olaf Olsen was a twenty-three year old farmer who lived on the east side of Manndalen River. A strong youth, a hard worker, dependable and persevering, he felt honored to be asked to help with Jan.

Nils Brustrøm lived on his farm, Brustrøm, highest up in the interior of Manndalen valley. All four were anxious to get Jan to Sweden, knowing that his health was deteriorating rapidly. The men agreed to meet at the usual place just above the tree line at 11 p.m.

That afternoon the wind picked up. They had all hoped for a reprieve from the stormy weather conditions for a few days; after all it was spring.

Towards evening, the wind increased to a moderate gale with a strong storm in the wind gusts.

The four men thought they might still manage the ascent, but the violent snowdrifts blinded them. They arched themselves against the snow and the wind as they inched their way upward. Higher up in Kjerringdalen Valley, the wind increased to such a velocity that it was near impossible to breathe or to keep one's balance. There were no options - they had to return to the valley floor.

Peder and Nigo had promised Jan they would return on this night. But it was impossible; they would not be able to keep their word. In Manndalen to keep your word was a virtue of necessity; it was unthinkable not to. The overpowering weather made it impossible for the young men to follow through on their promise.

Restless, the men could not stop thinking about Jan up on the plateau, helpless and trapped behind the "Gentleman stone."

Later, they tried several different routes, but each ended in disappointment. It was impossible. They could not see their own feet. The wind and the full-blown whiteout forced the four men to turn back. Concern for Jan weighed heavy on all of their minds. In these weather conditions, though, he was better off right where he was – in the snow cave.

May 1, 1943: The storm raged on. The men tried to reach the plateau by a different route. It was no use. They had to turn back.

May 2, 1943: The stormy weather continued. They did not stand a chance of making it. Peder and Nigo worried constantly about Jan, but they were powerless against the tempest.

May 3, 1943: The storm screeched through the valley. The wind howled around the house corners and it was impossible for any human being to be outside. This was the fourth day; none could remember such spring weather. The men decided they had to try to reach Jan. Again they tried an alternate route, but the storm pounded them. No living creature could make it up on the plateau in such weather. Defeated, they returned to the valley. They began to doubt that Jan could have made it through such weather. Anxious as they were for a let-up, they could do nothing but wait inside.

It might cost me my life,
but what of it? You have to
say 'Yes' or 'No' to life.

— Marius Grønvoll

JAN'S SOLITUDE

ENCOURAGED, JAN settled back down by himself after Peder and Nigo had left. Little bursts of happiness ran through him. He looked forward to the new happenings and the plans for his final rescue.

He started thinking about the near future. He decided a large tub filled with hot water and soap was top priority for him. He wanted to soak for hours.

Clean clothes were next on his list. The smelly, filthy clothes he was wearing had long since lost their usefulness. Delicious foods came to his mind - Sweden would have it all. There were many things for his mind to ruminate on. Time would pass quickly; possibly the night would slip by and he would be able to enjoy some sleep. The new day would dawn and quickly turn into night and his friends would return for him.

He discerned that the snow cave darkened early, and thought it amazing how quick night was descending. Soon after came the screeching wind and then he realized it was another Arctic spring storm. The wind came from somewhere behind the boulder and whirled around his snow cave. The darkness thickened and he knew night had come. The wind kept barreling down. The hours hardly moved.

There was no reprieve from the storm. Jan realized the men could not come for him in such weather. It would be impossible for them to fight their way through. Hour after hour snailed by - the storm persisted.

Jan forced himself to think of other things: his family, friends, hikes in the mountains in his youth, his military training, and his hopes for the future.

Jan listened to the wind. Like a raging giant, it took a deep breath, giving him a few seconds of silence; then, with roaring fury, the giant exhaled and the tempestuous wind shrieked with added force around the boulder. The snow whipped around his cave.

Jan lay in his snow-covered bed, listening to the storm; it raged on for four days. He realized he was being buried alive as the wind forced the snowdrift around him up against the boulder. He could not distinguish day from night any longer and the storm became muted. At long last a disquieting stillness settled in. The only sound was his breathing.

The icy cold forced him to keep turning within the sleeping bag so as not to freeze to death. Because of this shifting, painful blisters and raw sores developed on his body. His feet were aching, his toes infected. His body went from shivering to overheating with intermittent fever attacks and sweating, back to freezing. The cold was agonizing. Sleep was impossible. During these fitful days, superficial, shallow periods of sleep for ten to fifteen minutes at a time were his only relief. They recurred when he was too fatigued to fight any longer.

Jan's sufferings continued for three days. Foods and liquids were gone. The men had planned to return within twenty-four hours and Jan had been well supplied for that period. No one had imagined a spring storm of this magnitude. In his wretchedness he was sapped of physical strength and mental fortitude. Rapidly losing weight, an overriding helplessness engulfed him.

As time went on, he heard church bells pealing. At first Jan noticed the barely audible sounds coming from afar, then the volume increased and he became aware that the resonant sound of chiming bells came from the highest mountain peaks. They bounced out across the wilderness and echoed back from a facing mountaintop. The beautiful sounds were muted or intensified depending on which mountain peak sent the melodic sounds back. Church bells had never sounded this celestial before. Jan strained to hear. He did not know he was hallucinating and that the end was near for him.

RESCUED FROM
THE SNOWCAVE

TUESDAY, MAY 4, 1943: The Manndalen men anxiously watched the weather. Early on the morning of May 4 they were able to attempt another climb up to the tundra. There were some Germans in the neighborhood that morning, but nothing could hold the four back now that the weather had cleared.

The route up the steep mountain was tricky and exhausting. With all the new snow, there was a risk of spring avalanches. The four men rubbed their skis with paraffin wax, which made the going easier, but which also gave the skis a tendency to slip backwards. Within three hours they stood in front of the "Gentleman stone."

Hastily they slipped out of their ski-bindings and began removing armsful of snow at a time, continually shouting out the password, "Hello Gentleman!" Soon Jan came into view. He was alive but wretched.

"Jan, we have come to take you to Sweden!"

"There are four of us, and this time we will get you there."

Jan gave a weak smile and the thumbs up sign.

His rescuers were anxious for Jan's welfare after his nine days in the snow cave. Moreover they knew that they were in plain view of Furuflaten and Lyngseidet, where many Germans with powerful binoculars were stationed.

They removed Jan from the sleeping bag and emptied it, hurriedly cleaned him up and put him back in to ward off the cold. Hot soup, bread and coffee revived him once more. They made the soldier comfortable on the sled as best they could, and then fastened him down.

"Si fra, er du klar Jan?," Are you ready Jan?, they asked.

"This is the very moment I have lived for!"

"Are you comfortable?"

"I am anxious to see the Swedish border!" Jan smiled.

The men fastened their skis, put on their knapsacks, and tied the ropes from the sled around their waist. The four worked out how they could best work in unison, braking downhill and pulling together more effectively uphill.

"We are on our way to Sweden!"

"Off to Sweden we go!"

"Off we go to Sweden!" A much weaker but enthusiastic voice came from the sleeping bag.

Ridges and extended valleys made the going across the whole plateau strenuous. In various places, the tundra rolled like waves on a storm-tossed sea, up a knoll, down a dip, then up again.

They moved in a southeasterly direction. Far down on their right, Lyngenfjord reflected steel-gray clouds gathering, and on their left was the precipitous downgrade toward Manndalen Valley.

The most difficult passages were the sharp downward slopes when the sled had a tendency to take off and the men in the back endeavored to slow it down. Drenched with sweat, they stopped for a short breather when they came to some fairly even land.

"How about something hot to drink, Jan?"

"Ja takk."

"Are you okay? You don't say much."

"I am not the one struggling." Jan attempted to flash his handsome, but now tired smile.

His pallid, haggard face told its own story but the only feelings Jan expressed were of gratitude.

On they pushed!

After the men traveled for about four hours toward the border, the wind pounced.

A thick snow squall bore down and engulfed them in a white torrent of flakes. The tips of their skis disappeared in the whiteout. It became difficult to hold their balance. Being familiar with the spring weather conditions in this area, the men from Manndalen knew the storm could stop as suddenly as it had begun. Olaf bent over, "Jan I am going to cover your whole face." Jan nodded.

Unable to see, the men lost all sense of direction. They were fully aware, however, that the three thousand-foot drop to Manndalen Valley was somewhere near and on the other side was Skibotn, filled with Germans. They could only hope they would not stray in that direction.

"Jan, we need to leave you awhile to go and get oriented to our position."

Jan indicated agreement. The Manndalen men discovered they were lost. After about forty minutes they turned back.

Olaf Olsen

While on the way back to Jan, the storm stopped momentarily. Far below them lay Manndalen. They now knew where they were and hurried to get Jan. The wind and snow had erased most of their tracks, making it difficult to find the way back. About an hour after leaving they came to a slight rise. Jan had been snowed under! Some sixty feet from him they stopped cold.

"In all the world... what is this?" Peder pointed to new tracks in the snow – two pairs of fresh ski tracks the wind had not erased yet. The men looked around but they were alone. It was evident the tracks had been made by two German soldiers on a search. None but Germans would be up in the mountains during such weather conditions. The men stood in speechless amazement and watched each other. They backed off from Jan to lay plans.

"No doubt, these tracks were made by Germans. But they are only two, and we are four!"

"If they should come back, let us surrender – Jan also. And when we are led away, let's look for the right opportunity. I'll shout 'Hei!' then we'll overthrow them. We all have knives." Nigo had it all figured out. The others agreed. Their knives were not particularly sharp, but good enough to complete the job, if necessary.

"There is no need for us to tell Jan about this incident," said Peder. All were of the same mind. They continued on to Jan.

Someone removed the snow, then the covering from his face. "We are back, Jan!"

"I've never been so happy to see anyone!" Jan beamed.

"You knew we'd be back, didn't you?"

"That's not what I mean. Only moments ago I thought I heard German voices."

The men gaped.

"I was petrified thinking you had become their prisoners."

"How could we get you to Sweden then?" Nigo quipped. They all laughed, but they did wonder why the Germans had not smelled Jan.

The men were grateful the snow squalls had completely covered Jan. If the Germans had seen him, the sled must have just appeared as one of the many snow-covered rocks scattered across the tundra.

Neither Jan nor the men knew at the time that the Germans had increased their patrols and fortified their forces within the inner Troms District and along the Swedish border. For some time the Germans had had indications that someone in the area was trying to escape. The document case retrieved from the waters in Toftefjord contained several papers which revealed certain escape routes toward Sweden. The Germans were convinced it would be in the area of Troms. For that reason, orders had been sent down from German High Command to fortify and intensify the patrols and to be vigilant at all times.

In the mountains, Wednesday, May 5, 1943: The four Manndalen men picked up the ropes and continued further into the wide expanse. The rough terrain slowed them and progress was difficult. They'd pull uphill, then abruptly had to brake going down a steep incline.

It was nearing 5 a.m. The men were on the plateau in upper Manndalen Valley. For twenty hours they had been on the move. It was time to rest and grab something to eat. Quickly they produced from their knapsacks nourishing bread, cured meat, beverages and of course, coffee and cigarettes. They unbuckled Jan and helped him sit up to eat and view the landscape. Suddenly hundreds of reindeer rushed past. These beautiful animals with their broad antlers gather in enormous throngs and at that very moment the clouds parted.

"Majestic! Majestic!" Jan was thrilled.

"Just wait, things will get even better for you, Jan!"

"I have no complaints. You men are my inspiration."

"And you are ours!"

The men had realized for some time that it would be impossible to reach Sweden in one big leap with still another fifteen or twenty miles to go. They discussed how best to work their way to the border. When they had finished eating and packed things away, Nigo suddenly popped up. "I am taking off for Sweden. I have some Sami friends over there, two brothers, and they will probably be able to help us with reindeer transport on the last leg of the journey."

"Nigo you're delirious!" Olaf chuckled. "You are talking about another 85 miles round trip to your Sami friends. You want to ski that by yourself after these twenty hours? "

"No problem. I'll do it!"

They briefly discussed Peder, Nils and Olaf bringing Jan down the Avzevaggi valley a bit where they would keep him until Nigo returned with the reindeer transport from Sweden.

Nils Brustrøm

He took off without provisions of any sort. This was typical Nigo, with more endurance than any of them. He didn't give his friends a chance to dissuade him. All they could do was watch his silhouette diminish on the horizon. Like a light-footed reindeer, Nigo disappeared among the mountain ridges.

When Nigo left, the three men fought their way back some three miles on the plateau uppermost in Avzevaggi, a side valley on the southwest side of Manndalen Valley. Here they began their descent.

They labored to bring Jan downward a distance but the rugged terrain was almost impossible to traverse. The ropes tied to the sled were too short, and several times they had to gingerly lower the sled, letting it hang and sway in the open air. In other places, two of the Manndalen men took a few careful steps down the precipitous mountain while the third lowered the sled after them.

This time Jan suffered excruciatingly, moaning and twisting.

Despite the cold air, the sweat poured off the men.

Foot by foot they descended the rock-ribbed height until they reached a point where a bold-faced wall protruded skyward. The vertical wall blocked the view to the west but it was wide open in all other directions, and it gave shelter from the wind.

Peder, Nils and Olaf were drained. Helpless, they dropped into the snow.

"We probably could go on another little piece, Jan. But we're exhausted and maybe it's best that we leave you here until the reindeer transport comes," said Nils.

"It's just fine here. I am sure I'll be all right for the short while until the reindeer transport comes."

The men built a snow wall around the sled to protect Jan should the wind pick up.

They emptied two of their knapsacks of food, drinks, and cigarettes, putting the items into the other knapsack, which they placed close to Jan.

Jan did not mind sleeping under the open sky. He thought it rather exhilarating after his experience in the snow cave. The men agreed this was the best place for him for the next few hours.

They said their good-byes and left, totally spent, yet encouraged by Jan's upbeat mood. The arduous decent down to the Brustrøms' farm uppermost in Manndalen Valley took them six hours. They arrived in the early afternoon after thirty hours of hard labor in the mountains. Disappointed in the outcome – different than what they had planned – but Jan was a little closer to his goal.

The men flopped as soon as they entered the Brustrøm home. They slept the rest of the day and into the night. Peder and Olaf got up and left in the middle of the night. They walked a few feet from the Brustrøm house and into the icy Manndalen River to avoid leaving any tracks.

BENEATH THE SKY
IN AVZEVAGGI

AVZEVAGGI, MAY 6, 1943: Jan stirred and slowly opened his eyes to the bright morning sun. From his sled beneath the black vertical wall, he could see the mountain bluffs nearby and the snow-capped peaks on the horizon. The beauty and splendor of it all filled him with hope and wonder.

He was not sure which mountain the sun was climbing over; he only appreciated its light and its warmth. His happiness was short lived. As the Arctic spring sun raised the temperature, it melted the snow on the ridges and outcrops on the mountain wall above him. The melting snow dripped incessantly down on him and the sleeping bag all through the day. Soon he was soaked, as if covered with a drenched blanket. And when the sun sank behind the mountain crests and the night rolled over him, the melted snow water froze. The sleeping bag became a tomb of ice from which he could not free himself.

The next day the scenario recurred. He cursed the sun that had welcomed him on the first morning and filled him with hope. This was too much. This was more than should be asked of anyone.

Weakness and cold replaced his courage and the warmth. What was left of his toes ached – their putrid smell told him they were rotting away – and he was too weak to do anything about it. The thought of food nauseated him, and he lost still more weight. His mind could not make any sense of it all. Jan was rapidly deteriorating.

Thursday, May 7, 1943: Peder had been up for a couple of hours when he heard the sound of rushing skis in the snow outside his home. As it was mid-morning, Peder assumed it was drunken Germans on their way back to their quarters after an all night brawl. Peder was wrong. It was Nigo returning from his thirty hour, 85-mile trip to Sweden. He had met with his Sami friends, who gave him some food and coffee, but that was all he had eaten since he had left his friends.

Fifty hours of skiing with only a short break in Sweden – Nigo was unbeatable! But even after all his struggles, his Sami friends could not promise him help. The Germans had fortified their borders along the road to Finland and it was the only way into Sweden. The Samis found it too dangerous to transport Jan past the German guards under the circumstances.

Peder Isaksen indicates the place where they left Jan.

Avzevaggi as it appears from Manndalen Valley. The arrow indicates where Jan was left.

THE SPIRIT OF THE SAMI

IN THE village of Birtavärre, brothers Leif and Rolf Bjørn were the contact persons for the resistance. The brothers had several business interests including a large lumber business, which supplied several areas in the Troms District. In addition, they were shipping agents and had many local contacts. Organizing the escape routes into Sweden from Kåfjorddalen Valley, four miles from Birtavärre, fell to them.

During the war, the Bjørn brothers and Hjalmar Steinnes, a thirty-year-old bachelor in Kåfjorddalen, had developed a close working relationship. Their mutual goal was to defeat Germany. At the time of the German invasion of Norway, Hjalmar was working at Spitsbergen in the Svalbard Islands, a Norwegian possession in the Arctic Ocean. The islands lie about midway between Nordkapp, the northern tip of Norway, and the North Pole.

Long before the invasion of Norway, Hjalmar had developed a hatred for Hitler and all Nazism stood for. Their atrocities caused him to detest Hitler's very name and anything related to him.

Hjalmar Steinnes

A born patriot, Hjalmar was anxious to return to the mainland to fight against the German tyranny. With many others he was mobilized at Svalbard. A tramp steamer brought him back to Narvik, south of Tromsø, and he soon involved himself with the resistance movement.

Following the outbreak of the war in northern Norway, a steady stream of refugees crossed the border to Sweden. Hjalmar guided many of them. Kåfjorddalen was isolated but the distance to the Swedish border was only 45 miles. Conversely, precipitous mountains bordered Kåfjorddalen. Refugees had to climb these mountains before reaching the plateau and setting out for Sweden. Kåfjorddalen Valley became one of the main refugee routes across the Norwegian and Finnish wilderness into Sweden.

Border patrols were usually stationed some distance apart and it was not too dangerous to cross. In the early war years, the German soldiers seldom came to Kåfjorddalen Valley. This changed after the Germans confiscated the document case in the battle of Toftefjord and learned that sabotage work was planned against them. Almost immediately, they increased and strengthened their border patrols. After that time the fugitives had to be extremely cautious.

Furthest up in Kåfjorddalen Valley at the lowermost part of Ankerlia Mountain, the Germans had confiscated a small hut owned by the Bjørn brothers, left from the copper mining days. They stationed guards there to keep a lookout for refugees. The forested mountainside was steep, but the trees shielded fugitives and guides climbing the mountain near the hut.

The elongated valley begins at the Kåfjord and stretches eight miles inland. At its narrowest point it is only 450 feet across, but spreads out to about 1000 feet at the widest place. Nearly perpendicular mountains reaching heights of 2700 feet enclose the valley, except to the west where it skirts the fjord.

Winter begins when the first snow falls early in November. The snow stays until April, sometimes May. The heavy downwind from the mountains plays havoc with the snow and forges huge piles several feet high. Torleif Lyngstad says in his book, "Kåfjord – mennesker, administrasjon og politikk" that "nature is a master the people of Kåfjord have always accepted."

In 1943 only a few hundred people resided in the valley. The nearest store was three-and-a-half-miles away, Leif and Rolf Bjørn's in Birtavärre.

Birtavärre: Hjalmar and the Bjørn brothers had learned of Jan Baalsrud soon after his arrival in Furuflaten. Messages had been exchanged between established contacts. The Bjørn brothers asked Hjalmar to assist them in securing Sami reindeer transport for the soldier when the time was right.

Some nomadic Samis make Kautokeino their winter home. Their reindeer roam the nearby plateaus. Kautokeino is located in Finnmark County, which borders the Troms District in Northern Norway. In the spring, the Kautokeino Samis move their reindeer to the coast.

The area where the Samis and their reindeer herds roamed is known as Lapland, a vast territory that included the extreme north of Norway, Sweden, Finland and the Kola Peninsula of the Soviet Union. Lapland has no borders and the Sami are free to follow their reindeer herds. The area of Lapland is commonly regarded as the area within the Polar Arctic Circle. The higher, Alpine types mountains in northern Norway and Sweden are known as the tundra, with marshes, moors, dwarfed birch trees and rich pastureland which feeds the huge reindeer herds.

Birtavärre, Wednesday May 5, 1943: Hjalmar and the Bjørn brothers held exhaustive discussions on possible solutions on how to best help Jan. They considered bringing him to Kåfjorddalen by boat, but decided it was too chancy. Hjalmar hit on another idea.

"I'll ski over the mountains to find out exactly where they keep him hidden. Then we'll take the next step."

The Bjørn brothers agreed.

Across a narrow country path, a short distance from Hjalmar's home, stood a small red-painted cottage. The cottage stood at the foot of a 2100-foot mountain. John Olav Ballovarre, Hjalmar's faithful helper, lived here with his parents and eight siblings. With his new assignment, Hjalmar headed straight for John Olav's home to ask for his assistance.

John Olav and Hjalmar set off to the mountains that very day for Manndalen, thirteen miles west of Kåfjorddalen. They carried their skis on their shoulders up steep Ankerlia Mountain. When they reached the uplands, they put the skis on and set out across the plateau.

One thing the Sami and others in the North Country enjoy is their coffee. It is said that the Samis do not measure journeys in miles but rather

Rolf Bjørn

in the number of coffee breaks required. Hence, when these two men reached Moskugaise Mountain up on the plateau they had their first coffee, Rika, a coffee substitute made from grains, and the only thing available during the war.

From Moskugaise, they took the path toward the uppermost part of Manndalen. A roughly sketched map of the place where Jan was hidden had been given them.

Nearing Olmmaivaggi, a sudden blinding snowstorm overpowered them. The thick snow made it impossible to see even their ski tips.

"We had best turn back. Maybe we'll make it back to the hut in Moskugaise," John Olav yelled above the howling wind.

After the copper mines closed down in 1919, outdoor lovers had maintained a small hovel from material left after the copper-mining days. Hunters and fishermen alike stopped there for coffee breaks when they came to the uplands.

"Let's do it. We won't find Baalsrud in this soup."

They turned and, with the help of the compass, made their way back to the hut.

The storm increased and nearly lifted the hut off its foundation.

"We can't stay, Hjalmar. Let's try again when the weather clears."

"I agree. It's a terrible night. Let's try to get back down into the valley."

Safely home, the storm stopped abruptly. Hjalmar was exhausted and hungry after the challenging outing. He grabbed a quick bite, changed into dry clothes and set out for the Bjørn brothers in Birtavärre. Deeply disturbed over his report of the unsuccessful trip, the brothers promised to contact him further.

Shortly after Hjalmar's arrival home, two attractive girls from Lyngen visited. Some time earlier he had met them and a young quisling on the ferry from Tromsø. (Vidkun Quisling was a Norwegian Nazi party leader and traitor during WWII. He was executed in 1945. His name is used a label for a person who betrays his or her country by aiding an invading enemy.) Suspicious of Hjalmar's involvement with fugitives and hoping to trap him, the young quisling sent the girls as decoys. The girls told Hjalmar the young man had been called up to the Eastern Front and had asked them to come and see him. "Would he be able to help get the young man to Sweden?"

Uneasy, Hjalmar sensed something seriously wrong. "I'm only a fisherman. I work in the mines," he said. "All those who knew the mountains have escaped already."

"Can't you do anything for him?"

"I don't know what. Let's hope the war ends soon and your friend can return home."

Birtavärre

Three Samis in traditional costume. Nils Siri is in the center.

AT CROSS PURPOSES

MANNDALEN, THURSDAY, May 6, 1943: Peder, Nils and Olaf, the Manndalen men, had descended from Avzevaggi the day before Nigo returned from Sweden. Nigo hadn't received a promise of help because the Sami felt the risk was too great at this time. Realizing there would be no Sami transport, they sent an immediate message to the Bjørn brothers in Birtavärre. "Jan is seriously ill, can you help with reindeer transport, now?" The Bjørn brothers forwarded the pressing communication to Hjalmar.

"Please arrange for reindeer transport – post haste!"

By chance, while in Birtavärre, Hjalmar had run into his Sami friend, Nils Juuso, who had just come from Sweden. He relayed that the Siri brothers were camped near Jierta some 35 miles east in the direction of the Reisafjell Mountains. The brothers, who were from Kautokeino, were on the move with their reindeer herd. Hjalmar knew these Sami brothers well. Per and Nils Siri were dependable, honorable men about his own age. He expected they would help him with reindeer transport. At this point, Hjalmar had no idea that Nigo had been to Sweden attempting to get help.

The Bjørn brothers told Hjalmar that Jan was on a ski-sled in Olmmaivaggi.

Manndalen stretches in a southeasterly direction from the country settlement up into the wilderness, which divides into three more side valleys. Jan was not in any of these valleys but on his sled out in the open in Avzevaggi at the highest point of the four side valleys on the opposite side of the Manndalen Valley, in the southwest.

A terrible misunderstanding had taken place.

Hjalmar willingly accepted the assignment to find reindeer transport for Jan. He only asked that the Manndalen men meet him at the place and time they had agreed to, the night between May 9 and 10. Hjalmar skied nearly 90 miles round trip in his search for the Siri brothers' camp, close to Kautokeino. If they were able to come, the Samis needed time to gather their reindeer.

"Tell the Manndalen men not to leave the place in case I am delayed. I am on my way."

Before Hjalmar left, he and the Bjørn brothers discussed the need to compensate the Samis fairly for transporting Jan to Sweden – and for risking their lives. They decided that 3000 kroner ($400) was a fair price. Rolf and Leif Bjørn provided the money.

Hjalmar brought with him two of his neighbors, Mons-Peder Gundersen and Einar Løvli, both active in the resistance, as he set out to find the Sami.

The Arctic spring with its light evenings was fast approaching. Soon there would be no darkness at all. Hjalmar was equipped with a rough outline of a map showing where Jan lay hidden. The men carried their skis up through the rugged woodland until they drew above the tree line. From there they continued upland until they reached the plateau. They set out toward Jierta and the Reisafjell Mountains. The snow was crusty, enabling them to move quickly.

By Carajavre, they took their first break in an old turf-hunting hut. Within minutes, fire burned in the old granite pit and they heated the ever-present Rika. Thick slices of homemade rye bread spread with churned butter disappeared quickly.

Satisfied after their break and meal, the men continued their journey. Several hours later, they passed Jierta. But they found neither tracks nor traces of the Sami or their reindeer. Not until they neared Miehtavarri did they see the first lavvo, Sami tent. Yelping dogs greeted them and stayed with them until they reached the tent opening.

Inside, Magnus, the oldest of the Siri brothers, sat close by a coal-black steaming kettle of coffee.

Magnus greeted them. "Boris, boris!" Welcome, welcome!

His brothers Per and Nils Siri sat on birch branches and shaggy goatskins further back in the tent. They arose and greeted them eagerly.

This time they were served real coffee smuggled in from Sweden and delicious Swedish bread. Out came dried reindeer meat. Wielding his sharp hunting knife, Magnus cut the meat into thin slices. After many hours on the plateau, the food tasted fantastic and the men's ferocious appetites were satisfied. It felt good to be among the brothers.

"What brings you to us?" Nils queried.

"I am looking for reindeer transport for a very ill Norwegian soldier hidden in the mountains. He is hunted by the Germans and needs to get to Sweden," Hjalmar explained.

The brothers offered to help without hesitation. Because of his unmarried status, Nils was designated to be the driver. Fatigued after their eight hours in the upland, Hjalmar and his friends slept for five hours while Nils and Per gathered three strong reindeer bucks.

Nils and Hjalmar readied the reindeer bucks and packed the pulks with plenty of cured meat, bread and coffee. Pulks are canoe-shaped sleds built from birch wood, set on runners and lined with reindeer skin. They headed for Manndalen to pick up Jan.

With only a moderate mountain breeze and decent snow conditions, they made good time. Nils drove the reindeer further west and closer to the Finnish border than Hjalmar and his friends had come.

By Sumajavrre stood a newly restored cottage the border police used. Hjalmar knew the four police stationed there. They were true jøssinger, Norwegian patriots during WWII. The resistance workers still detoured, not wishing to take unnecessary chances on their top-secret mission.

In spite of good weather conditions, riding in a reindeer sled was strenuous. At Smuolkojavret they took a break. Food and coffee always seemed more delicious out on the plateau, especially after an arduous trip. From their resting place, Olmmaivaggi, the side valley where they believed Jan was hidden, was only eight miles away.

Birtavärre, May 9, 1943: While Hjalmar and Nils were in the mountains, the Bjørn brothers, not aware that Nigo had been in Sweden seeking help, sent a message to the Manndalen men: "Reindeer transport from Kautokeino will arrive this coming night. Meet them on the plateau and show them the way to the soldier."

Jan still was at Avzevaggi on the west side of Manndalen Valley. Hjalmar and Nils Siri were on their way to Olmmaivaggi, on the east side of the valley.

MANNDALEN, MAY 9, 1943: The Manndalen men were happy to receive the message of the upcoming reindeer transport.

That evening, Peder Isaksen and Peder Pedersen were on their way up to Avzevaggi Plateau to meet with the reindeer transport from Kautokeino. As it was Sunday evening, the two bachelors met people along the road enjoying a stroll.

"Where are you young men going so late on a Sunday night?"

"We are just meeting some young ladies up in the valley."

They all laughed together and there were no more questions.

FOLLOWING SEVERAL hours of strenuous climbing they reached Jan. This time the men noticed an emotional change in him. Jan had always been warm and friendly, even in his most difficult moments, but now he seemed to have lost hope.

"I heard church bells chime again. This time they seemed far away," Jan muttered.

They were at a loss for what to tell him, but they tried to cheer him up. They had brought hot coffee and soup in thermoses, but it wasn't enough to warm his spirits.

"We are on the way up to the plateau to meet the Sami. They'll bring you to Sweden, Jan."

Jan's ashen face, hollow cheeks and overgrown black beard frightened them. He had lost weight since they saw him last. His lifeless large blue-gray eyes, framed by thick black eyebrows, manifested his torment all too clearly.

"Will it really happen this time?" A slight hope brushed across Jan's face.

"Yes, Jan. Before long you will be in safety in Sweden. You will get the medical care you need."

Thanks," he whispered, forcing a slight upturn of his lips.

"We're going up to the plateau to meet them and before too many hours we will be back."

Filled with misgivings, the men left Jan, but felt calm knowing the Sami transport would join them on the way down.

IN THE mountains, Evening, May 9, 1943: Hjalmar and Nils continued to make good time, and arrived early at the agreed upon place. They set the tent up. Coffee in hand made the long wait more pleasant. The kerosene stove was produced and the coffee pot filled with snow. Nils had brought a leather pouch with more of the good Swedish coffee.

Nils' good-natured remarks made him a jovial fellow to be around. Though his mother tongue was Sami, he communicated well in broken Norwegian. When he relaxed, he liked to joik, a Sami monotone chant that tells the story of a person or past event.

The reindeer were tied to stakes near bare spots in the snow where there was plenty of silver gray lichen, reindeer moss, for them to eat.

Reindeer bucks scrape away snow with their antlers to find food during the winter. After the older bucks shed their antlers they use their hooves to paw away the snow to get to the lichen if the snow is not too deep. The obtain water by eating snow.

Time dragged on and the Manndalen men did not come. Hjalmar and Nils grew uneasy. They could not understand the delay. At last they began their own search for Jan. For hours they searched in ever-widening circles. The plateau with the scattered boulders stretched out pure white for miles. They found no tracks. No sign of life.

They searched all the way down to the tree line, but to no avail. Repeatedly they studied the rough drawing. They believed they were in the right place. The reindeer were getting restless; the two men moved the animals to better pasture. Worn down from long hours of skiing and intense searching, the men finally went to sleep on the reindeer pelts in the tent.

In the early morning hours of May 10, they started exploring anew. No matter where they skied, or how much they called out, there were no answers. Not a trace of a human being.

"What's the use? They're not in this area," Hjalmar said toward evening. "We need more information."

"Nils, will you wait here while I make a run back to Birtavärre to contact the Bjørn brothers? They can contact the Manndalen men and find the cause." Hjalmar was downcast.

"What are you thinking of Hjalmar? That's a 26-mile round trip. It doesn't make any sense to wait way out here on the plateau. How could I explain a reindeer transport out here should the German patrols show? It's best I return to my camping ground."

Hjalmar understood his friend. They had hunted and waited for nearly forty-eight hours without success.

"I see your point. We'll try again once I've found the exact location?"

"Jaja, ja. I'll work with you."

Past midnight, Hjalmar helped Nils hitch up the reindeer. He paid him the previously agreed upon salary, and they parted. Saddened and exhausted, Hjalmar watched his friend disappear in among the mountain boulders. What had gone wrong? Attaching his own skis, he started on the long way home.

LATE EVENING, May 9, 1943: After leaving Jan, the Manndalen men climbed up to the Avzevaggi Plateau and went another three miles south to where they understood they were to meet the Sami.

The Samis had not arrived yet when Peder and Peder reached the tableland. Chill night winds blew and the men flapped their arms back and forth to keep warm. They continually scanned the landscape. No one was near. And they saw no one coming from afar. They dared not think the worst; as a result they just waited – and searched.

They could not have known that in a side valley two other men spent desperate hours searching also. Their hope rose every time they came around boulders, up bumps, around knolls, or down in dips, only to fall again. They tried to find the man they wanted to get to Sweden.

Peder and Peder waited until early in the morning of the 10th.

Two dispirited young men, nearly overcome with cold and emotional defeat, climbed silently down toward Avzevaggi and Jan.

By the time they returned from their fruitless search for the Sami, Jan was barely able to converse with them.

The men were distraught to see Jan's condition. They could see that Jan needed both medical help and to be gotten out of the weather. Jan's courage to press forward had diminished, and the men determined that Jan had to be moved quickly or they would lose him.

"There will be no reindeer transport." Peder Isaksen had difficulty speaking.

"In time there will be, Jan. Just not yet."

Jan stared into space. A hopeless look crossed his face and his despondency grew. At that moment they felt him disassociating himself from them and his surroundings.

They promised him that the following evening four men would come up with provisions and other necessary things they were able to carry up here to the upper valley.

Something snapped; Jan had reached the end of his tolerance. The five days in Avzevaggi had turned into a prolonged nightmare.

"It is enough," his dejected voice was almost inaudible. "I can't anymore. Let's call it quits. It is more than I can bear."

Watching him filled them with empathy. He was right. The suffering and loneliness he had been through, the uncertainty and the loss of his friends, pain and illness was more than most people could have coped with. Yet he had taken his hard knocks unflinchingly and with heroic valor. And now when he needed them, all they could do was to look down at him, powerless to help.

Except for their presence, they had no meaningful comfort to offer. They tried as best they could to encourage him not to give up.

"We'll stand by you Jan, until you are across the border."

Anguished and frail, Jan lay there helpless and without hope. He just stared out in space. His friends grew resolute. They would save him no matter what the cost.

Peder Isaksen and Peder Pedersen did not have four men ready to make the trip to Sweden at that point, but they also knew something had to be done, and soon. And they knew they would have no difficulty finding such men in the valley. Again they were able to ignite a spark of hope and life in Jan. They started their six-hour downward climb.

BIRTAVÄRRE, MAY 10, 1943: When Hjalmar did not return when expected, the Bjørn brothers sent his friend John Olav a message, "Please come and see us at the store in Birtavärre."

"John Olav, what do you think has happened? Do you think the Germans have caught them?" Leif asked with great concern.

"It is hard to know. Maybe after such a long time they have reached Sweden. But even at that they should have been back."

"John Olav, would you mind acting as our liaison and try to find the cause?"

"I'll go. But on my last outing I broke my skis."

"Come back to my house tonight and I'll have skis for you," Rolf said.

When John Olav returned that evening, many guests filled the Bjørn home. Rolf brought him over to a corner in the ante-room filled with shoes and boots. Rolf picked out his own boots. "Use these, and here are my skis."

"Before you leave, come down to the store and I'll have some tobacco for you, John Olav."

"I'll take the road along the riverbed."

He headed for the store on the way home.

Before long he became aware of two Germans behind him on bicycles.

"Now," he thought. "Now it is over! What will I tell them about carrying skis with no snow in the valley?"

But the Germans bicycled right past him. Most likely, John Olav concluded, they were "trading-Germans." From time to time German soldiers came from Spåkenes, a large German fortification. It was not unusual for them to bicycle the 20 miles to Birtavärre to trade their tobacco for home churned butter, mittens and other knitted goods.

Rolf met Hjalmar at the store, and immediately called one of the contact men in Manndalen. He wanted to know if Jan had been brought to Sweden yet.

"Has the fish been picked up?"

The answer was not clear, though it sounded as if Jan hadn't been picked up yet, but soon would be.

"Jan has not been picked up yet." Rolf turned to John Olav. "It is best you go searching. Here is some tobacco, both twist-tobacco and pipe tobacco for you. Good luck!"

John Olav stopped home to prepare for the outing. Without delay, he changed clothes and packed his knapsack. He loved cold, cold milk and always took a quart whenever he went on outings. Next best, he liked to sink his teeth into homemade whole grain bread. The other "must" he carried was a bottle of hard liquor. He did not drink, but it was good to have close by should the need arise. It was always in his sack with his bread and milk, and Rika coffee.

John Olav had never told his parents that he was involved in illegal activities, and they did not pry, but they were suspicious and a little unnerved. Fear of the Germans was very real, something most families learned to live with. John Olav wanted to protect his parents and siblings. Should the Germans come searching their home, his family could with good conscience tell them they did not know his whereabouts.

"Don't wait for me. I do not know when I will return." They asked no questions.

He left the little cottage around 9 p.m. A neighbor saw him and shouted through the window, "Are you heading into the mountains, John Olav?"

"Ja. I am heading for Vaddas (a plateau some distance from John Olav's home) to see if the Sami have returned." The Samis' return to the plateaus above Kåfjorddalen Valley was a sure sign of spring.

Skiing along on the upland he noticed a silhouette coming toward him from the direction of Manndalen. He could not make out who it was and thought it might be a German. "Let that be as it may, I will make out," he told himself.

Coming closer he was happy to see it was his friend Hjalmar. He was discouraged and worn out. "We did not find Jan Baalsrud. Nils Siri has promised to wait in upper Manndalen." Hjalmar expressed great concern.

"Do you have any tobacco John Olav?"

"Ja da, I can give you some tobacco. Rolf gave me some."

"Do you have any liquor as well?"

"Ja, but that you can't have until you have drunk some milk." Hjalmar drank about one fourth of the bottle.

"Tasty! Just what a weary body needed."

"Now my friend, since you've got some milk in you, have a nip so you don't fall asleep." John Olav handed him the bottle. "And don't wait for me, if I don't come home for a while, I have probably gone on to Sweden."

Kåfjorddalen, Monday, May 10, 1943: Hjalmar continued on his way homeward and arrived early the following morning. As soon as he had eaten and changed clothes, he set off toward the Bjørn brothers in Birtavärre. He told his fatiguing, discouraging story. They fell silent at the news. At the same time they knew the Manndalen men had gone up in the mountains to meet them, also in vain. Hjalmar was irritated and frustrated with the miscommunication. He was convinced that the place he and Nils had searched was not the correct one. As usual, the Bjørn brothers remained calm and said they would get to the bottom of it all. He would hear from them.

Hjalmar pondered how the communication between the valleys worked. He knew there were many links and that it was difficult to arrange such a dangerous mission in the midst of spying Nazis, German troops and control points. The Brattholm affair was well known, but Jan's escape had to be kept top secret.

SPRING PUSHED forward and with it, the always-radiant midnight sun. But for the men in Manndalen Valley, the moments of darkness were more precious, especially since the Arctic spring robbed them of several minutes of shadows daily.

The Manndalen men's breeding gave them fortitude and resilience. They had gained their strength and character from the rugged mountains enclosing their valley and from the stormy seas. In their homes as children they had been taught honesty, dependability and hard work. They, to a man, had been taught not by words, but by the actions of their parents. By watching the people in the valley they had learned that living meant loving and caring for one another, and that to be a man was more than physical prowess and a flawless personality. A real man was tender and giving and filled with selflessness as well as strength

Manndalen, May 10, 1943: In the lower part of Manndalen, a side valley from where Jan was lying in the open air, the men knew of a cave in the mountain wall from earlier times, located nearly 200 feet up a steep incline from the Manndalen River. Jan's helpers had decided to bring him here until they could arrange the final transport to Sweden.

The resistance members in Manndalen had been working extremely hard when they learned of Jan's misfortune. As soon as they decided to transfer him down to the cave in Skaidijonni, men and women worked to make him as comfortable as possible. The most important for his weary body, they felt, was a good bed. The men began braiding together thick bundles of birch branches. They covered the top of this "mattress" with leaves and hay to make it soft and relaxing. The bed was placed right up against one of the inside walls of the cave, making it impossible to see the mattress from the outside. One had to come into the cave before one discovered anything made by human hands. They felt certain of Jan's safety here.

Aslak Fosvoll went to his sister Helene Mikalsen to ask her assistance. Helene was a widow with three children ranging in age from two to ten years old. She was also an expert at making grener – the woven woolen covers that the valley of Manndalen is famed for. Today these grener are mostly used for decorative wall hangings. But in days past, the nomadic

Sami people would use them as coverlets in their tents. Helene was a Sami, as was Aslak, and the tradition of her people making these grener go back hundreds of years in the district of Troms. They were made in the natural colors of the wool, white, gray and black.

"Helene, I need for you to make us two Manndalsgrener as soon as possible. They are for a wounded Norwegian soldier. We are bringing him to Skaidijonni, and we need to keep him warm."

Helene went right to work, never questioning her brother's judgment. She bedded her children down and set up her work in her little kitchen. She worked straight through the night and the next day, stopping only to feed the animals and to meet of her children's basic needs. The first one was ready the day after Jan arrived in the cave, because, as she said, "It is important for him to have a warm cover as soon as possible."

A few days later, the second cover was ready for him. Now he had one to sleep on and one to cover him.

AVZEVAGGI, MAY 11, 1943: When the four Manndalen men reached Jan they tied him securely to the sled and fastened the long ropes. They knew this would be extremely difficult for him and they tried to be encouraging and told him of all the preparations made for him by many people in Manndalen Valley.

"We want to make you as happy as possible"

"And you will have a mattress! Well, maybe not as good as in Grand Hotel in Oslo. But the birch branches are braided with love and we think you will be comfortable."

Jan forced a smile. The last thing he wanted to do was to hurt these generous people. But the truth was he had given up.

The five hour descent from Avzevaggi to the cave in Skaidijonni was torturous for both Jan and the Manndalen men. His painful feet, made worse when the sleigh hung almost vertically downward, were unbearable. He was frozen and hungry but unable to eat. And the Manndalen men were tested to the limit as they inched their way down over the craggy, slippery outcrops struggling to handle Jan and the sled with care to minimize his pain and discomfort.

Once they had come down the precipitous mountain in the north, they came directly upon a gentler birch-forested downgrade. It brought them to the edge of another steep incline where the Manndalen River in the valley bottom bordered the bold-faced mountain on the other side. At the edge of the downgrade, a thirty-foot perpendicular gradient led them down to a three-foot wide shelf. They traversed carefully, clinging to dwarfed birch trunks so as not to slip with the sled over the narrow shelf and down into the river far below. The narrow path turned slightly to the left and about another sixty feet ahead was the opening to the cave.

Jan's spirit was bankrupt of hope. Livsgleden, the joy of life, had come to naught. Everything seemed futile and he did not care what happened anymore. He allowed his friends to make all the decisions and he let them transport him wherever they wished. Did it really matter? Everyone now knew he would never experience Sweden and freedom again. He pitied his friends who had cared and slaved for him, knowing their dream for him could never be.

Entrance to the cave in Skaidijonni.
The Manndalen River is down the incline on the left.

CONCEALED IN A CAVE
IN SKAIDIJONNI

SKAIDIJONNI, MAY 11, 1943: Jan was taken to the Skaidijonni cave. The cave had been formed from a large crevice in the interior of the mountain, and it was high enough that a grown person could almost stand upright. It was twenty feet long and had two apertures; the first was within a few feet of the thirty-foot incline they had brought Jan down. This gap was the smallest and most difficult to use as an entrance. At the opening in the lower end, huge boulders formed a natural camouflage in such a way that it was impossible to discover the cave until one was right on top of it.

The roomy cave would be a good shelter from the spring storms. Jan's helpers also felt it was a secure place away from the Nazis. From his bed he had a partial view of the sky and some trees growing near, and from the opening in the back, shafts of light entered the cave. There was room to lay his clothes on the rocks to dry, and when his helpers came, there was enough space for a couple of them to sit on the rock close by him.

The day after Jan was taken to the cave, Peder Isaksen and Aslak Fosvoll made the trip from Manndalen to bring him food and other provisions. Aslak looked forward to meeting the soldier he had heard so much about.

Peder introduced Aslak to Jan. The two men instantly connected. Peder had warned Aslak about Jan's condition, but Aslak was still shocked to see how scrawny and sickly Jan looked with his sunken cheeks and eyes ringed in black.

"If you have a wish or a need, please don't hesitate to let me know," Aslak offered.

The upper entrance to the cave in Skaidijonni

Inside the cave. Jan lay close to the left wall with his feet toward the left corner of the picture.

"Thanks, I appreciate it, but my needs are filled with this great bed and sheltered cave."

"We brought clean clothes for you, and we'll help you get cleaned up if you wish."

"It will be good to be clean and dry. Thanks!"

Already a good night's rest had strengthened Jan, and the care given and the kindnesses shown him brought hope back again in small doses.

Aslak helped Jan remove his dirty socks, but the one on his wounded foot was bonded to scabs and dried up blood clinging to his foot – the skin was bluish-black. In Avzevaggi Jan had become aware that what was left of his toes had rotted away. Without a moment's hesitation, Jan took his knife from his pocket and cut off the tissue that clung to the sock and the extra scar tissue left on his foot. He did it without a word.

Aslak and Peder realized Jan was a remarkable man, uncommon in his capacity to tolerate pain and to survive traumatic experiences. They also realized his unique ability to make necessary decisions even in his wretched condition, and to cope with burdens too heavy for many.

They observed how seriously ill he was and wondered how to best handle the crisis. Somehow they had to find a doctor who could come and help Jan, or at least give them advice.

Once back in Manndalen, Aslak and Peder consulted with teacher Nordnes. Manndalen did not have a doctor. The nearest one, who was known as a patriot, kept an office in Lyngseidet. Nordnes' sister worked for the doctor in his office, which gave Nordnes an idea. One morning Nordnes called in and said his sister was ill and she needed for the doctor to come and give her a check up. The doctor intended to do so, but he missed the ferry.

The following day Nordnes called again and said his sister's condition had taken a turn for the worse, and would he please come quickly? When the doctor received the phone call, he called the sheriff, a Nazi, and asked for permission to take the doctor boat across the fjord to see a sick patient in Manndalen. Gasoline was rationed and the Germans maintained strict control of all the comings and goings. Permission was granted and he was on his way.

The doctor found the school in Manndalen and went straight to teacher Nordnes. He handed the teacher Jan's medication, along with a prescription, in case more was needed. Nordnes was also instructed on how best to treat and care for Jan's feet, and how to wrap them. Jan's helpers took him the medication and cared for his feet, following the doctor's instructions.

IN THE upper part of Manndalen Valley lived Nils Brustrøm with his wife Signe and their three children. To the south of their Finnish-style cottage, a secluded place quite some distance from the nearest neighbor, the valley stretched upward into the foothills, and steep mountains bordered the narrow plains on each side of the house. The Manndalen River flowed a few feet from the cottage and was filled with salmon. Wild fowl and animals lived in the forest. From time to time, reindeer appeared on the horizon high up in the mountains. For the Brustrøm children the place was pure paradise.

Signe and Nils Brustrøm

One evening, that paradise changed forever. Hanna, the youngest child, was four and a half years old at the time. She remembers how she sat close by her father's chair while he was reading the newspaper by the kerosene lamp. He looked up and said to her mother, "The war is coming closer."

"We had better gather as much food as we can then," answered her mother.

Food had been rationed for some time and commodities were scarce. Some people watched to make sure no one got more than their share.

The war caused many to be covetous. Nils was able to buy some sacks of flour and a few other staples.

Many a night little Hanna woke up to the clatter of knitting needles and saw her mother sitting up in bed knitting mittens, socks, and stockings. Nils caught salmon in the river and they traded it for other staples: sugar, grains, flour, and other foods.

They had a few sheep and cows that gave them milk. Signe churned butter and made cheese and gomme. They dried and salted their lamb, and during the summer they picked wild strawberries. When fall came, they roamed through the woods and gathered blueberries and lingonberries. From these, Signe made juice and jam. Since they lived close to the wilderness and were an industrious family, they were better off than many, and shared generously with others.

The war moved steadily closer to their valley. When Jan Baalsrud was brought to the cave in Skaidijonni, Nils Brustrøm became involved with helping him, and he began to disappear from the house at regular intervals. Signe constantly prepared food. Hanna's mother stood by the kitchen counter, which was just about Hanna's eye level, pouring food into the transport pails. Nils took the pails and skied up into the valley, sometimes toward the south, other times toward the east up the mountainside, and now and again he crossed the fields straight toward the steep mountain to the west of the valley. It was all a decoy to fool anyone who might see him. The food and provisions were taken to Jan in the cave.

Nils was among the group of helpers that regularly visited Jan with food and other supplies. He was an energetic and happy fellow who loved to tell stories and sing all types of songs both for his family and for Jan. His bright outlook on things was a boon to Jan's sagging spirit and loneliness.

Signe became known as "the cook," since she cooked most of Jan's food. Several other women in the valley helped with the cooking or brought their food to her to be cooked, but Signe prepared it all for transport, and Jan was the grateful recipient. They gave him of the best they had, soups made from fish, dried meat, salted lamb, milk and homemade breads.

Jan expressed concern to his helpers that he was taking the food away from the children and that he would be happy with fiskesø, the water that the fish was cooked in. They assured him they had enough to go around.

The helpers liked to have two men go together for safety, but sometimes Nils went by himself. During those times he spent a little extra time visiting with Jan. They talked about family and the news of the war and everyday things. From time to time Nils and the other helpers brought Jan ukeblader, weekly magazines, or books to shorten the hours when he was alone. And Nils taught Jan some lively songs, making their times together memorable.

Typically the trip up and back from the cave took about four hours from the Brustrøm house. For safety the trips were most often taken late in the evening, and these excursions often lasted the whole night through.

It was rough and dangerous terrain and provisions hampered their progress occasionally. Usually the helpers took a path close along the out-of-the-way river until they reached just below the cave, where they secured their skis in the snow by the river's edge, then climbed the steep slope up to the cave.

Jan always looked forward to hearing the helpers call out the password, "Hello Gentleman!"

"Hello, hello!"

He was armed since he never knew who might be calling on him. When he heard someone coming he became tense and alert. One could never be sure that the enemy had not followed and spied on his helpers. Jan's gun was beginning to rust because of his swim in the salt water at Toftefjord.

"Nils what are the chances that you can restore this gun?"

"I would think they are pretty good," Nils winked at his friend. He took it home, cleaned and polished the gun and brought it back. Jan's happy countenance when he saw the gun was reward enough for Nils.

"Tusen, tusen takk!" Thousands and thousands of thanks!

When Jan's helpers left, he listened to the last sound of their movements until the stillness of the vast wilderness blended with his own solitude. The sounds of the wind rustling the trees around the cave and the Manndalen River babbling below lightened his burden. A fondness for the place and its people was kindled and Jan felt a new desire to live emerge from somewhere deep within.

Jan had a lot of time to think and often rehashed the events which led to Brattholm's mission.

Jan thought of what a difference Eskeland, Blindheim, Salvesen, and he could have made toward the war effort with their planned sabotage actions against the German installations had they not been betrayed. The soldier wanted another chance to fight the Germans. He had to get to Sweden and then back to England. He was beginning to trust that the Manndalen people would be able to get him the rest of the way to freedom, and then he would fight again.

The Germans had an inkling that secret activities were taking place in the inner Troms District, but they had never been able to pin them down. Periodically they sat for hours in secluded areas with their binoculars, scouting for fugitives on their way to Sweden.

One morning, German soldiers crowded into the little Brustrøm house in the upper Manndalen Valley. They had come to arrest Nils but he had gone to take food to Jan with Olav Fossum. When the soldiers spoke to the children in broken Norwegian, the children pretended to not understand them. Signe was told to go and milk the cows. She protested and said they had been milked a short while ago and that there was no more milk. One of the officers reached for his gun belt. Signe grabbed a pail and ran down by the fence to milk the cows. The Germans drank the unstrained hot milk as fast as she could milk it. She was forced to pull the udders until every drop of milk was gone and the animals became fidgety.

Olav's father, Ole, was visiting the Brustrøm farm. In the confusion, he slipped away unnoticed on horseback. He galloped along the river until he reached the valley floor where he knew Nils and Olaf would be returning. On a piece of birch bark he wrote, either in Sami or Finnish, a warning that the Germans were approaching. Nils and Olav discovered the bark and hid in the thick forest. A short while later they heard the Germans as they passed them on the way up the valley. The Germans never returned to look for Nils.

To secure food for Jan every day and to bring him clean and dry clothes was a big operation. His helpers felt that it was important that they stay awhile to break the monotony for him. All involved had their assigned work. They were careful not to send the same people through the valley every day, eliminating the cause for suspicion.

Not only did the men in Manndalen contribute to Jan's welfare but the women did as well. In addition to Helene Mikalsen, who wove the coverlets for Jan, and Signe Brustrøm, who became known as the "cook," there was Eliva, who later married Peder Isaksen. She was a courageous and trustworthy woman who knew about the operation all along and supported the men, as well as helped to obtain food and to cook.

And there were Marie Olsen, Olaf Olsen's sister, and Marie Holm down in Samuelsberg, a small hamlet in Manndalen. She and her husband had run a small grocery store together. When he died, she continued on alone. She was a tremendous help in gaining access to groceries so that the women could prepare food for Jan.

Together with several other women, they all participated in this dangerous work, always performed in secret. A slip of the tongue, one false move, and all their work could unravel before their eyes. The whole village could be burned to the ground.

Isak Solvang

Peder Pedersen

Marie Fossen Olsen

Nils Nilsen

Marie Holm

Eliva (Hansen) Isaksen

At left: Helene Mikalsen and her three children, Magne, Anton and Ella.

At right: The Nilsen brothers. From left: Nigo, Ole and Hans.

THE SHERIFF'S ASSISTANTS

LYNGSEIDET, MAY 1943: The tranquil village of Lyngseidet reposes amidst small farms and mountain slopes on three sides; to the west it fringes Lyngenfjord. It is the largest and most populated village in the area, and until the war, a place where tourists loved to come.

During the war, Lyngseidet swarmed with Germans. They were quartered at the village's two schools.

While Jan lay hidden in the cave at Skaidijonni, knowledge of him and the activities surrounding him had somehow seeped out. No one to this day knows how it came about.

Nonetheless, one day during May 1943, a black-clad lady was aboard one of the local ferries writing a letter. When finished, she quickly sealed and stamped it and dropped it in the ferry's mailbox.

The next day a letter arrived at the sheriff's office in Lyngseidet. Three men worked in the office – the sheriff, who was a Nazi, and his assistants, Halvard Halden and Hans Larsen.

On this particular day the sheriff was out of the office when the mail arrived. The two assistants noted the letter that had no return

Halvard Halden, one of the sheriff's assistants

address and had been posted on the ferry. They became suspicious and discussed back and forth how to handle it.

Halvard asked, "What shall we do with this letter?"

"Let's open it," said Hans.

DEFIANT COURAGE

"You know the consequences?"
"Jaja. Open it!"
Carefully they opened the letter and removed it contents. They huddled together. It read:

Dear Sheriff,

I want to inform you of a happening in Manndalen, which should be of great interest to you.

Somewhere in the Skaidijonni Mountains, I have been told, a wounded English soldier lies in a cave. Several men and women in Manndalen are nursing him back to health. Daily they take turns bringing him food and provisions.

I believe I know who some of them are and will be happy to share this information with you.

Sincerely,

Fru........................

The two men fell silent and still.
"The sheriff must not see this letter," said Halvard.
"You're absolutely right!" answered Hans.
"Let's take a moment to get our wits about us."
It was a rather chilly day and the black wood burning stove in the corner crackled cheerfully. The same thought occurred to each of them and they nodded to each other.
"Let's burn it!"
"If we do, we must act as if such a letter never arrived in this office."
"I know nothing."

298

The flames instantly engulfed the letter. Nothing more was heard from the mysterious writer.

The spontaneous, daring decision made by the two patriotic men, Halvard Halden and Hans Larsen, saved Jan Baalsrud and many men and women in Manndalen from certain death. Since so many in Manndalen were involved, many people would have been executed and most likely the village would have been burned to the ground.

Ironically, in the fall of 1944 when the Germans retreated from the Troms District, they followed a "scorched earth" policy. Tore Hauge says in his book, They Burned Our Homes, "No one believed that Manndalen would be burned and it came as a shock to all. But the Germans systematically went to work with their gas cans and matches! Within a few days Manndalen was no more."

The one thing the people of Manndalen could be grateful for, despite the suffering and heartache the people endured, was that no lives were lost. And they had the inner satisfaction of having played a major role in Norway's longest escape story from World War II.

None of Jan's benefactors in Manndalen knew anything about the letter. But they were concerned about people noticing the many trips the helpers made up into the mountains, always with filled knapsacks.

Far up in the valley there lived a man who liked to talk. He freely conversed with anyone on any subject, and especially about things which were not his business. It was obvious to Jan's helpers that he was a dangerous man. One of the resistance men, Ludvik Nilsen, visited his home one day for the purpose of getting this man to keep his mouth shut.

Ludvik Nilsen

"I have learned that you spread rumors about things that are not your business," said Ludvik. "When the sheriff and the Germans come to question you, I am telling you here and now what you are to say. Listen carefully, and then repeat after me verbatim. If you say as much as one word that I have not instructed you, I will return with some men. Your days will be numbered!"

An angry Ludvik dictated, and the man repeated sentence after sentence, verbatim. The man clearly understood what Ludvik meant.

In spite of all the careful planning, the rumors of all the trips the men in the village were making further up into Manndalen still reached Sheriff Marvold's ears in Birtavärre from other sources. Sheriff's assistant Hans Larsen was asked to make the trip across the fjord to Manndalen to try and find the cause of the rumors. According to the rumors, Peder Isaksen was one who had to be investigated.

Hans Larsen came to Peder's home. "Do you know Aslak Fossvoll, Peder Isaksen?"

"Yes, I know Aslak, at least well enough so that when we meet, we visit for a minute or two."

"I have heard that the two of you go into the mountains from time to time. I am not sure what you do up in the mountains, but I assume that you are hunting for the mentally ill man that disappears in the mountains from time to time? Is that right?"

Hans Larsen was a good man and did not want Peder to get in any trouble. Hans was suspicious that Peder was involved in something top-secret, but he tried to help him out of the tough spot by planting another thought in his mind.

"You are right," Peder said. "We continually have to go hunting for the deranged man that disappears all the time."

The sheriff's assistant was satisfied. Once again he had saved Manndalen from a catastrophe.

The village buzzed with whispered rumors. Some guessed some things were going on, others knew. The situation worsened when two quislings from Lyngseidet arrived a couple of days after the sheriff's assistant had been in Manndalen. They came hunting fugitives. They requisitioned a horse down in the valley and started on their way.

What could have been a bad day for Manndalen gave the village people a story to chuckle over for some time.

A young girl was coming down the road, and the quislings asked her for directions to one of the people they planned to interrogate.

"Don't ask me. I don't know anything. I am just a child," the girl said and skipped away.

Next they met an elderly lady on her way to the store. They stopped her and asked if she knew an Olav Olsen. He had escaped from a German camp in Skibotn.

"No. I have lived in this village all my life, but I am not familiar with that name."

The woman was Olav Olsen's mother.

The men continued upwards into the valley and came to a small farm where a man was sawing wood. On one of his feet he had a boot and on the other a kommag, a soft boot made of reindeer hide and worn by the Sami. The man was known in the village as a man who was a little confused and muddled.

"We understand you have several sons. Where are they?" the quislings asked.

"Ja, I have five sons, and they have all escaped to Sweden. Soon I will follow them." The man was a bachelor and did not have any children.

The men continued up into the valley to find the man who was the easy talker (the same man whom Ludvik Nilsen had visited with a warning). The man himself was not home, but his wife was. The quislings asked when she expected him home.

"That man is crazy, and there is no reason to question him," she said. "He just talks nonsense, and he can be real dangerous if he is pressed. If you're wise you will think twice before you interrogate him," she continued.

The quislings decided to call it a day. They returned the horse to the owner and they confided to him that they thought most of the people in Manndalen were screwballs.

The Brustrøm's home

*The old wood-burning stove on which
Signe Brustrøm cooked Jan's meals*

DO NOT ASK ME THIS

FOLLOWING ONE of his pleasant visits with Jan, Nils Brustrøm was about to leave the cave.

"What can I bring you the next time I come, Jan?"

"I am remembering Signe's delicious fish soup, maybe with a couple of nibbles of meat?"

"No problem."

"And..." For a split second Jan hesitated.

"Yes Jan? You know we will try and do anything for you."

Jan looked at him pensively.

"Will you cut my rotten toes off?"

Nils' face paled. His mind raced. Speech left him. He just stared at this ill, suffering man who needed help. He weighed it all in his mind. Several times. Quietly he spoke up.

"Oh, Jan! You know I'll do anything for you. But please... don't ask me this. I don't have the heart."

"It's okay. But you'll bring me a sharp sheath knife then?"

"I'll do it."

Nils reflected upon the reason Jan wanted a sharp knife while he plodded homeward along the river. He had no problems guessing how he would use it. Jan soon had both his wishes fulfilled. Nils brought both the delicious fish soup and the sheath knife on his next visit.

Jan devoured the soup with gusto. Both Nils and the other Manndalen men had noticed how Jan, almost imperceptibly, was gradually gaining strength and becoming healthier and more jovial every day. Nils watched him with satisfaction. It was good to see their labors paying off with such a meaningful dividend, though they all realized he was still a very sick man.

Their friendly visit ended, and when Nils parted with Jan, he left the sharp knife.

On his way down from the mountain Nils spotted a German patrol coming up the valley. How could he get out of this tight spot? There was no easy way to explain what errand he had been on - and what about his tracks? He grappled for a solution.

The war had taught Nils to be extremely resourceful. Quickly he removed his knapsack and the transport pail and buried them in a snow heap. He owned a small section of the forest and he started searching for a nice size willow tree. Finding one, he chopped it down, tied it to the rope he always carried with him, and dragged it behind him erasing his own ski tracks. Then he set his path straight in the direction of the Germans.

They saw him coming and the lieutenant raised his arm and signaled him to stop.

"What is your errand here in the woods?" he questioned in broken Norwegian.

Nils smiled with questioning eyes as he studied them. He turned and looked at the tree then turned back and looked at them. Pointing to the tree, and acting somewhat amazed at the question, Nils said, "Surely, you can see for yourselves? I am bringing some nourishment to my sheep. They love the willow bark."

The Germans huddled together in conversation. Nils grew concerned. He could see they were suspicious. A thought hit him like a lightning bolt.

"Follow me to my farm if you have doubts. It is close by. Then you may see for yourself."

The Germans joined him as he moved further down in the valley, away from Jan's cave and toward the Brustrøm farm. Nils gloated inside, thinking what a curious sight they made – him dragging a willow tree and behind him following seven German soldiers on skis with their rifles hung loosely over their shoulders.

Once back at the farm, Nils removed the rope and cut some of the branches off the tree. Luckily for him the sheep gathered quickly as he spread the limbs out on the ground. They wasted no time before they nibbled at the boughs.

"Sehr gut, sehr gut!" Very good, Very good!

The Germans' suspicions had been laid to rest.

UP IN the cave Jan made the final plans for his self-operation. What he had started at Hotel Savoy he was about to finish here in the cave in Skaidijonni. As he laid in the open in Avzevaggi, he realized from the feelings in his feet and the stench that the rest of his toes were rotting away. At that time though, Jan was too ill to do anything. He had neither the physical strength nor the unswerving mental resolve needed for such a task.

Over the last few days, though, Jan had been well nursed and fed, and his friends came up from the valley at regular intervals. He was comfortable in his dry bed, and he gained courage and strength from his caring friends. To feel the joy of life return was a source of great encouragement to him. As a result, Jan's basic human character traits also returned.

He clearly understood that the rotten tissue could infect his toes, and this could spread to his lymph glands and cause blood poisoning. He was also fully aware that if blood poisoning set in while he lay here in the cave far away from a doctor's care, he would die.

He knew exactly what to do. Jan had had plenty of time to plan the amputation during the long hours of solitude. He picked up the sharp knife Nils left and started his self-operation anew.

He removed seven toes down by the main joint. The eighth he cut off at the middle joint. The rotten, dead tissue was loosely attached to the knucklebones and just fell off as Jan touched the toes. He was relieved to see the bleeding was not as heavy this time.

Through his ordeals, Jan had become like tempered steel. His conviction that his operation had saved his life strengthened him and left him at peace with himself.

He wrapped his foot in the old rags the men had already brought to the cave and which they used when they changed the bandages on his foot.

Exhausted, Jan lay back on his bed of birch branches. He covered himself up with the wool covering Helene had woven for him. It comforted him.

During the quiet moments that followed, his mind wandered backward in time, which it so often did at these times of solitude. The saboteurs' mission to stop the German bombing of the convoys to the Soviet Union had failed. Jan sorrowed over the many additional crews who by now had probably lost their lives because of it. When he contemplated the failed mission, his fallen comrades always came to mind. Remembering them, his whole being mourned.

It was unavoidable for Jan to think of his comrades without his thoughts drifting homeward to his family and friends in Oslo. What he would not give to just have one word from them, just to know that they were safe. Missing them, his brother Nils and his sister Bitten, made his solitude especially agonizing.

As he lay distressing, he earnestly sought to cope with his physical pain, sorrow and isolation. As so often before, Jan became aware of the wind rustling the trees on the mountainside near to the cave and the murmuring river at the valley bottom – and his spirit calmed.

THE GERMANS IN PURSUIT

NEARLY TWO weeks had passed since Hjalmar and Nils' unsuccessful attempt to find Jan.

One evening, Petter Pettersen, an employee at the Bjørns' store, came to Hjalmar with another urgent message for him to meet the brothers at their store. He learned that Jan had been moved to the east side of lower Manndalen Valley, and he was still awaiting transport.

"Will you be willing to take on the assignment one more time?"

"Of course I will." Hjalmar was not a man to say no when he was needed.

That same night he was on his way up Ankerlia Mountain, staying hidden in the forest behind the German hut. On his last trip he had concealed his skis above the tree line. The snow on the mountainside was wet and heavy, but on the upland the ski conditions were good. He needed to reach the Siri brothers before sun-up, and he only stopped once to rest.

Per and Nils Siri greeted him with the usual Sami friendliness. Nils expressed concern about taking on the assignment to transport Jan this late in the season. The ice on the river bordering Sweden was no longer safe and the road above Kilpis in Finland lay wide open for long stretches. Several German military movements had been seen from time to time.

"I recently crossed over to Sweden with seven fugitives," Hjalmar explained. "We were told the Germans military movements usually come in convoys, and far between."

"Well, let's get a map out and see how we can do this then," Nils ventured.

They mapped the route across occupied Norway and Finland and on into neutral Sweden. Out of necessity they sometimes had to cross the wide-open spaces, but whenever possible, they mapped the way through thickets and shrubs.

Nothing but the strongest and fastest reindeer would do. Their trained eyes picked out two of the best among the many.

Early in the morning they harnessed the reindeer to the pulk, and each man crawled into his canoe-shaped sled. With good snow conditions holding, they made excellent time and were ahead of schedule. They even had time to eat and relax a little while the reindeer grazed along the way. As they neared the plateau above Manndalen, a flock of about thirty reindeer and some men came into view in the distance. They hurried onward to see who it might be.

Coming closer, they noticed two Sami sleds. The men were running back and forth into the tent. One man in one of the sleds seemed to be getting all the attention. Hjalmar stopped a little ways off while Nils continued on so he could talk with the men. The sled with the man who had drawn all the attention was put in the center of the reindeer flock. Another Sami climbed into the pulk with him. Then the entourage of sleds, reindeer and barking dogs began to move.

Somewhat bewildered, Nils returned to Hjalmar to explain.

"One of the men in those sleds is Jan Baalsrud. Aslak and Per Thomas Baal are bringing him to Sweden."

Nils and Hjalmar were astounded. Extremely disappointed, after their best efforts, their many hours of struggles came to naught. Yet in the midst of their discontent they were gratified that Jan had been taken care of and was on his way to Sweden.

The friends shook hands and said farewell to one another. Nils took the reindeer and the sleds and headed east, and Hjalmar noticed the early morning glow of the sun as he attached his skis and headed for home.

Before reaching Kåfjordalen Valley he hid his skis among the trees in Ankerlia Mountain and trudged the rest of the way home. His mother awoke as he entered. By the time he had cleaned up and changed into clean clothes, his mother had breakfast ready for him. He shared the happenings of the last few hours with her and then went to bed in his room in the attic.

Hjalmar had no sooner pulled the covers up when he heard the sound of a motorcycle. It puzzled him. There were connecting roads between Kåfjorddalen to Birtavärre, but none to Olderdalen. Whoever the visitor was, he must have come by boat and motorcycled from the docks up to his home. Hjalmar jumped out of bed and ran to the window. He stiffened as he saw a motorcycle with a sidecar. Two German soldiers walked toward the house and another stood watch by the motorcycle.

Hjalmar jumped into his clothes, grabbed the inner works of the Tandberg battery-super-radio and stuffed it in his jacket. Downstairs loud German voices mingled with his mother's calm voice. Concerned the old floor would creak, he stood as if nailed to the floor for a few seconds. Like a prowling cat, he moved quietly down the steps toward the first floor. His mother and the Germans were now in the living room and he snuck out the front door where the third soldier still held his gun ready by the motorcycle. Though Hjalmar's body felt like a tightrope, he nonchalantly walked toward the barn, hid the radio works in the corner of one of the horse stalls and kicked some hay over it. He came back out and again moved unhurriedly toward the summer barn that lay 120 feet closer to the edge of the forest. While walking this distance, he was within open view of the German guard. He continued in the direction of the forest and sprinted toward the trees as fast as he was able. In the outlying fields there was a hay barn well hidden by the trees. He prepared himself a bed in the hay. Lying there he finally began to relax and fell asleep.

After many hours of sleep he awoke in the middle of the night. His thoughts wandered and he realized what peril he had been in. Had he been arrested and brought in for interrogation and torture, the whole Baalsrud affair might have unraveled. He shuddered at the ghastly circumstances that would have followed, and how many people might have suffered.

His concern grew as he thought of his mother. Had the Germans arrested her? He left the hay barn and carefully moved from the forest toward the farmyard staying extremely alert to his surroundings. He crawled through a window in the back of the house and found his mother still in bed.

The Germans had ransacked every room in the house including the attic. They had opened every closet and searched through every drawer.

"Who else lives here?" the Germans asked.

"I have a husband and a son, but both have been called to work for the Germans in the district of Finnmark (the neighboring district). They very seldom get leave to come home," Hjalmar's mother had told them.

Hjalmar shared the experience of his escape and how he had slept in the summer barn. His mother had only one comment, "The one God wants to preserve is without danger."

Hjalmar knew the only way the Germans had been able to come to Kåfjord with the motorcycle was by boat. He also realized there must have been rumors about Jan Baalsrud and that someone had revealed that Hjalmar had a part in the affair. It was obvious that they had come to pick him up. For now he had been able to escape, and Jan Baalsrud was on his way toward safety in Sweden. Once again, Jan's benefactors were a step ahead of the Gestapo.

EN ROUTE TO FREEDOM

JAN HAD been in the Skaidijonni cave for seventeen days. In Avzevaggi his life had hung by a fragile thread. The intent of the people of Manndalen had been to nurture him back to a better physical condition. They never wavered in their purpose, but they gave so much more. Daily the men trudged the five miles through the rugged snow-covered terrain to bring him nourishing food prepared lovingly by their women, dry clothes, medical supplies, and reading material. More importantly, they brought him the commodity he needed most of all, the comfort and warmth of their own spirits. They nurtured him back to life by giving him of their time, friendship and their selfless love.

It was now the end of May, and time was running out. The warmth of the midnight sun was melting the snow cover. Jan had to be moved before the good snow conditions disappeared.

Manndalen, Thursday, May 28, 1943: Without notice, a man appeared in the lower Kjerringdal Valley in Manndalen. He was Aslak Baal, one of the two Sami brothers whom Nigo had contacted on his 80 mile round trip to Sweden on May 5.

Aslak's brother, Per Thomas, had remained up on the plateau making ready to bring the soldier across the border. They believed they had found a way to fool the German border guards and were now willing to take the risk to bring Jan to Sweden.

Sami Aslak Baal

Five men, Aslak Fossvoll, Nigo Nilsen, Hans Nilsen, Isak Solvang and Nils Brustrøm

Sami Per Thomas Baal

made their way up to Jan's cave during the night of May 28. They carried long ropes to help them with the steep climb to take Jan up to the plateau to meet the Baal brothers. Jan had little desire to leave the safety of the cave and the comfort of his friends' love to face another horrendous climb and uncertainty up on the plateau.

"Is it possible to postpone the leaving a day or two?" he asked.

"Jan this is your chance for freedom. We have to grab it."

Jan knew his friends were right, and he mustered his courage. "I'm ready."

They carried him out to the waiting sled, and again he was securely strapped down.

The memory of the prior suffering he had endured on the sled was still vivid. Jan did his best not to let the others know the fear that abruptly gripped him and nearly overwhelmed him.

The exhausting climb took several hours and morning had dawned when they reached the plateau. Three of the Manndalen men felt the need to leave right away, because all were concerned that someone would start to ask too many questions. The emotional farewell was difficult for all of them.

"The day we hear you are safely in Sweden will be a special day for all of us here in Manndalen, Jan."

"Thank you. I am looking forward to it, but I will miss all of you good people."

They tried to be jovial. "All the women wanted to come up to the plateau to see you off. But we felt someone needed to mind our homes and the youngsters." Everyone laughed.

"Take care, Jan. We're going to miss you dreadfully."

"After this atrocious war is over, you've got to come back to Troms. We'll throw a party out in the open!"

"I look forward to that. How do I thank all of you? Please take care and be safe," said Jan. His voice trembled with emotion. As he said farewell to his rescuers, his eyes grew moist. These people had given so much to him, a stranger. They had given him shelter and food. And they'd given him friendship and hope.

"You too, dear friend. Have a safe journey." They all shook his hand. Jan was unable to do anything but whisper, "Tusen, tusen...tusen takk," Thousands and thousands and thousands of thanks.

The men started down toward Manndalen.

May 29, 1943: Jan remained in the mountains with Aslak Baal, Nils Brustrøm and Nigo Nilsen.

Per Thomas went to gather the reindeer flock. The reindeer would follow Jan all the way to the border. Jan would be hidden in the midst of them and the animals would be his shield and erase the tracks from his pulk.

During the night, Jan was brought into the Baal's laavo, their Sami tent, to get some good sleep before the final journey.

Saturday, May 30, 1943: In the early morning hours, Aslak and Per Thomas Baal dressed Jan in the traditional Sami fur winter clothing with its bright colorful trimmings of red, yellow, white and cornflower blue. They placed a Sami hat on his head; typical of the Finnish and Norwegian Sami, with four floppy points, it was known as the "hat of the four winds."

The vast white tundra stretched out before them. Jan was tense and fearful that the German patrols would discover them.

"Don't you worry, Jan. We will get you safely to Sweden this time."

Aslak and Per Thomas had their carbine rifles hidden at the bottom of their pulks.

"If the Germans should approach us, would you use that gun, Aslak?"

"Absolutely! I will not only shoot, but I will hit my mark as well. Remember, I have been shooting reindeer for years."

"If you should have to kill some Germans and you returned safely to Norway, are you not afraid they will come chasing you?"

"Maybe so, but don't forget Jan, we live in the mountains a lot."

Around 2 a.m. on May 31, the men placed Jan, too ill to manage a pulk by himself, with Per Thomas. The men left their encampment and headed south. At this time of the night the snow was at its firmest and they could make better time. The midnight sun had returned to northern Norway on May 21 and would not set again until July. There was no darkness.

Sitting low in his pulk, with Per Thomas, Jan was surrounded by reindeer nostrils snorting hot breath at top speed. The reindeer spread their sure feet wide. Close to Jan's head, their pounding hooves whipped the snow into a small blizzard. Above the snow Jan saw nothing but bouncing reindeer horns, which resembled thick bare tree branches enduring a snowstorm.

The first stretch of their journey brought them to Didnojarvi Lake, about midway between the Manndalen plateau and the Swedish border. They rested here and gathered a few roots to build a fire for their black coffee pot. They also heated up some broth that they enjoyed with some heavy rye bread. The entourage had been able to maintain a nice speed, making good time and they decided to rest out the day in the higher elevation.

Up on the highest plateau, the snow conditions were best and they had a good overview of their surroundings. The reindeer would have a chance to rest and eat before the final push across the border. They expected to cross into Sweden under good conditions in the early morning hours. The men reasoned they had about another four hours or so to travel before they reached the border.

The sun had been dazzling throughout their journey, making the snow crystals sparkle like highly polished diamonds. The unending white upland shimmered. When Aslak gathered roots for the fire for late afternoon-coffee he suddenly went snow blind. The intense pain made him unable to scoop up the snow for the coffee pot. Jan knew well what his friend was experiencing and was filled with empathy.

The three men discussed this new development. Per Thomas said if they were going to get Jan across the border, they had to continue as planned, and leave Aslak behind. Per Thomas would come for him on the way back. Aslak fully agreed, though Jan felt terrible about the situation.

June 1, 1943: The next morning at two, Jan and Per Thomas readied to leave. The snow conditions were holding good and the wind was tolerable. This close to the Finnish border they were nearing the danger zone. The German patrols were stationed within close vicinity of each other and they were on the alert for fugitives.

It was a difficult time for Jan in light of the physical suffering and loneliness he had endured during the last two months, and all that his helpers had sacrificed. Would it now all come to naught as they neared the border?

"Per Thomas, if the Germans come, we cannot, under any circumstances, be taken prisoners." Jan fondled his gun.

"I understand. Take my gun Jan, it is better than yours." He dug out the carbine rifle from the bottom of his pulk, and they exchanged weapons.

"And here is my knife. It is sharp and will cut straight through!" He handed Jan the knife.

The men agreed that if a situation should arise where there was no hope for them, Jan should first shoot Per Thomas and then himself. With mixed feelings Jan and Per Thomas left Aslak behind. A mixture of emotions swept over all three of them. They were so close, and yet they could not predict what the next few hours held in store for them.

"På gjensyn," so long, a somber Jan waved, but Aslak could not see.

Coming from the east, they continued south down Sørhellinga toward the lower plateau. In the early morning the reindeer herd reached Lake Coahppejåvri where they stopped for their last rest near the Finnish border. They left the reindeer herd. From here on it would only be Per Thomas and Jan in the one pulk and three of the strongest and fastest reindeer bucks. The third reindeer was brought in case an accident should happen to one of the others.

The two men descended around the Saana Mountain's extended valley. Lake Kilpisjårvi, the last stretch of the crossover to Sweden, was in sight. The men's nerves were taut. Only a few miles to freedom, surely they would make it now. Per Thomas bore down on the bucks; they whizzed headlong across the snow.

Shots rang out!

Again and again the shots flew through the air. Jan twisted around to get a look. "They will never catch us Per Thomas, they are too far behind!"

"May you be right!"

Per Thomas walloped the reindeer with his whip and they lurched forward at breakneck speed.

They came out by Saamivaarat on the Finnish side of the border. A short distance away flowed a brook with a bridge crossing over.

"The Germans have a patrol station close to that bridge," Per Thomas shouted over the pounding hooves.

The Germans, some distance behind them, kept firing as they sped across the snow. "They're lousy skiers!" Per Thomas shouted. He had observed the guards skiing on previous trips.

He set course for the frozen Lake Kilpisjårvi and whooshed onto and over a narrow protruding headland. Another short distance on the lake and they would be in Sweden.

"Freedom! Freedom Jan! You are right, they could not catch us!"

Overwrought with emotion, Jan covered his face in the fur raiment. His body trembled.

PER THOMAS took Jan to the home of his Sami friends, the brothers Per and Aslak Juhso in Kommavopio, Sweden. From here the brothers took him to Sweden's northernmost farm in Keinovopio, where the August Jensen family warmly received him. These hospitable people had helped many a fugitive in the past.

Jan was tended and fed before he was placed in a sleeping bag, lifted into a riverboat, and carefully tied down. The boat rode low in the water and they wanted him secure. Two men sat in the bow and two in the stern; each rowed with one oar. They followed the river along the Finnish border-river Konkama down to Saarikoski. The rowers had a difficult time maneuvering the strong current between the ice floe and rocks. Jan did not like this trip; he felt uneasy tied down and unable to move. After all he had experienced, he feared that this river trip would not have a happy ending.

The boat made its way through many obstacles until it reached Saarikoski, where the Konkama River widened and turned into a narrow lake. A seaplane had been called in and was on its way. The frozen-over river had to be cleared of ice to enable the plane to land.

Dr. Englund from Vittange, Sweden had been brought in earlier to watch over Jan and he stayed with him while several men worked to keep the ice from closing in.

The plane came in low, landed without mishap and Jan was put aboard. The men had to work quickly - the river was icing up fast and all involved were nervous. A disaster seemed imminent. But the pilot, Norberg, was well seasoned and he pulled the plane up at the last second. He and his navigator, Arne Sundquist, flew to Boden in northwest Sweden, where an ambulance was waiting.

Boden Gardisjon Hospital was under blackout during the night because of the war in neighboring Norway. Nurse Barbro Morin was on duty. A message had preceded Jan, that a fugitive in critical condition would be brought in from Norway sometime during the night.

Jan was lifted from the ambulance onto a stretcher and hurriedly wheeled through the hospital doors down the long, dim corridor. A kerosene lamp burned at the end of the corridor. Barbro Morin watched as Jan was

Nurse Barbro Morin

rolled through the doors. He was lying on his back with his arms under his head. Weary and thin with an ashen face, his long coal-black beard nearly covered all his face but his eyes. He lay there smiling. His chalk-white teeth nearly lit up the corridor.

A robust young soldier when he landed in northern Norway two months earlier, Jan now weighed only 80 pounds.

The attendants unraveled the rags that Jan's feet were wrapped in. Next was a layer of newspapers, a layer of reindeer hair and another layer of newspaper. The stench from his feet nauseated those in attendance. Nurse Barbro and the other hospital personnel were concerned about inflicting pain on Jan as they removed the bandages, but Jan never complained. He only smiled and showed gratitude.

"Don't worry, you won't hurt me."

The condition of his feet was horrid. The putrid smell nearly overwhelmed the nurses. A surgeon with special knowledge in gangrene and transplantation was called in. All were under the watchful eye of Dr. Torben, the hospital's Medical Director. Jan's feet and legs were darkish-blue up to his knees, and his hands were in danger of needing amputation as well, as their color matched his legs and feet.

The doctors told Jan they did not know if they could manage to save his hands and feet, but they would do all they could. They removed as little as possible, then they had to wait and see. The wounds left on the toes Jan himself had amputated were cleaned and trimmed, making them ready for new skin transplantation. Skin from the inside of his thighs was removed to cover the protruding bones on his toes. They healed well and Jan was able to keep the remainder of his feet without further amputation.

"Jan, we had to burn your clothes. They were so filthy they would be impossible to clean. I apologize," the surgeon said when he returned the following day.

"By the way, Baalsrud, while I am here, who amputated your toes? That is one of the finest surgeries I have ever seen."

"Thanks, doctor. I was the surgeon," Jan smiled broadly while the doctor looked at him in stunned silence.

The Swedish police came to question Jan, but the medical director refused because the patient was too weak. Jan was given two weeks, and during this period he prepared his story. The last time he was in Sweden he had been asked to leave and he now decided to tell his story as it was. In the meantime he called the Norwegian consulate in Stockholm and let them know one man from M/K Brattholm had survived.

During the several weeks Jan recuperated in the Swedish hospital, he faced many emotional struggles. He yearned for his family, yet he could not call them in occupied Norway. Jan also missed his deceased buddies, and often he thought of the many people in Troms who'd helped save his life.

The appreciation he felt for what the Manndalen men and women had done for him held no bounds. Often, in the solitude of the quiet evenings in his hospital bed, he remembered their many kind deeds and words, and their faces came to him one by one – Peder, Nigo, Nils, Olaf. He thought of the many women who had prepared his meals; he might never know who they all were.

Afterward his mind wandered to his dear friends in Furuflaten, Marius, Alvin, Agnete, Ingeborg, Gudrun and all the others who had risked their lives for him.

And then he remembered his fallen comrades again and the horrors that had taken place in Toftefjord - and he anguished.

Even in Toftefjord helping hands had been outstretched toward him, the Idrupsens and the Pedersens. Jan retraced his steps through the mountains and remembered the Heikas and the stalwart Sørensen men, the Løvlis, and dear Peder Nielsen who carried him on his back. And the Samis Aslak and Per Thomas Baal who had snatched him right out of the Germans' grip and gotten him to Sweden.

The list was overwhelming. His heart swelled with gratitude and he cried soundlessly for the love and selflessness that these people had shown him, a total stranger. These stalwart people had risked their own lives and families and their villages and had shared all they had. How could he ever repay them?

The people of Troms had proven to him that evil could never conquer goodness. Hitler's might and the power of his armies, and the horrors of their brutality, were no match against such people. Evil did not have the muscle to crush the goodness and the decency of the people of northern Norway. Jan had seen freedom in their eyes.

In the end, as all through the world's history, he now knew of a surety, that the light of freedom would burst forth to dispel the darkness covering Norway. The land and its people, and all the other lands under the Nazi heel would rise again to the sounds of freedom.

Jan had learned firsthand from these simple, courageous people that evil can never be gruesome enough to chill the love of freedom, nor to stifle the inborn love for our fellow man.

Yes, We Love this Land
As It Rises
Furrowed, Weathered,
O'er The Sea with
The Thousand Homes...

Bjørnstjerne Bjørnson
Norway's National Anthem

EPILOGUE

JAN BAALSRUD'S story did not end when he reached freedom in Sweden.

The war's scars stayed with many of those involved throughout the rest of their lives, especially Jan. He had bouts of depression and nightmares, but Jan, determined and courageous, fought back.

When he returned to the Shetland Islands following his convalescence in Sweden, Jan taught marksmanship to the men of the Linge Company. At war's end, he returned to Norway in the Bergen area, and was involved in taking over the Russian prison camps from the Germans. In September of 1945 he left the Navy.

When Jan's fallen comrades were taken home to their final resting places, Jan traveled to be with each one of them as they were laid to rest.

In 1947 Jan and others originated The Linge Club, and became its first president, a position he held for many years. He was the first honorary

Jan in the Shetland Islands teaching marksmanship

member of Den Norske Krigs Invalid Forbund, the Norwegian War Invalid Confederation, and president of the same for eight years. Jan also served as vice-president of the World Federation of War Veterans for six years.

Jan was actively involved in the establishment of the Bæreia Veteran Recreation Institution for War Invalids at Kongsvinger. He was awarded Norway's St. Olav's Medal and the Most Excellent Order of the British Empire, MBO.

Jan suffered constant pain in his legs and feet after his ordeal in the Arctic. Because of this, he returned to the hospital each winter for treatment. It became apparent that Norway's cold winters were too difficult for him to tolerate, and he searched for a home in a warmer climate.

In 1951, Jan married Evie Miller, a Scottish lady from New York. They had one daughter, Liv. When Liv was five years old, Evie died.

In 1959 Jan married Terese Balmesita, a Spanish woman, and in 1962 they bought a farm on Tenerife, an island off the north African Coast.

Jan and Terese grew oranges on their farm. When Jan turned 50, his brother Nils Ivar and some friends in Norway sent him three sows and a boar and he became a successful hog farmer.

Jan died of cancer at Bæreia on December 30, 1987. Because of his many hours of service to the Institution, he stayed bedridden at Bæreia without cost for four months prior to his death.

Jan's wish was to be buried among his friends in northern Norway. His ashes were taken to Manndalen and buried with Aslak Fossvoll in his grave.

Tor Knudsen and Kaare Moursund, the Tromsø resistance leaders, were sent to a concentration camp in Germany where they both died.

Jernberg Kristiansen and Sedolf Andreassen, the half brothers from Grøtøy Island who offered to store Brattholm's cargo of explosives and other provisions, were tortured and sent to a concentration camp in Germany where they perished.

Edwin Wikan, the policeman who tried to forestall the telephone call about the Brattholm men to the Gestapo, today lives on the outskirts of

Tromsø. During the war, he was among the many Norwegian policemen who refused to bow to Hitler's regime. In August of 1943, he was sent to a German concentration camp near Stutthof, Poland.

Edwin was freed on May 3, 1945, and returned to his work as a policeman in Tromsø. During the late summer of 1945, he was placed in charge of excavating the Brattholm men slain at Grønnåsen Rifle Range.

Peder Nilsen, who in Tyttebærvika waded from the rowboat to the shore with Jan on his back, lives at Herakleum Retirement Home in Tromsø. He is 87 years old.

Following the war, Peder continued his work as a fisherman and a small farmer. He also worked at a fish processing plant until his retirement. After the death of their first son Norman, Peder and his wife had three more children.

On the day of Norway's Liberation, Peder fixed breakfast and brought it to his wife, who was still in bed. That was the first time she learned of Peder's involvement with Jan Baalsrud.

Einar Sørensen, from Bjørnskar, preceded both his wife and father in death. He died on March 24, 1953. Bernhard lived another seven years until February 2, 1960, and Einar's wife Elna lived until June 12, 1990.

Marius Grønvoll and Agnete Lanes married. They had five children and built another house on the Grønvoll farm at Furuflaten. Marius continued to be a leader in his village and went into business with Alvin Larsen. He worked with their company until his death. Agnete still lives at Grønvoll Farm in Furuflaten.

Eliva Hansen and Peder Isaksen were married in October 1943. They had four children. When the Germans scorched the earth in 1944, Peder and Eliva escaped to a mountain cave not far from their home. The Germans did not burn all the homes at the same time. When the Isaksens returned three days later, they found Germans in their home.

One young soldier found the bed that Peder had built very attractive and wanted it. Peder was furious. "That is my bed!" said Peder, as he yanked the linens off and started dismantlingthe bed. He and Eliva wrapped it carefully and took it, with a few other belongings, aboard the ferry which evacuated the Manndalen people.

When Peder and Eliva returned to Manndalen after the war, they rebuilt their home and Peder continued as a fisherman and small farmer. Because he was a skilled carpenter, he spent many years helping to rebuild Manndalen. Today Eliva and Peder, both 80 years old, live in Manndalen.

Alvin Larsen married his sweetheart Erna Lanes in October 1943. They had eight children. He continued fishing until 1952. Circumstances changed dramatically after the war and fishing became less profitable. With his two brothers and Marius Grønvoll, Alvin started his own construction company, working on projects all over northern Norway. According to Alvin, they "wanted to help rebuild Norway and be able to feed their families." At 82 years old, Alvin is the same jovial fellow and lives in Furuflaten with his wife.

Haakon Sørensen, the merchant from Bromnes, was given twelve years at hard labor for his betrayal. His citizenship was revoked for ten years and he was ordered to pay back the 5000 kroner the Gestapo awarded him. Haakon was released after four years in prison. Until his death in 1990, he lived in Bromnes with his wife. They had no children.

For his betrayal, Sheriff Hoel of Karlsøy was sentenced to fourteen years at hard labor. His citizenship was revoked for ten years and he was ordered to return the 500 kroner the Gestapo had given him. Both the merchant and the sheriff were ordered to pay the court costs. Aldor Ingebrigtsen, a member of the parliament, helped to get Sheriff Hoel's sentence appraised and he was freed in 1950, having served less than half his sentence. He was 88 years old when he died in 1975.

JAN BAALSRUD always said, "I am not the hero. The people in Troms are." It was his lifelong wish that all the people who had helped him would be honored. That has been the goal of the co-authors of this book, to honor the unsung heroes of the Troms district. As we do, we are fully aware that there are so many others throughout Norway and the world who willingly sacrifice to help others, and that Jan and his benefactors are only a symbol of those many others.

Jan Baalsrud Foundation
"Many risked their lives and helped
one to freedom"

On June 19, 1989 the Jan Baalsrud Foundation
was organized. Established as a private foundation, it
received public acknowledgement on October 11, 1990
from the Troms District Governor. The foundation is
jointly administered between four municipalities, Kåf-
jord, Storfjord, Karlsøy and Lyngen. Each community
is equally represented in the foundation's leadership
and the general assembly.

Jan's brother Nils Ivar Baalsrud, co-founder of the
foundation, has served either as president and vice-
president since the organization's inception.

The foundation has established Jan Baalsrud-
Marsjen, a permanent and annual re-creation of Jan's
125-mile trek through the mountains, with historical
markers along the route. The Foundation has also
established memorials to the M/K Brattholm *men;*
a stone monument in Toftefjord and a monolith and
memorial birch grove near the University of Tromsø.

MAP 1— Jan's escape route from
Toftefjord to Mikkelvik.

X   *Brattholm* explodes
I   Swim
II   Swim
III   Swim
--- Walking
— By Boat

MAP 2 — Escape route from Toftefjord to Veggefjord toward Karanes

X   *Brattholm* explodes
---   Walking
—   By Boat

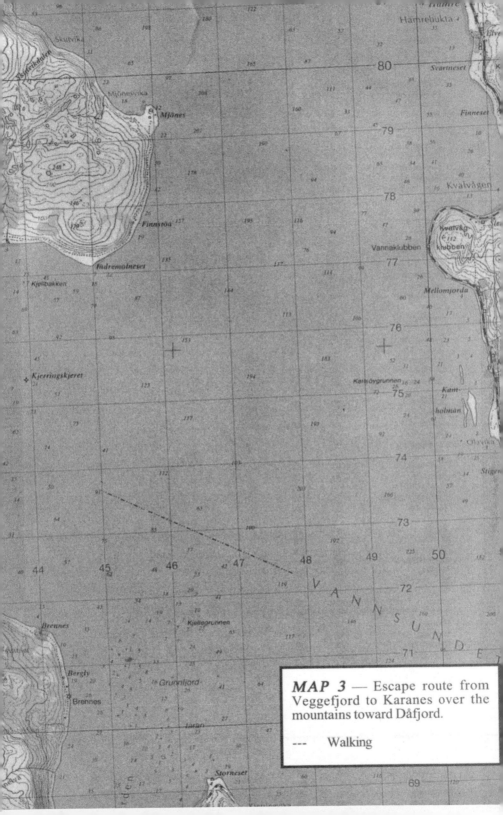

MAP 3 — Escape route from Veggefjord to Karanes over the mountains toward Dåfjord.

--- Walking

MAP 4 — Escape route from the mountains to Dåfjord and continuing over the mountains to Kopparelv.

--- Walking
— By Boat

MAP 5 — Escape route from Kopparelv to Bjørnskar across Grøtsundet Sound to Løvli and into Ullsfjord.

---   Walking
—   By Boat

MAP 6 — Escape route from Ullsfjord to Tyttebærvika on to Lyngseidet and up into the mountains.

--- Walking
— By Boat

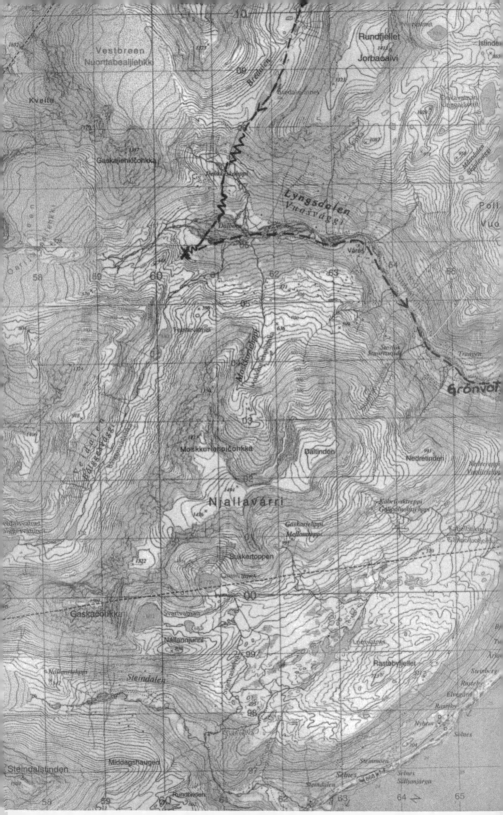

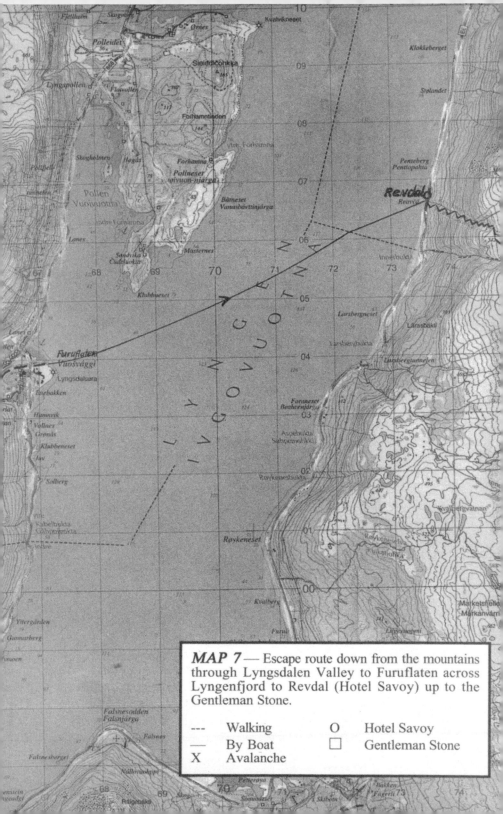

MAP 7 — Escape route down from the mountains through Lyngsdalen Valley to Furuflaten across Lyngenfjord to Revdal (Hotel Savoy) up to the Gentleman Stone.

- - -   Walking   O   Hotel Savoy
——   By Boat   □   Gentleman Stone
X   Avalanche

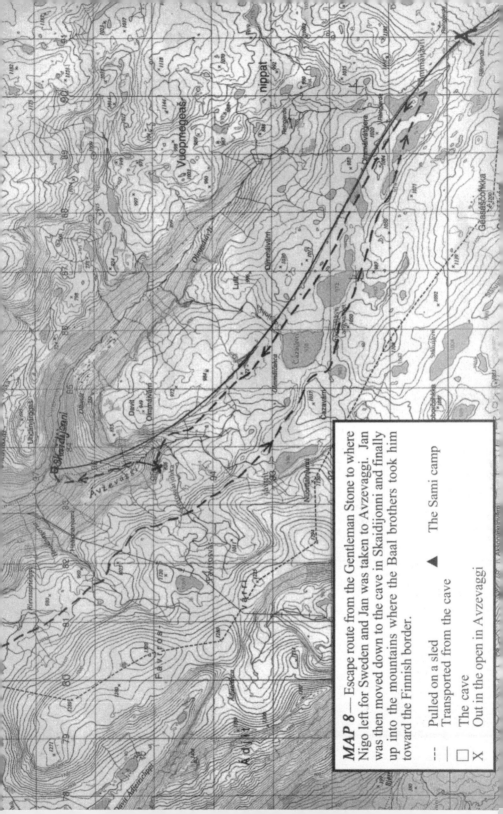

MAP 8 — Escape route from the Gentleman Stone to where Nigo left for Sweden and Jan was taken to Avzevaggi. Jan was then moved down to the cave in Skaidijjomni and finally up into the mountains where the Baal brothers took him toward the Finnish border.

- - -   Pulled on a sled
———   Transported from the cave
▲   The Sami camp
☐   The cave
✗   Out in the open in Avzevaggi

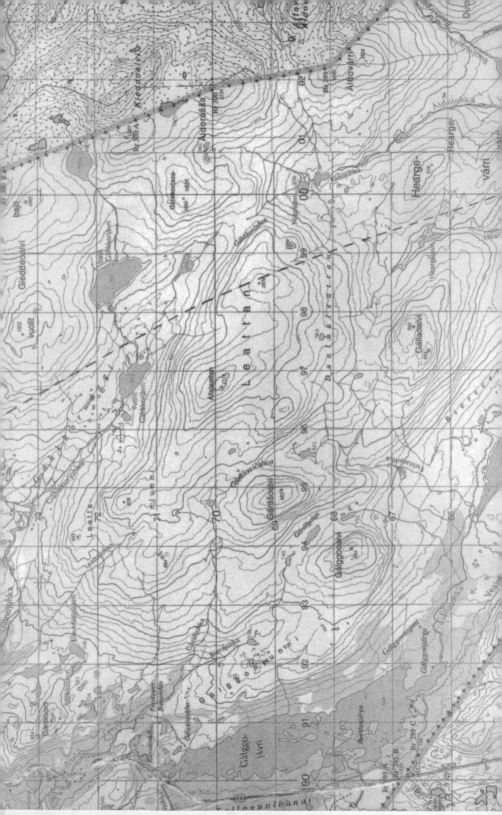

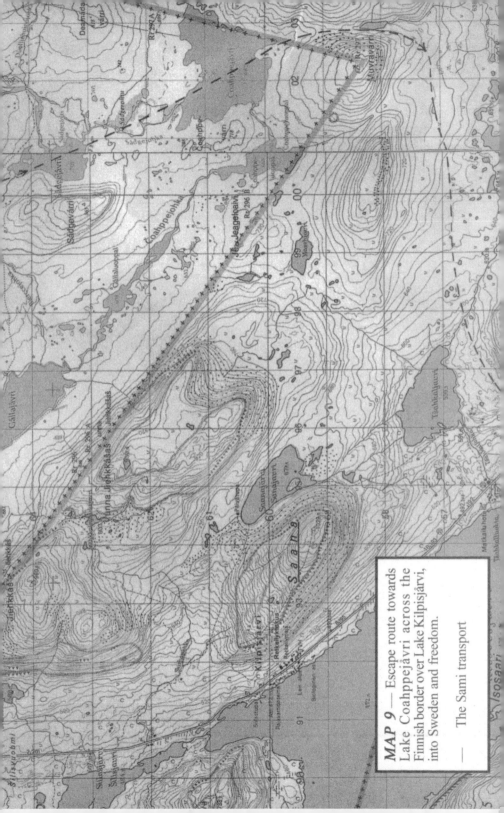

MAP 9 — Escape route towards Lake Coahppejávri across the Finnish border over Lake Kilpisjärvi, into Sweden and freedom.

— The Sami transport

MAP 10 — Jan's escape route from Toftefjord to Saarikoski, Sweden, where he was picked up by seaplane and flown to the hospital in Boden, Sweden.

SOURCES

Documents:

Jan Baalsrud's report, 1943, Norway's Resistance Museum, Oslo, Norway

Krigsdokumenter, 1943 Bundesarchiv, Militaerarchiv, Freiberg, Germany.

Krigsdokumenter, 1943. Prof. Dr. Peter von Rueden, Militaergeschichtliches Forschungsamt, Potsdam, Germany

Operation Instructions for Martin, 20th March,1943

Articles:

"Hallo, Gentleman!" Holger Raste. Jan Baalsrud Festivalen 8 -15. August 1987

Baalsrud flukt over Ringvassøy, Holger Raste Jan Baalsrud Festivalen 8 -15. August 1987

Grene-vevtradisjon i Nord-Troms, Vårt blad, 8/98

Mange av oss ble aldri tatt, Vi Menn, Nr. 13, May 8, 1979, Kjell Fjørtoft

Med Verdens beste kjørerein, Holger Raste, Jan Baalsrud Festivalen, August 8-15, 1987

Rettsreferat, Avisen Tromsø, September, 18-20 1946

Spreng Bardufoss flyplass og Lyngen-ferga, Vi Menn, Nr.13, March 27, 1979, Kjell Fjørtoft

Books:

Årbok for Karlsøy, Ulf L. Vinje, 1996

Bygd og By i Norge,Troms, Gyldendal Norsk Forlag, Oslo, *Under redaksjon av* Ivan Kristoffersen

De brente våre hjem, Nord-Troms Museum, 1995, Tore Hauge & Anders
Ole Hauglid
Den annen verdenskrig, J.W. Cappelens Forlag, Oslo, 1949, Winston S.
Churchill
Greneveving, Kåfjord kommune med hjelp av Manndalen Husmaflidslag
Kåfjord – mennesker, administrasjon og politikk, Torleif Lyngstad
Kompani Linge, Første bind, Gyldendal Norsk Forlag, Oslo 1949, Er-
ling Jensen, Per Ratvik, Ragnar Ulstein
Kompani Linge, Annet Bind, Gyldendal Norsk Forlag, Oslo 1949, Er-
ling Jensen, Per Ratvik, Ragnar Ulstein
Lensmen i Karlsøy, Ulf L. Vinje, 1995
Militær motstand i nord 1940 –1945, Universitetsforlaget, 9001 Tromsø
*Svensketrafikken–3, Flyktningar til Sverige frå Trøndelag og Nord-
Norge 1940-1945,* Det Norske samlaget,1977, Ragnar Ulstein
Våre Falne, Første bok, Bind-1-4, Grøndahl & Sønn, Oslo 1951, Den
Norske Stat

Interviews:
Andersen, Ingeborg, Bø in Vesterålen, Norway
Andreassen, Alvin, Asker, Norway
Antonsen, Hjalmar, Rebbenes, Norway
Bål, Per Gustav, Troms, Norway
Bål, Sigrid, Troms, Norway
Baalsrud, Nils Ivar, Vormsund, Norway
Ballovarre, John Olav, 9147 Birtavärre (in Sami w/Mikkel Bongo)
      Nordisk Samisk Institutt, Kautokeino, July 13, 1978 Translated
      to Norwegian by Torleif Lyngstad, April 1999, Translated to
      English by Astrid Karlsen Scott
Ballovarre Vilhelm, Kåfjordalen, Norway
Bergmo, Asmund, Olderdalen, Norway
Bergmo, Erling, Birtavärre , Norway
Brustøm, Gudbrand, Manndalen, Norway
Dalhaug, Asbjørn, Furuflaten, Norway
Dalhaug, Lasse, Furuflaten, Norway

Fjørtoft, Kjell, Tromsø, Norway
Grønnslett, Arvid, Rebbenes, Norway
Grønnvoll, Helge, Furuflaten, Norway
Grønvoll, Agnete, Furuflaten, Norway
Hågensen, Olaug, Tromsø, Norway
Halden, Halvard, Lyngseidet, Norway
Halden, Hans, Lyngseidet, Norway
Hansen, Ragnhild, Dåfjord, Norway
Hauge, Tore, Oteren, Norway
Heika, Arvid, Kopparelv, Norway
Heika, Viggo, Kopparelv, Norway
Henriksen, Thorleif, Tromsø, Norway
Hoel, Grethe, Tromsø, Norway
Idrupsen, Dagmar, Tromsø, Norway
Idrupsen, Halvor, Rebbenes, Norway
Idrupsen, Idrup, Rebbenes, Norway
Isaksen, Eliva, Manndalen, Norway
Isaksen, Peder, Manndalen, Norway
Isaksen, Magne, Trondheim, Norway
Larsen, Alvin, Furuflaten, Norway
Leivseth, Gudrun, Bergen, Norway
Lyngstad, Torleif, Birtavärre, Norway
Mikalsen, Aud, Manndalen, Norway
Mikalsen, Magne, Manndalen, Norway
Morin, Barbro, Kalix, Sweden
Nilsen, Peder, Tromsø, Norway
Olsen, Harald, Dåfjord, Norway
Pedersen, Gunnar, Tromsø, Norway
Raste, Holger, Tromsø, Norway
Ratvik, Johan, Ålesund, Norway
Siri, Berit Anne, Kautokeino, Norway
Solberg, Alf, Tromsø, Norway
Sønsteby, Gunnar, Oslo, Norway
Sørensen, Odd, Tromsø, Norway

Ulstein, **Ragnar**, Ålesund, Norway
Wikan, Edvin, Kvaløyvågen, Norway

Institutions:
Norway's Resistance Museum, Oslo, Norway
Sameinstituttet, Kautokeino, Norway

Letters:
Brustrøm, Gudbrand, Samuelsberg, Norway
Reinøy, Julius, letter to Magnar Olsen, July 28, 1985, regarding *M/K Brattholm*
Solvang, Hans, letter to Ingolf Sjursnes, Sjursnes, August 8, 1991
Stilnes, Hanna Brustrøm, Oppegård, Norway
Vågseter, Aud Brustrøm, Skåla, Norway

Maps:
National Geographic
Statkart, Oslo, Norway LA82011 R88334

Photographs:
Kompani Linge, Annet bind, Gyldendal Norsk Forlag, Oslo, 1949, Erling Jensen, Per Ratvik, Ragnar Ulstein: Fishing barrels with machine guns
Kompani Linge, Første bind, Gyldendal Norsk Forlag, Oslo, 1949, Erling Jensen, Per Ratvik, Ragnar Ulstein: Martin Linge, Scalloway Harbor
Krigen i Norge fra Sola til Tromsø, Gyldendal Norsk Forlag: Reichskommissar Terboven in Svolvær
Lennsmenn i Karlsøy, Ulf L. Vinje, 1995: Sheriff Hoel
Norwegian Resistance Museum, Oslo, Norway: Josef Terboven
Så vi vant vår rett, Frihetskampen 1940-1945: Nasjonalhjelpen til Frihetskampens ofre, E. Ancher, Hanssen
Våre falne – Første bok, Grøndahl & Son, Oslo 1949, Utgitt av den norske stat: Lt. Sigurd Eskeland, Sgt. Per Blindheim, Sgt.Gabriel Salvesen

Baal, Aslak Family: Per Thomas Baal, Aslak Baal

Baalsrud, Nils Ivar: Jan Baalsrud (Cover), Jan Baalsrud in Shetland Islands

Ballovarre, Vilhelm: John Olav Ballovarre

Brustrøm, Gudbrand: Nils Brustrøm, Signe and Nils Brustrøm

Dahlhaug, Asbjørn: Lyngsdalen, Amandus Lillevoll, Olav Lanes, Alvin Larsen and Marius Grønvoll, Alfon Hansen

Grønnslett, Arvid: Ludvik Nilsen

Hågensen, Olaug: Haldis Idrupsen, Peder Idrupsen, Olaug Hågensen, Dina Pedersen, and Dagmar Idrupsen, Anna Pedersen, Idrupsen's home

Halden, Hans: Halvard Halden

Haug, Dr. Tore: The Bromnes store and Anaton Pedersen's house, Toftefjord, Island and rock by Vårøya where Jan swam to, Vårøya Island, Idrupsen home, Jacoba Jensen's home

Isaksen, Eliva and Peder: Aslak Fossvoll, Teacher Nordness, Peder and Eliva Isaksen, Nils "Nigo" Nilsen, Olaf Olsen, Peder Pedersen, Isak Solvang, Marie (Fossen) Olsen, Marie Holm, Ludvik Nilsen

Iversen, Leif Erik: Police station in Tromsø, *M/K Brattholm* twisted skeleton on bottom of Toftefjord, Memorial Plaque infront of Gestapo Headquarters, Gestapo Headquarters, Veggefjord, Solvatnet Lake, Arvid and Viggo Heika and Astrid Karlsen Scott, Lyngsneset, The dock at Løvli, Peder Nilsen, Workbench at Solhov School, Replica of sled, The Gentleman Stone, Gentleman Stone seen toward the East, Entrance to Skaidijonni Cave, Upper entrance to Skaidijonni Cave, Inside Skaidijonni Cave, The Brustrøm home, Brustrøm's old wood-burning stove

Leivseth, Gudrun: Marius Grønvoll, Ingeborg Grønvoll

Lyngstad, Torleif: Ankerlia with Moskugaise, Birtavärre , Kåfjord, The hut in the mountains

Mikalsen, Magne: Peder Isaksen by mountain wall in Avzevaggi, Helene, Magne, Anton and Ella Mikalsen

Morin, Barbro: Barbro Morin

Eliva Isaksen, Nils E. Nilsen

Raste, Holger: Astrid Karlsen Scott (Cover)

Scott, Astrid Karlsen: The Ballovarre home, Tore Haug (Inside back
    cover), Kåfjorddalen Valley, the Steinnes home, Kåfjord, the
    Sørensen home, Bjørnskar, Toftefjord, Toftefjord where the sabo-
    teurs came ashore

Steinnes, Inger: Hjalmar Steinnes

Wikan, Edwin: Edwin Wikan, excavation photos of the *Brattholm's*
    men's graves